D1265103

introduction to

MULTIVARIATE ANALYSIS

introduction to

MULTIVARIATE ANALYSIS

GEORGE H. DUNTEMAN

SAGE PUBLICATIONS
The Publishers of Professional Social Science
Beverly Hills London New Delhi

Copyright © 1984 by Sage Publications, Inc.

All rights reserved. No part of this book may be reproduced or utilized in any form or by any means, electronic or mechanical, including photocopying, recording, or by any information storage and retrieval system, without permission in writing from the publisher.

For information address:

SAGE Publications, Inc.
275 South Beverly Drive
Beverly Hills, California 90212

SAGE Publications India Pvt. Ltd.
C-236 Defence Colony
New Delhi 110 024, India

SAGE Publications Ltd
28 Banner Street
London EC1Y 8QE, England

Printed in the United States of America

Library of Congress Cataloging in Publication Data

Dunteman, George H. (George Henry), 1935-
Introduction to multivariate analysis.

Bibliography: p.
Includes index.
1. Multivariate analysis. I. Title.
QA278.D86 1984 519.5′35 83-19139
ISBN 0-8039-2176-4

FIRST PRINTING

Contents

Preface

This book is the second in a two-volume set. The first volume, *Introduction to Linear Models,* covers basic statistical concepts, elementary matrix algebra, and the basics of linear statistical models. It provides the background for this volume. Together, the two books present a comprehensive coverage of linear models and multivariate analysis at an elementary level. This two-volume series is virtually self-contained because it has comprehensive chapters on basic statistical concepts and elementary matrix algebra. Understanding of the material presented requires only a course or two of noncalculus introductory statistics. Broad coverage and penetrating discussions of advanced concepts (such as generalized inverses and reparameterization) are presented in an intuitive and nonrigorous manner. All techniques are illustrated step by step on small, hypothetical, yet meaningful data bases. Applied examples are also provided, as well as a discussion of computer software. Many of the problems at the ends of the chapters involve actual data sets taken from the literature. In addition, each of the two books contains an appendix of actual data on a sample of 300 high school seniors from a large national survey.

The reader who diligently works his or her way through this book will have a basic understanding of statistical model building that can be used as a stepping-stone to advanced study. Furthermore, the reader should be able to carry out statistical analysis and comprehend statistically oriented articles in his or her discipline.

The suggested audiences for this book include advanced undergraduate and graduate students in the behavioral and social sciences and social science researchers and research administrators in both the government and applied research organizations. This volume should also be useful for broad survey courses taught in departments of statistics. Although the examples are set in a behavioral and social science framework, this book should be useful in other disciplines as well.

This book was made possible through the generous support of the Research Triangle Institute (RTI). Special thanks are due to George R. Herbert, President, and Dr. William C. Eckerman (now deceased), former Vice President for Social Sciences, for creating the atmosphere conducive to this difficult undertaking. Secretarial support over the years was provided by Nita Blake, "Pete" Pender, Linda Hoffman, and Frances Heald. Nita Blake, Administrative Assistant for Social Sciences Administration at RTI, was the key person responsible for preparing the manuscripts for both volumes. Without her competent help in typing complex material, these two volumes would not have been completed.

Thanks are also due to my wife, Rosarie, and my children, George and Elizabeth, for tolerating "lost" evenings and weekends over a period of several years.

1 Introduction

As mentioned in the Preface, this book is the second in a two-volume series. The first volume, *Introduction to Linear Models,* provides the necessary background for mastering the content of this volume. *Introduction to Linear Models* is a relatively self-contained elementary treatment of linear statistical models. It begins with a review of basic statistical concepts, progresses through elementary matrix algebra, and culminates in a comprehensive discussion of the elements of linear statistical models. While I feel that *Introduction to Linear Models* provides the best preparation for this volume (because of continuity of treatment), the mastery of the material presented in that volume from other sources will certainly suffice.

All of the models described in *Introduction to Linear Models* contained one continuous dependent variable. The models discussed in this volume contain two or more continuous dependent variables. Hence a framework must be developed to characterize the joint distribution of two or more continuous variables. Under certain conditions, the joint distribution of two or more continuous variables can be described by their means, their standard deviations, and the correlations among them. The reader will see that the multivariate normal distribution (Chapter 2), an analogue of the univariate normal distribution, is a convenient way to summarize the simultaneous distribution of two or more continuous variables, if certain assumptions can be met.

In Chapter 3 the properties of linear composites of variables are explored. For example, we may want to derive a total test score, y_1, that is an equally weighted linear combination of verbal ability (x_1), mathematical ability (x_2), and spatial relations ability (x_3). Our linear composite would be $y_1 = x_1 + x_2 + x_3$. The properties of y_1 (such as mean and variance) can be derived from a knowledge of the properties of x_1, x_2, and x_3 (for example, means, variances, and covariances) and the weights attached to each component (1 in the present example).

Multivariate regression (Chapter 4) is a generalization of the regression models with a single dependent variable discussed in *Introduction to Linear Models*. The basic difference is that the multivariate regression model concerns itself with simultaneously modeling two or more continuous dependent variables that are themselves related. As in the regression models presented in that volume, the dependent variables can be modeled as additive combinations of continuous, categorical, and interaction variables. Each dependent variable in the dependent variable set is modeled as a linear combination of the same set of independent variables. The primary difference is that statistical hypotheses concerning the parameters of two or more regression equations, one for each dependent variable, have to be tested simultaneously. For example, two dependent variables may be reading and math achievement, y_1 and y_2, respectively. The common set of independent variables might be intelligence (x_1), socioeconomic status (x_2), and school quality (x_3). We then have two regression equations, one for each of the correlated dependent variables:

$$y_1 = \beta_{01} + \beta_{11}x_1 + \beta_{21}x_2 + \beta_{31}x_3 + \epsilon_1$$
$$y_2 = \beta_{02} + \beta_{12}x_1 + \beta_{22}x_2 + \beta_{32}x_3 + \epsilon_2$$

The errors associated with each equation (ϵ_1 and ϵ_2) are assumed to be correlated; this leads to the multivariate analysis formulation of the problem. Also, the model allows the regression coefficients associated with the first equation to be different from the regression coefficients associated with the second equation as signified by the second subscript attached to each regression coefficient. The problem again is to estimate the parameters simultaneously in each equation and test various hypotheses about them. For example, one might desire to test simultaneously whether both regression coefficients attached to x_1, intelligence, are zero, that is, $\beta_{11} = \beta_{12} = 0$.

Chapter 5 describes procedures for discriminating among two or more populations on the basis of two or more common variables measured on a random sample of individuals or units from each population. In addition, the related problem of determining procedures for assigning an individual or unit to membership in a particular population on the basis of a set of variables is explored. For example, a clinical psychologist might develop classification rules for assigning a new patient to a psychotic, neurotic, or normal population on the basis of measures from a multidimensional psychological test battery.

The idea behind principal components, discussed in Chapter 6, is to summarize a set of variables by finding a smaller set of variables, called principal components, that are linear composites of the original variables and have certain desirable statistical properties. We shall see that these properties are that the principal components or linear composites have maximum variance and are uncorrelated with one another. In addition, the number of principal components should be considerably less than the number of original variables. The goal of factor analysis (Chapter 7) is similar to that of principal components analysis. In both principal components and factor analyses no distinction is made between the variables in terms of independent or dependent variables as in regression models. The variables are considered as a single set to be summarized by a smaller and more basic and meaningful set of "underlying" variables.

Canonical correlation analysis, discussed in Chapter 8, distinguishes between two sets of continuous variables and summarizes the interrelationships between the two sets of variables. In each set a linear composite is formed by weighting the variables in each set in such a way that the correlation between the two linear composites is the highest possible. Again, independent and dependent variables are not distinguished; the two sets of variables have equal status. The technique is similar in spirit to principal components and factor analyses, but in this case the goal is to simplify the relationships between two sets of variables. For example, a psychologist might be interested in summarizing the relationship between a set of personality measures (x_1, x_2, and x_3) and a set of interest measures (y_1, y_2, and y_3). A canonical correlation analysis will yield linear composites $x = ax_1 + bx_2 + cx_3$ and $y = a'y_1 + b'y_2 + c'y_3$ such that the correlation between x and y is the highest possible. Instead of looking at the many cross-correlations or relationships between the sets (x_1, x_2, and x_3) and (y_1, y_2, and y_3), we can concentrate on one pair of canonical variables whose characteristics can shed light on the nature of the relationship between x and y. Sometimes more than one pair of canonical variables is needed to summarize adequately the interrelationships between two sets of variables.

2 The Multivariate Normal Distribution

2.1 INTRODUCTION

Most of the previous discussions (*Introduction to Linear Models*) have been concerned with examining or making inferences concerning various aspects of univariate distributions. The characteristics of discrete distributions and continuous distributions such as the normal distribution were examined. The univariate normal distribution was emphasized for two major reasons: (1) Theoretical considerations would lead us to assume normality in a large number of situations because of the central limit theorem, and (2) most of sampling distribution theory (for example, t, F, and χ^2 distributions) is based upon normality assumptions. In reference to the first point, for example, a reasonable assumption is that since academic ability is the sum of a large number of relatively independent sources (various genes, various childhood experiences, various school experiences, and so on), the central limit theorem would suggest that academic ability should be normally distributed. Empirical distributions of aptitude and achievement test scores support this assumption. Other distributions such as a 0, 1 binary variable are clearly not normally distributed.

In this chapter, we shall generalize our discussion from the univariate case to the multivariate case. We will be primarily concerned with the multivariate analogue of the univariate normal distribution, which is known as the multivariate normal distribution. The reason for emphasizing the multivariate normal distribution is that most of the machinery needed to test various multivariate hypotheses is based upon assumptions of multivariate normality.

In section 2.2 the multivariate normal distribution is defined. It is an analogue to the univariate normal distribution, but involves the distribution of a vector instead of a single variable. Accordingly, more parameters are needed to describe the multivariate normal distribution. Further similarities between the univariate and multivariate normal distribution are noted in section 2.3, especially the concept of generalized variance. Generalized variance is a summary measure reflecting the variance of a vector and as such is an analogue of the variance of a single variable. Like the univariate normal distribution, the multivariate normal distribution has an associated distribution function (section 2.4). It is defined for a vector of variables rather than a single variable. Marginal and conditional distributions for bivariate distributions were discussed in *Introduction to Linear Models*. The concepts are extended to the multivariate normal distribution and are discussed in sections 2.5 and 2.6, respectively. The estimation of the parameters of the multivariate normal distribution (that is, the mean vector and covariance matrix) is straightforward and is described in the final section.

2.2 MULTIVARIATE NORMAL DISTRIBUTION

We have previously seen (see *Introduction to Linear Models*) that the density function for the univariate normal distribution can be expressed as

$$f(x) = \frac{1}{\sqrt{2\Pi}\,\sigma} e^{-\frac{1}{2}\frac{(x-\mu)^2}{\sigma^2}}$$

This equation tells us that the density of the univariate normal distribution can be characterized by the two parameters, μ and σ^2. That is, if we know that the density is in the normal family, then the density, f(x), for a specific value of the random variable, x, is known if μ and σ^2 are known. We shall see that more parameters are needed to characterize the multivariate normal distribution and that the number of parameters is determined by the dimension of the vector representing the multivariate observation. Let us now discuss the notion of a random vector.

In the univariate situation, the random variable x would represent just one characteristic or measure of the set of objects under consideration. For example, if the objects were people, the random variable x could represent the mathematical aptitude for people. In many applied research situations, however, we are interested in measuring more than one characteristic of an object. We might be interested in measuring verbal aptitude, space perception, psychomotor coordination, and mechanical aptitude in addition to mathematical aptitude. If we measure a number of characteristics such as these simultaneously on the object of interest (for example, people), then we may characterize our observation as a random vector, $\mathbf{x}$, where $\mathbf{x}' = [x_1, x_2, x_3, \ldots x_p]$ has dimension, p, equal to the number of measured characteristics under consideration for the randomly selected object. Like x, in the univariate case, the random vector $\mathbf{x}$ can also be expressed in terms of a density function, f(x). Under assumptions analogous to those of the univariate normal situation, the vector, **x**, can be assumed to be distributed in a multivariate normal form. The multivariate density function is expressed as

$$f(\mathbf{x}) = f(x_1, x_2, x_3, \ldots x_p) = \frac{1}{(2\Pi)^{\frac{p}{2}} |\mathbf{V}|^{\frac{1}{2}}} e^{-\frac{1}{2}(x-\mu)'\mathbf{V}^{-1}(x-\mu)}$$

where **V** is the covariance matrix of the vector, **x**, and μ is the vector of the means corresponding to the components of **x**.

In order to obtain a better understanding of the general case expressed above, it might be informative to examine the multivariate normal distribution for the specific case of **x** having two components. When $\mathbf{x}' = [x_1, x_2]$, the vector **x** is said to have a bivariate normal distribution. The density in this case is

$$f(\mathbf{x}) = f(x_1, x_2) = \frac{1}{(2\Pi)^{\frac{2}{2}} |V|^{\frac{1}{2}}} e^{-\frac{1}{2}(x-\mu)'V^{-1}(x-\mu)}$$

$$-\frac{1}{2}(x_1-\mu_1, x_2-\mu_2)\begin{bmatrix} \sigma_1^2 & \rho\sigma_1\sigma_2 \\ \rho\sigma_1\sigma_2 & \sigma_2^2 \end{bmatrix}^{-1}\begin{bmatrix} x_1-\mu_1 \\ x_2-\mu_2 \end{bmatrix}$$

$$= \frac{1}{2\Pi \begin{vmatrix} \sigma_1^2 & \rho\sigma_1\sigma_2 \\ \rho\sigma_1\sigma_2 & \sigma_2^2 \end{vmatrix}^{\frac{1}{2}}} e$$

$$= \frac{1}{2\Pi\sigma_1\sigma_2\sqrt{1-\rho^2}} e^{-\frac{1}{2(1-\rho^2)}\left[\frac{(x_1-\mu_2)^2}{\sigma_1^2}\right.}$$

$$\left. + \frac{2\rho(x_1-\mu_1)(x_2-\mu_2)}{\sigma_1\sigma_2} + \frac{(x_2-\mu_2)^2}{\sigma_2^2}\right]$$

The reader can verify this expression by noting that

$$|\mathbf{V}| = \begin{bmatrix} \sigma_1^2 & \rho\sigma_1\sigma_2 \\ \rho\sigma_1\sigma_2 & \sigma_2^2 \end{bmatrix} = \sigma_1^2\sigma_2^2 - \rho^2\sigma_1^2\sigma_2^2 = \sigma_1^2\sigma_2^2(1-\rho^2) \text{ and hence,}$$

$$|\mathbf{V}|^{\frac{1}{2}} = \sqrt{\sigma_1^2\sigma_2^2(1-\rho^2)} = \sigma_1\sigma_2\sqrt{1-\rho^2}.$$

Also,

$$\mathbf{V}^{-1} = \begin{bmatrix} \sigma_1^2 & \rho\sigma_1\sigma_2 \\ \rho\sigma_1\sigma_2 & \sigma_2^2 \end{bmatrix}^{-1} = \frac{1}{\sigma_1^2\sigma_2^2 - \rho^2\sigma_1^2\sigma_2^2} \begin{bmatrix} \sigma_2^2 & -\rho\sigma_1\sigma_2 \\ -\rho\sigma_1\sigma_2 & \sigma_1^2 \end{bmatrix}$$

$$= \frac{1}{\sigma_1^2\sigma_2^2(1-\rho^2)} \begin{bmatrix} \sigma_2^2 & -\rho\sigma_1\sigma_2 \\ -\rho\sigma_1\sigma_2 & \sigma_1^2 \end{bmatrix} = \frac{1}{1-\rho^2} \begin{bmatrix} \dfrac{1}{\sigma_1^2} & \dfrac{-\rho}{\sigma_1\sigma_2} \\ \dfrac{-\rho}{\sigma_1\sigma_2} & \dfrac{1}{\sigma_2^2} \end{bmatrix}$$

Making these substitutions into the matrix expression of the bivariate normal distribution, we have the scalar representation presented above.

Let us look at the number of parameters needed to characterize the bivariate normal distribution by examining the expanded (scalar) formula for the normal bivariate density function. In order to specify the density of a particular bivariate observation, we need to know μ_1, μ_2, σ_1^2, σ_2^2, and ρ. That is, given that $[x_1, x_2]$ has a bivariate normal distribution, then for any realization such as $[1, 2]$ of $[x_1, x_2]$ we can determine its density, $f(1, 2)$, if we know the above five parameter values. In other words, we must be able to assign particular values to each of the five parameters before we can determine the density of a particular observed value of $[x_1, x_2]$.

In order to specify the density of an observation, $[x_1, x_2, x_3]$, from a trivariate normal distribution, we need to specify the mean vector for the random vector $[x_1, x_2, x_3]$ and the variance-covariance matrix associated with the random vector $[x_1, x_2, x_3]$. The expectation (mean) of a random vector $[x_1, x_2, x_3]$ is denoted as

$$E \begin{bmatrix} x_1 \\ x_2 \\ x_3 \end{bmatrix} = \begin{bmatrix} \mu_1 \\ \mu_2 \\ \mu_3 \end{bmatrix}$$

where μ_1, μ_2, and μ_3 are the means of the components x_1, x_2, and x_3, respectively. The variance-covariance matrix for the random vector $[x_1, x_2, x_3]$ is

$$\text{var}\,\mathbf{x} = \text{var} \begin{bmatrix} x_1 \\ x_2 \\ x_3 \end{bmatrix} = \begin{bmatrix} \sigma_1^2 & \rho_{12}\sigma_1\sigma_2 & \rho_{13}\sigma_1\sigma_3 \\ \rho_{21}\sigma_2\sigma_1 & \sigma_2^2 & \rho_{23}\sigma_2\sigma_3 \\ \rho_{31}\sigma_3\sigma_1 & \rho_{32}\sigma_3\sigma_2 & \sigma_3^2 \end{bmatrix}$$

In order to specify the density function $f(x_1, x_2, x_3)$, we need to know the values of the following parameters: $\mu_1, \mu_2, \mu_3, \sigma_1, \sigma_2, \sigma_3, \rho_{12}, \rho_{13}, \rho_{23}$. In other words, we have to know the mean for each of the three variables, the standard deviation for each of the three variables, and the three correlations that represent the relationships among the three variables. This means that we have to specify the values for nine parameters in order to obtain the density for a particular observation $[x_1, x_2, x_3]$ from a trivariate normal distribution.

In the general case of a p component random vector $[x_1, x_2, \ldots, x_p]$, which has the multivariate normal distribution, we will need to specify the p means, p standard deviations, and $[(p)(p-1)]/2$ correlations among the variables in order to calculate the density of an observation $[x_1, x_2, \ldots, x_p]$. For example, a multivariate normally distributed vector with five components has a total of $5 + 5 + 5(4)/2 = 20$ parameters that have to be specified.

2.3 GENERALIZED VARIANCE

Let us now look more closely at the similarity in form between the univariate and multivariate density functions. In order to do this, we shall first slightly alter the form in which the univariate density function is normally written. That is, let

$$f(x) = \frac{1}{\sqrt{2\Pi}\,\sigma} e^{-\frac{1}{2}\frac{(x-\mu)^2}{\sigma^2}} = \frac{1}{(2\Pi)^{\frac{1}{2}}(\sigma^2)^{\frac{1}{2}}} e^{-\frac{1}{2}(x-\mu)(\sigma^2)^{-1}(x-\mu)}$$

Looking again at the form of the general multivariate density function

$$f(\mathbf{x}) = f(x_1, x_2, \ldots, x_p) = \frac{1}{(2\Pi)^{\frac{p}{2}}|\mathbf{V}|^{\frac{1}{2}}} e^{-\frac{1}{2}(\mathbf{x}-\mu)'\mathbf{V}^{-1}(\mathbf{x}-\mu)}$$

we can immediately notice certain similarities. The analogue of σ in the multivariate normal case is $|\mathbf{V}|^{1/2}$ and the analogue of $(\sigma^2)^{-1}$ is $\mathbf{V}^{-1}$. For the univariate case, if σ^2 is small, this signifies that the distribution of x is concentrated close to the mean or is clustered tightly on the line representing x. For the multivariate case, if the value of $|\mathbf{V}|^{1/2}$ is small, this means that the multivariate density is concentrated in a small area of Euclidean p space where p is the number of components in the random vector. For this reason $|\mathbf{V}|^{1/2}$ is sometimes referred to as the "generalized variance" of the multivariate normal distribution. This situation might best be illustrated through the use of a few

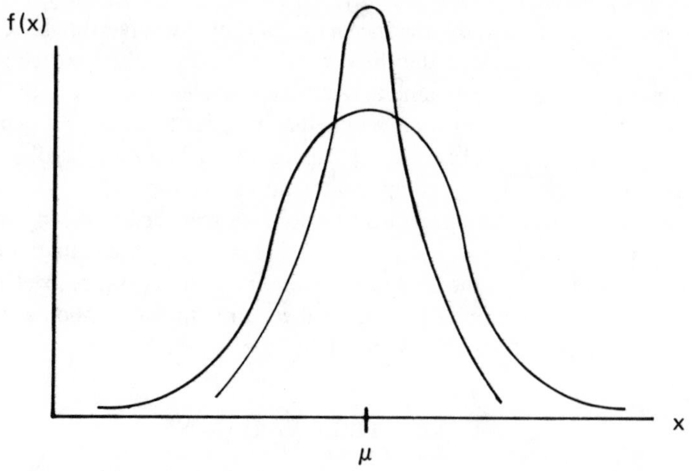

Figure 2.1 Two Univariate Normal Distributions with Identical Means but Differing in Variances

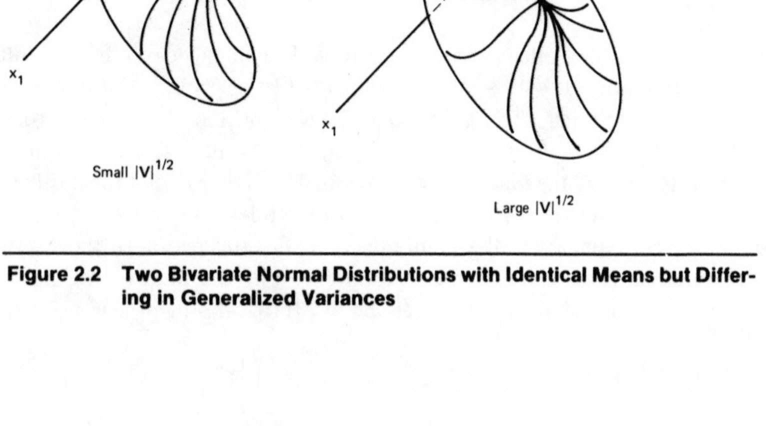

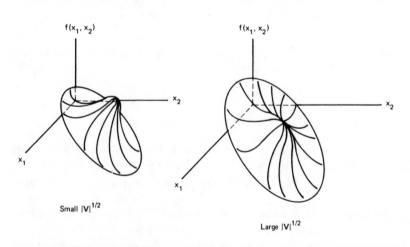

Figure 2.2 Two Bivariate Normal Distributions with Identical Means but Differing in Generalized Variances

figures. Figure 2.1 contrasts a univariate normal distribution with relatively small variance with a univariate normal distribution with relatively large variance. Figure 2.2 contrasts a bivariate normal distribution with relatively small generalized variance (that is, $|\mathbf{V}|^{1/2}$) with a bivariate normal distribution with relatively large variance.

If we look at the left-hand side of Figure 2.2, we can see that the vectors $[x_1, x_2]$ tend to be concentrated in a smaller region of the x_1, x_2 plane compared to the figure on the right. The figure on the left portrays a bivariate normal distribution that has a small variance on both of the components x_1 and x_2 and a larger correlation between x_1 and x_2 than the figure on the right. Since

$$|\mathbf{V}|^{\frac{1}{2}} = \begin{vmatrix} \sigma_1^2 & \rho\sigma_1\sigma_2 \\ \rho\sigma_2\sigma_1 & \sigma_2^2 \end{vmatrix}^{\frac{1}{2}} = \sigma_1\sigma_2\sqrt{1-\rho^2}$$

it is obvious that this value has to be smaller for the figure on the left than for the figure on the right. We can say that the vectors $[x_1, x_2]$ tend to be closer to $[\mu_1, \mu_2]$ for the figure on the left. Note that $[\mu_1, \mu_2]$ is in the x_1, x_2 plane and would be located directly under the peak of the bivariate distribution.

Another way of portraying the density of a bivariate normal distribution geometrically is shown in Figure 2.3. Each of these figures summarizes the concentration of the bivariate normal distribution. The ellipses indicate the proportion of the vectors $[x_1, x_2]$ (that is, observations) that are contained within the ellipses. For example, the interior ellipse in the figure on the left identifies the region in which .20 of the random vectors $[x_1, x_2]$ are contained. If we compare the set of ellipses from the figure on the left to the set of ellipses from the figure on the right, we can easily see that a larger area of the x_1, x_2 plane is needed to contain a given proportion of vectors $[x_1, x_2]$ for the figure on the right as compared to the figure on the left.

These generalizations apply to multivariate normally distributed random vectors of any arbitrary dimension, p. However, we cannot portray these relationships geometrically for random vectors that have more than two components (one axis is needed for the density), for we live in a three-dimensional world. We can see that in the case of a bivariate normal distribution the magnitude of the generalized variance is a function of the magnitudes of the two variances and the intercorrelation between the two variables. An increase in the variances and/or a decrease in the intercorrelation results in an increase of the generalized variance. This observation can be generalized to the case of a multivariate normal distribution of arbitrary dimension, p. As the intercorrelations among the variables decrease and/or the variances increase, the generalized variance will increase.

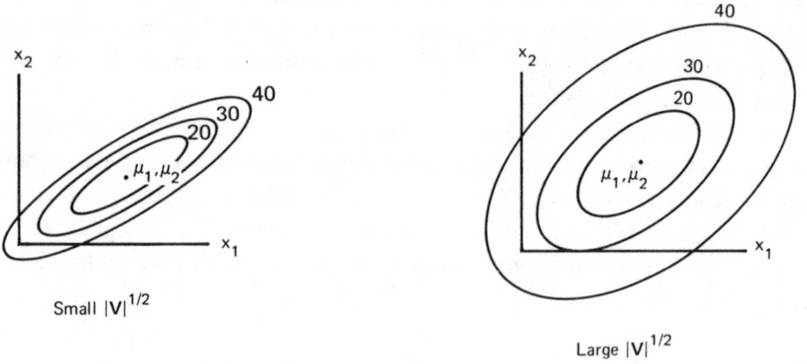

Figure 2.3 Bivariate Density Contours for Small and Large $|V|^{1/2}$

2.4 MULTIVARIATE NORMAL DISTRIBUTION FUNCTION

There are a number of other similarities between a univariate and multivariate normal distribution. The volume contained under the surface of $f(x_1, x_2, \ldots x_p)$ can be expressed as

$$\frac{1}{(2\Pi)^{\frac{p}{2}} |\mathbf{V}|^{\frac{1}{2}}} \int_{-\infty}^{\infty} \int_{-\infty}^{\infty} \cdots \int_{-\infty}^{\infty} e^{-\frac{1}{2}(\mathbf{x}-\boldsymbol{\mu})'\mathbf{V}^{-1}(\mathbf{x}-\boldsymbol{\mu})} dx_1 dx_2 \ldots dx_p = 1$$

The volume equals 1 since it represents the probability of the event that the random vector, **x**, lies somewhere in p dimensional space, which is 1. This is a formidable formula, but it is analogous to the univariate case, where

$$\frac{1}{\sqrt{2\Pi}\,\sigma} \int_{-\infty}^{\infty} e^{-\frac{1}{2}\frac{(x-\mu)^2}{\sigma^2}} dx = 1$$

In the univariate case, the integration symbol

$$\int_{-\infty}^{\infty} \ldots dx$$

signifies that we are solving for the area under the curve or density function

$$f(x) = \frac{1}{\sqrt{2\Pi}\,\sigma} e^{-\frac{1}{2}\frac{(x-\mu)^2}{\sigma^2}}$$

while in the multivariate case, the integration symbol

$$\int_{-\infty}^{\infty}\int_{-\infty}^{\infty}\cdots\int_{-\infty}^{\infty}\ldots dx_1, dx_2, \ldots, dx_p$$

means that we are solving for the volume under the surface of the multivariate density function

$$\frac{1}{(2\Pi)^{\frac{p}{2}}|V|^{\frac{1}{2}}}e^{-\frac{1}{2}(x-\mu)'V^{-1}(x-\mu)}$$

The multivariate normal density function, like the univariate density function, has a unique distribution function associated with it. However, the multivariate distribution function indicates the probability of a random vector having each of its components satisfying the relationship $[X_1 \leqslant x_1, X_2 \leqslant x_2, \ldots X_p \leqslant x_p]$ where the large X's signify the random variable in general and the small x's indicate particular realizations or observed values. Sometimes the vector $\mathbf{x} = [x_1, x_2, \ldots x_p]$ will represent a random vector in general; other times it will represent particular values of the random vector. The meaning will be clear from the context. If a distinction needs to be made, then the distinction in the previous sentence will be used. For example, we might be interested in the probability of a vector falling into the region of p space defined by $[X_1 \leqslant 2, X_2 \leqslant 5, \ldots, X_p \leqslant 10]$. For the bivariate case we can show a region on the x_1, x_2 plane as illustrated in Figure 2.4, where $[X_1 \leqslant 5, X_2 \leqslant 3]$.

The shaded area extending infinitely below the line $x_2 = 3$ and to the left of the line $x_1 = 5$ indicates the area for which we want to find the probability of observing a random vector $[x_1, x_2]$. The probability of observing a random vector satisfying these conditions for this bivariate case can be written as

$$F(5, 3) = \frac{1}{2\Pi|V|^{\frac{1}{2}}}\int_{-\infty}^{5}\int_{-\infty}^{3} e^{-\frac{1}{2}(x-\mu)'V^{-1}(x-\mu)}\, dx_1\, dx_2$$

which has a specific value (probability) if the parameters are known. For any arbitrary $[x_1, x_2, \ldots, x_p]$, the probability of $[X_1 \leqslant x_1, X_2 \leqslant x_2, \ldots, X_p \leqslant x_p]$ is given by the distribution function

$$F(x_1, x_2, \ldots, x_p)$$

$$= \frac{1}{(2\Pi)^{\frac{p}{2}}|V|^{\frac{1}{2}}}\int_{-\infty}^{X_1}\int_{-\infty}^{X_2}\cdots\int_{-\infty}^{X_p} e^{-\frac{1}{2}(x-\mu)'V^{-1}(x-\mu)}\, dx_1 dx_2 \ldots dx_p$$

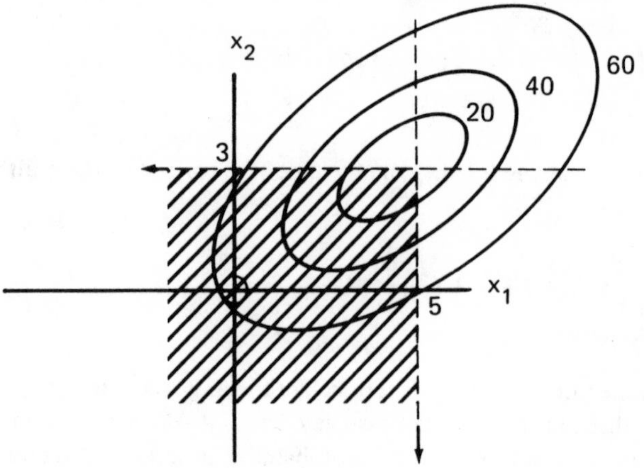

Figure 2.4 Region of the x_1, x_2 Plane Where $X_1 \leq 5$, and $X_2 \leq 3$

The above multidimensional integral indicates the probability of observing a vector $[X_1, X_2, \ldots, X_p]$ with components satisfying the restrictions that $[X_1 \leqslant x_1, X_2 \leqslant x_2, \ldots, X_p \leqslant x_p]$.

2.5 MARGINAL DISTRIBUTIONS

All possible marginal distributions of a multidimensional normal distribution are also normally distributed. It turns out that we may determine the marginal distribution for a subset of the components of $[x_1, x_2, x_3, \ldots, x_p]$ by taking the elements of $\mathbf{V}$ and $\mathbf{x} - \mu$ corresponding to the components of interest and substituting them in the multivariate density or distribution function.

For example, the marginal distribution function of x_1 for a trivariate normal distribution is defined as

$$F(x_1) = \frac{1}{(2\Pi)^{\frac{3}{2}} |V|^{\frac{1}{2}}} \int_{-\infty}^{x_1} \int_{-\infty}^{\infty} \int_{-\infty}^{\infty} e^{-\frac{1}{2}(x-\mu)' V^{-1} (x-\mu)} dx_1 dx_2 dx_3$$

where we have integrated (or, loosely speaking, summed) the trivariate density function over the remaining 2 components, x_2 and x_3. In a sense, we have projected the mass of x_2 and x_3 onto the real line corresponding to x_1. If we performed this double integration we would find that the marginal distribution function for x_1 reduces to

$$F(x_1) = \frac{1}{\sqrt{2\Pi}\,\sigma} \int_{-\infty}^{x_1} e^{-\frac{1}{2}\frac{(x_1-\mu_1)^2}{\sigma_1^2}}\, dx$$

which we can readily recognize as the form for the univariate normal distribution. Consequently, any univariate marginal distribution from a multivariate normal distribution is normally distributed with mean and variance equal to the mean and variance of the corresponding component of the multivariate vector. In the example above, x_1 was found to be normally distributed and the distribution function was found to involve only the parameters μ_1 and σ^2, the mean and variance corresponding to component or variable x_1. We took σ_1^2 from the variance-covariance matrix **V** and $x_1 - \mu_1$ from the vector $[\mathbf{x} - \mu]$ and substituted them into the formula for the univariate density function. There are two other univariate marginal distributions that can be obtained from the trivariate normal distribution. They are the univariate distributions for x_2 and x_3. Besides the three univariate distributions, there are three possible marginal bivariate distributions, $[x_1, x_2]$, $[x_2, x_3]$, and $[x_1, x_3]$. We can derive the density or distribution function for any one of these three bivariate distributions by following the principle illustrated above. For example, the marginal bivariate distribution function for $[x_1, x_2]$ is given by

$$F(x_1, x_2) = \frac{1}{(2\Pi)^{\frac{3}{2}} |\mathbf{V}|^{\frac{1}{2}}} \int_{-\infty}^{x_1} \int_{-\infty}^{x_2} \int_{-\infty}^{\infty} e^{-\frac{1}{2}(\mathbf{x}-\mu)'\mathbf{V}^{-1}(\mathbf{x}-\mu)}\, dx_1\, dx_2\, dx_3$$

Integrating or summing over the third variable, the reader can take it upon faith that this reduces to

$$F(x_1, x_2) = \frac{1}{2\Pi |\mathbf{V}_{1,2}|^{\frac{1}{2}}} \int_{-\infty}^{x_1} \int_{-\infty}^{x_2} e^{-\frac{1}{2}(\mathbf{x}-\mu)'_{1,2}\mathbf{V}^{-1}_{1,2}(\mathbf{x}-\mu)_{1,2}}\, dx_1\, dx_2$$

where $[\mathbf{x} - \mu]_{1,2}$ is the subvector involving the first two components of $[\mathbf{x} - \mu]$, that is, $x_1 - \mu_2$ and $x_2 - \mu_2$, and $\mathbf{V}_{1,2}$ is the submatrix of **V** involving x_1 and x_2. In other words, we have partitioned the variance-covariance matrix,

V, and vector $[\mathbf{x} - \mu]$ as below and taken the 2×2 submatrix as $\mathbf{V}_{1,2}$ and the 2×1 vector as $\lfloor \mathbf{x} - \mu \rfloor_{1,2}$.

$$\left[\begin{array}{cc|c} \sigma_1^2 & \rho_{12}\sigma_1\sigma_2 & \rho_{13}\sigma_1\sigma_3 \\ \rho_{21}\sigma_2\sigma_1 & \sigma_2^2 & \rho_{23}\sigma_2\sigma_3 \\ \hline \rho_{31}\sigma_3\sigma_1 & \rho_{32}\sigma_2\sigma_2 & \sigma_3^2 \end{array}\right] \left[\begin{array}{c} x_1 - \mu_1 \\ x_2 - \mu_2 \\ \hline x_3 - \mu_3 \end{array}\right]$$

The above results generalize to multivariate distributions of any arbitrary dimension. For example, if the vector $[x_1, x_2, x_3, x_4, x_5]$ is multivariate normally distributed, then it has normally distributed marginal distributions for $[x_1, x_2, x_3, x_4]$, $[x_2, x_3, x_4]$, $[x_3, x_5]$, and so on.

While the formulas look forbidding, the principles are identical to those discussed in relation to discrete variables in Chapter 2 of *Introduction to Linear Models.* That is, we sum over all the other variables not included in the marginal distribution to obtain the density or distribution function.

Perhaps we can gain a better intuitive understanding of this concept for continuous variables by examining a univariate marginal distribution obtained from a bivariate distribution as portrayed in Figure 2.5. The figure attempts to portray the projection of the bivariate density onto the line x_1 where this projected mass forms a univariate normal distribution. For example, the bivariate mass portrayed by the darkened normally shaped area under the surface of $f(x_1, x_2)$ is projected onto the line x_1 at the point a. The height of the line at point a, which represents the univariate density of x_1 at point a, signifies that relatively little mass is contained in the bivariate density on a line perpendicular to point a_1 in the x_1x_2 plane. As we move toward the middle of the bivariate density where more mass is contained, more bivariate mass is projected onto x_1 and consequently the univariate density becomes relatively large at the corresponding point of the x_1 line. For higher-dimensional situations we cannot geometrically portray the situation, but the conceptualization is analogous. For example, the univariate distribution of x_1 from the multivariate distribution $[x_1, x_2, x_3, x_4, x_5]$ can be formed by projecting the mass contained under the surface of $f(x_1, x_2, x_3, x_4, x_5)$ perpendicularly onto the line x_1.

2.6 CONDITIONAL DISTRIBUTIONS

Multivariate normal distributions also have conditional distributions for subsets of the components of **x**. These conditional distributions are also normally distributed. "Conditional distribution" refers to the density function or distribution function of certain components of **x** given that the remaining

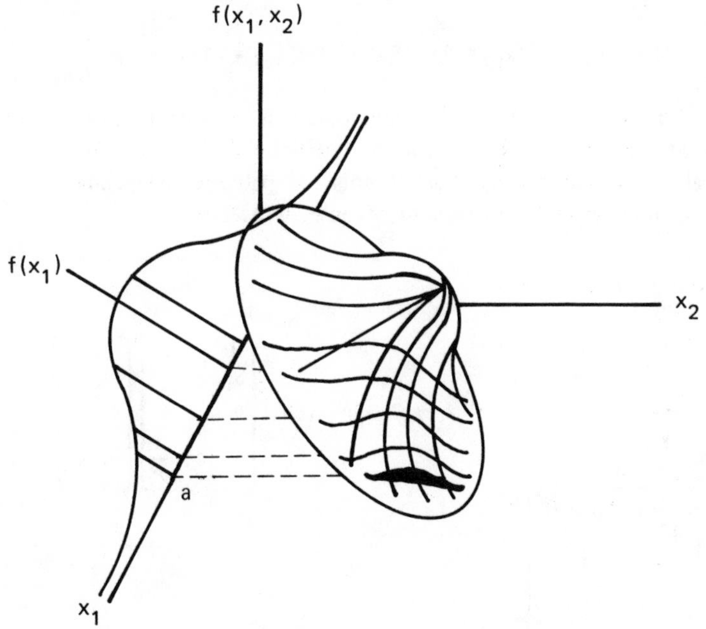

Figure 2.5 Univariate Normal Marginal Distribution from a Bivariate Normal Distribution

components of **x** take on certain specific values. For example, in the bivariate case, we might be interested in the distribution of x_2 given that x_1 has the observed value of 5. In a higher-dimensional case, we might be interested in the density function of $[x_1, x_2, x_3]$ given that $x_4 = 5$ and $x_5 = 0$.

We might surmise from our earlier discussion on probability (in Chapter 2 of *Introduction to Linear Models*) that if the components of the vector $[x_1, x_2, \ldots, x_p]$ are independent of each other, then the density function of any components of $[x_1, x_2, \ldots, x_p]$ are independent of the values that the remaining variables may take. The components of $[x_1, x_2, \ldots, x_p]$ are, however, independent of each other only if the variance-covariance matrix is a diagonal matrix. That is, all covariances among the components are zero. (For multivariate normal distributions, zero correlations imply independence among the variables. This is not true generally for nonnormal multivariate distributions.)

From our previous discussion of probability, we know that if the components of $[x_1, x_2, \ldots, x_p]$ are independent, then

$$f(x_1, x_2, \ldots, x_p) = f(x_1)f(x_2)\ldots f(x_p) = \prod_{i=1}^{p} f(x_i)$$

That is, the joint density of the components is equal to the product of the univariate densities. This can easily be illustrated algebraically for a trivariate normal distribution whose components are pairwise independent. In this instance, the trivariate normal density can be written as

$$f(x_1, x_2, x_3)$$

$$= \frac{1}{(2\Pi)^{\frac{3}{2}} \begin{vmatrix} \sigma_1^2 & 0 & 0 \\ 0 & \sigma_2^2 & 0 \\ 0 & 0 & \sigma_3^2 \end{vmatrix}^{\frac{1}{2}}} e^{-\frac{1}{2}[x_1-\mu_1, x_2-\mu_2, x_3-\mu_3] \begin{bmatrix} \frac{1}{\sigma_1^2} & 0 & 0 \\ 0 & \frac{1}{\sigma_2^2} & 0 \\ 0 & 0 & \frac{1}{\sigma_3^2} \end{bmatrix} \begin{bmatrix} x_1-\mu_1 \\ x_2-\mu_2 \\ x_3-\mu_3 \end{bmatrix}}$$

$$= \frac{1}{(2\Pi)^{\frac{3}{2}}(\sigma_1\sigma_2\sigma_3)} e^{-\frac{1}{2}\left[\frac{(x_1-\mu_1)^2}{\sigma_1^2} + \frac{x_2-\mu_2)^2}{\sigma_2^2} + \frac{(x_3-\mu_3)^2}{\sigma_3^2}\right]}$$

$$= \left[\frac{1}{\sqrt{2\Pi}\,\sigma_1} e^{-\frac{1}{2}\frac{(x_1-\mu_1)^2}{\sigma_1^2}}\right]\left[\frac{1}{\sqrt{2\Pi}\,\sigma_2} e^{-\frac{1}{2}\frac{(x_2-\mu_2)^2}{\sigma_2^2}}\right]\left[\frac{1}{\sqrt{2\Pi}\,\sigma_3} e^{-\frac{1}{2}\frac{x_3-\mu_3)^2}{\sigma_3^2}}\right]$$

$$= f(x_1)f(x_2)f(x_3)$$

Generalizing still further from the concepts of probability theory, the density of x_1 given x_2 can be expressed as $f(x_1|x_2) = f(x_1, x_2)/f(x_2)$. Assuming independence, we have shown above that $f(x_1, x_2) = f(x_1)f(x_2)$ so that

$$f(x_1|x_2) = \frac{f(x_1)f(x_2)}{f(x_2)} = f(x_1).$$

We can see that in the case of independence, x_2 provides no information concerning the density of x_1. For the trivariate normal distribution, the following conditional densities can be ascertained: $f(x_1|x_2, x_3)$, $f(x_2|x_1, x_3)$, $f(x_3|x_1, x_2)$, $f(x_1, x_2|x_3)$, $f(x_1, x_3|x_2)$, and $f(x_2, x_3|x_1)$ where, for example, $f(x_1|x_2, x_3)$ represents the density of the component or random variable x_1 given x_2 and x_3, and $f(x_1, x_2|x_3)$ represents the bivariate density of x_1, x_2 given x_3. If x_3 is independent of both x_1 and x_2, then

$$f(x_1, x_2|x_3) = \frac{f(x_1, x_2)f(x_3)}{f(x_3)} = f(x_1, x_2).$$

Similarly, if x_1 is independent of x_2 and x_3, then

$$f(x_1|x_2, x_3) = \frac{f(x_1)f(x_2, x_3)}{f(x_2, x_3)} = f(x_1)$$

and so on.

The notion of conditional distributions can be generalized easily to random vectors of any dimension. For example, let $\mathbf{x} = [x_1, x_2, x_3, x_4, x_5, x_6]$ be partitioned into $\mathbf{x}_1 = [x_1, x_2, x_3]$ and $\mathbf{x}_2 = [x_4, x_5, x_6]$, then

$$f(\mathbf{x}_1|\mathbf{x}_2) = \frac{f(\mathbf{x})}{f(\mathbf{x}_2)} \text{ and } f(\mathbf{x}_2|\mathbf{x}_1) = \frac{f(\mathbf{x})}{f(\mathbf{x}_1)}$$

For example, $f(x_1 = 8, x_2 = 6, x_3 = 7|x_4 = 9, x_5 = 2, x_6 = 3)$ equals

$$\frac{f(x_1, = 8, x_2 = 6, x_3 = 7, x_4 = 9, x_5 = 2, x_6 = 3)}{f(x_4 = 9, x_5 = 2, x_6 = 3)}$$

We simply substitute these specific values into the appropriate density functions and compute the unique value of $f(\mathbf{x}_1|\mathbf{x}_2)$. Conditional densities as well as marginal densities from a multivariate normal distribution are multivariate normal in form. If the correlations, ρ, among the variables were different from 0, then we would suspect that the conditional density of any variable would depend on the value of some or all of the remaining variables. For the bivariate normal distribution, $f(x_1|x_2) = f(x_1)$ and $f(x_2|x_1) = f(x_2)$ if the two components are independent of each other (that is, $\rho = 0$). However, if $\rho \neq 0$), then $f(x_1|x_2) \neq f(x_1)$ and $f(x_2|x_1) \neq f(x_2)$; the density of each random component depends upon or is conditional upon the particular value of the remaining component.

For example, if x_1 and x_2 are not independently distributed, then x_1 given x_2 (that is, $x_1|x_2$) is normally distributed with mean

$$\mu_1 + \frac{\sigma_1}{\sigma_2}\rho(x_2 - \mu_2), \text{ and variance } \sigma_1^2(1 - \rho^2).$$

On the other hand, if x_1 and x_2 were independent, then x_1 would be normally distributed with mean μ_1 and variance σ_1^2 for any value of x_2. We can see from the formula for the conditional mean that given $\rho \neq 0$ its value is dependent upon x_2. We can also see that the conditional variance of x_1 (that is, var $(x_1|x_2)$) is constant for all values of x_2, and that a large ρ results in a small conditional variance.

If we look closely at the formula for the conditional mean, we notice that the conditional mean $\mu_1|x_2$ can be written as $\beta_0 + \beta_1 x_2$ where

$$\beta_0 = \mu_1 - \frac{\sigma_1}{\sigma_2}\rho\mu_2 \text{ and } \beta_1 = \frac{\sigma_1}{\sigma_2}\rho.$$

The conditional mean $\mu_1|x_2$ is a linear function of x_2 and the constants β_0 and β_1 are the intercept and slope of a univariate regression equation, respectively. That is, we can find the conditional mean $\mu_1|x_2$ by regressing component x_1 on component x_2. The error or residual sum of squares associated with this regression is $\sigma_1^2(1-\rho^2)$. Consequently, the conditional variance of x_1 is less than the marginal variance of x_1. Conversely, the conditional mean of x_2 is

$$\mu_2|x_1 = \mu_2 + \frac{\sigma_2}{\sigma_1}\rho(x_1 - \mu_1)$$

and the conditional variance of x_2 is equal to $\sigma_2^2(1-\rho^2)$.

We can generalize to higher-dimensional cases. For example, if x_1 is dependent upon $x_2, x_3, \ldots, x_p$, then the conditional mean of x_1 (that is, $\mu_1|x_2, \ldots, x_p$) is $\beta_0 + \beta_1 x_2 + \beta_2 x_3, \ldots, \beta_{p-1} x_p$ where β_0 is the population regression intercept and $\beta_1, \beta_2, \ldots, \beta_{p-1}$ are the population regression coefficients. The conditional variance of x_1 (that is, $\sigma_{x_1}^2|x_2, \ldots, x_p) = \sigma_\epsilon^2$ is the population error variance for the regression model. It can be shown that these parameters can be estimated by multiple regression analysis. Note that the variance of the conditional variable is constant for all values of the conditioning variables while the mean of the conditional variable is a linear function of the conditioning variables.

2.7 ESTIMATION OF THE MEAN VECTOR AND COVARIANCE MATRIX

In many applied situations, we will not know the value of μ and $\mathbf{V}$ and we will consequently have to estimate the vector μ and the variance-covariance matrix **V** from the sample data. The estimators of the components of μ are simply the sample means corresponding to the respective components. That is,

$$\hat{\mu} = \begin{bmatrix} \hat{\mu}_1 \\ \hat{\mu}_2 \\ \hat{\mu}_3 \\ \cdot \\ \cdot \\ \cdot \\ \hat{\mu}_p \end{bmatrix} = \begin{bmatrix} \sum_{i=1}^{n} x_{1i}/n \\ \sum_{i=1}^{n} x_{2i}/n \\ \sum_{i=1}^{n} x_{3i}/n \\ \\ \\ \\ \sum_{i=1}^{n} x_{pi}/n \end{bmatrix}$$

The elements of **V** are estimated as

$$\hat{\mathbf{V}} = \begin{bmatrix} \hat{\sigma}_1^2 & \hat{\rho}_{12}\hat{\sigma}_1\hat{\sigma}_2 & \hat{\rho}_{13}\hat{\sigma}_1\hat{\sigma}_3 & \cdots \\ \hat{\rho}_{21}\hat{\sigma}_2\hat{\sigma}_1 & \hat{\sigma}_2^2 & \hat{\rho}_{23}\hat{\sigma}_2\hat{\sigma}_3 & \cdots \\ \hat{\rho}_{31}\hat{\sigma}_3\hat{\sigma}_1 & \hat{\rho}_{32}\hat{\sigma}_3\hat{\sigma}_2 & \hat{\sigma}_3^2 & \cdots \\ \cdot & \cdot & \cdot & \cdots \\ \cdot & \cdot & \cdot & \cdots \; \hat{\sigma}_p^2 \end{bmatrix} \text{ or } \begin{bmatrix} \hat{\sigma}_1^2 & \hat{\sigma}_{12} & \hat{\sigma}_{13} & \cdots \\ \hat{\sigma}_{21} & \hat{\sigma}_2^2 & \hat{\sigma}_{23} & \cdots \\ \hat{\sigma}_{31} & \hat{\sigma}_{32} & \hat{\sigma}_3^2 & \cdots \\ \cdot & \cdot & \cdot & \cdots \\ \cdot & \cdot & \cdot & \cdots \; \hat{\sigma}_p^2 \end{bmatrix}$$

which is computationally equivalent to

$$\begin{bmatrix} \frac{\sum_{i=1}^{n}(x_{1i}-\bar{x}_1)^2}{n-1} & \frac{\sum_{i=1}^{n}(x_{1i}-\bar{x}_1)(x_{2i}-\bar{x}_2)^2}{n-1} & \frac{\sum_{i=1}^{n}(x_{1i}-\bar{x}_1)(x_{3i}-\bar{x}_3)}{n-1} & \cdot \\ \frac{\sum_{i=1}^{n}(x_{2i}-\bar{x}_2)(x_{1i}-x_1)}{n-1} & \frac{\sum_{i=1}^{n}(x_{2i}-\bar{x}_2)^2}{n-1} & \frac{\sum_{i=1}^{n}(x_{2i}-\bar{x}_2)(x_{3i}-\bar{x}_3)}{n-1} & \cdot \\ \frac{\sum_{i=1}^{n}(x_{3i}-\bar{x}_3)(x_{1i}-\bar{x}_1)}{n-1} & \frac{\sum_{i=1}^{n}(x_{3i}-\bar{x}_3)(x_{2i}-\bar{x}_2)}{n-1} & \frac{\sum_{i=1}^{n}(x_{3i}-\bar{x}_3)^2}{n-1} & \cdot \\ \cdot & \cdot & \cdot & \frac{\sum_{i=1}^{n}(x_{pi}-x_p)^2}{n-1} \end{bmatrix}$$

These estimators of the mean vector μ and the variance-covariance matrix **V** have the desirable properties of being unbiased, efficient, and consistent.

2.8 PROBLEMS

(1) Using the sample data in the Appendix, estimate the mean vector and covariance matrix for variables 1 through 6 (ability).

(2) Write out the density function, $f(x_1, x_2, x_3, x_4, x_5, x_6]$, for these six variables.

(3) Write out the marginal density function $f(x_1, x_2, x_3)$.

(4) Calculate the density $f(x_1 = 46, x_2 = 57, x_3 = 58)$.

(5) Find the generalized variance for $\mathbf{x} = (x_1, x_2, x_3)$.

(6) Write out the density function for the conditional distribution of variable 1 given that variables 2, 3, and 4 take the values 58, 60, and 57, respectively.

(7) Compute the covariance matrix for the multivariate normally distributed vector $[x_1, x_2, x_3, x_4]$ given the following correlation matrix and vector of standard deviations.

	x_1	x_2	x_3	x_4	
x_1	1.00				$\sigma_1 = 9.8$
x_2	.47	1.00			$\sigma_2 = 6.4$
x_3	.24	.29	1.00		$\sigma_3 = 8.5$
x_4	.30	.21	.41	1.00	$\sigma_4 = 7.3$

(8) Compute the generalized variance from the covariance matrix found in problem 7.

(9) If the vector of means for the four variables in problem 7 is $[\mu_1 = 11.2, \mu_2 = 9.6, \mu_3 = 8.8, \mu_4 = 9.8]$, which vector of observations has the largest density: $[x_1 = 10.1, x_2 = 12.2, x_3 = 9.6, x_4 = 6.9]$ or $[x_1 = 10.0, x_2 = 9.2, x_3 = 9.1, x_4 = 9.2]$? Can you think of a meaningful way to compare two densities?

(10) What are the parameters associated with the marginal distribution of $[x_1, x_2, x_3]$ in problem 7? Use means from problem 9.

(11) Using data from problems 7 and 9, what is the density of $[x_1 = 9.2, x_3 = 8.8, x_4 = 5.8]$ given that $x_2 = 9.7$ (that is, $f[x_1 = 9.2, x_3 = 8.8, x_4 = 5.8 \mid x_2 = 9.7]$)? How does this compare to the unconditional density?

(12) Using data from problems 7 and 9, what is the conditional density, $f(x_1 = 9.2, x_4 = 5.8 \mid x_2 = 9.7, x_3 = 8.8)$?

(13) Using data from problems 7 and 9, find the formula for the conditional mean of x_4 given x_1, x_2, and x_3 (that is, $E[x_4 \mid x_1, x_2, x_3]$). What is the constant variance of this conditional distribution of x_4? Find $E(x_4 \mid x_1 = 13, x_2 = 11.5, x_3 = 9.5)$.

3 Linear Composites

3.1 INTRODUCTION

The purpose of this chapter is to discuss various aspects of linear composites of random variables. Much of the research conducted by behavioral and social scientists makes implicit or explicit use of linear composites of random variables. For example, a psychological test score is a linear composite of the test item responses; a socioeconomic status index is a weighted linear composite of various occupational, educational, and earnings information; and the decisions of a personnel psychologist regarding employment are often based upon a weighting of available information, including test scores.

In section 3.2, the mean and variance of a linear composite are derived and a number of uses are illustrated. Section 3.3 derives and illustrates the covariance and correlation between two linear composites. The reader shall see that the mean and variance of a linear composite and the covariance between two linear composites are functions of the statistical characteristics of the components making up the composite (for example, component means, variances, and covariances). The concept of a linear transformation is discussed in section 3.4. This concept is useful for discussing the situation in which a vector of scores is simultaneously transformed into two or more linear composites. The transformation matrix used to transform the components plays an important role in generating the covariance matrix of the transformed components. The covariance matrix of linear transformations is discussed in section 3.5. The reader will see that it is a generalization of the concepts discussed in sections 3.2 and 3.3. The material discussed in this chapter will be useful in the study of the remaining models in the book.

3.2 MEAN AND VARIANCE OF A LINEAR COMPOSITE

A linear composite of random variables can be expressed as $\mathbf{b}'\mathbf{x}$ where $\mathbf{b}$ is a vector of weights and $\mathbf{x}$ is a random vector from a multivariate distribution. The population mean of $\mathbf{b}'\mathbf{x}$ is $E(\mathbf{b}'\mathbf{x}) = \mathbf{b}'E(\mathbf{x}) = \mathbf{b}'\mu$, where E is the expectation operator and μ is the vector of means for the random vector $\mathbf{x}$.

The expectation operator, E, simply averages the values of the random variable across the population. If μ is not known, then substituting the vector of sample means for the population means will give an unbiased estimator of $\mathbf{b}'\mu$. As an example, let us assume that we want to construct an index of creativity on the basis of four creativity tests given to a large sample of schoolchildren. The means of the four tests are 10, 5, 15, and 20, and the researcher weights their relative importance as .5, 1.0, and .1, and .2, respectively. Then the mean of this composite would be

$$\mathbf{b}'\bar{\mathrm{x}} = [.5, 1.0, .1, .2] \begin{bmatrix} 10 \\ 5 \\ 15 \\ 20 \end{bmatrix} = 15.5$$

Let us now derive the variance of a linear composite of random variables. We will begin with a two-dimensional random vector and generalize to the case of an arbitrary dimension p. Since the population mean or expectation of $b_1x_1 + b_2x_2$ is $b_1\mu_1 + b_2\mu_2$, the variance of $b_1x_1 + b_2x_2$ can now be expressed as

$$\begin{aligned} E[b_1x_1 + b_2x_2 - (b_1\mu_1 + b_2\mu_2)]^2 &= E[b_1(x_1 - \mu_1) + b_2(x_2 - \mu_2)]^2 \\ &= E[b_1^2(x_1 - \mu_1)^2 + 2b_1b_2(x_1 - \mu_1)(x_2 - \mu_2) + b_2^2(x_2 - \mu_2)^2] \\ &= b_1^2E(x_1 - \mu_1)^2 + 2b_1b_2E(x_1 - \mu_1)(x_2 - \mu_2) + b_2^2E(x_2 - \mu_2)^2 \\ &= b_1^2\sigma_1^2 + b_2^2\sigma_2^2 + 2b_1b_2\sigma_{12} = [b_1, b_2] \begin{bmatrix} \sigma_1^2 & \sigma_{12} \\ \sigma_{21} & \sigma_2^2 \end{bmatrix} \begin{bmatrix} b_1 \\ b_2 \end{bmatrix} \quad \text{since } \sigma_{12} = \sigma_{21} \end{aligned}$$

where σ_{12} is the covariance between the two components of the random vector $[x_1, x_2]$.

For a three-component random vector $[x_1, x_2, x_3]$, the reader should verify that the variance of the linear composite $\mathbf{b}'\mathbf{x} = b_1x_1 + b_2x_2 + b_3x_3$ would be

$$\begin{aligned} & b_1^2\sigma_1^2 + b_2^2\sigma_2^2 + b_3^2\sigma_3^2 + 2b_1b_2\sigma_{12} + 2b_1b_3\sigma_{13} + 2b_2b_3\sigma_{23} \\ &= [b_1, b_2, b_3] \begin{bmatrix} \sigma_1^2 & \sigma_{12} & \sigma_{13} \\ \sigma_{21} & \sigma_2^2 & \sigma_{23} \\ \sigma_{31} & \sigma_{32} & \sigma_3^2 \end{bmatrix} \begin{bmatrix} b_1 \\ b_2 \\ b_3 \end{bmatrix} \end{aligned}$$

since the covariance matrix is symmetric. Generalizing from the two- and three-variable case, we can express the variance of a linear composite as $\mathbf{b}'\mathbf{V}\mathbf{b}$ where $\mathbf{b}'$ is a row vector of weights and $\mathbf{V}$ is the covariance matrix of the

TABLE 3.1 Creativity Test Covariance Matrix

	Test			
Test	1	2	3	4
1	25	10	30	50
2	10	50	40	30
3	30	40	100	60
4	50	30	60	125

TABLE 3.2 Items Means and Covariances for Five Test Items

$$\mathbf{p} = \begin{bmatrix} .20 \\ .40 \\ .30 \\ .60 \\ .10 \end{bmatrix} \quad \text{and} \quad \mathbf{P} = \begin{bmatrix} .16 & .10 & .08 & .12 & .11 \\ .10 & .24 & .15 & .20 & .10 \\ .08 & .15 & .21 & .06 & .08 \\ .12 & .20 & .06 & .24 & .12 \\ .11 & .10 & .08 & .12 & .21 \end{bmatrix}$$

random vector. Suppose that our four creativity tests had the covariance matrix as presented in Table 3.1. Then the variance of the linear composite $\mathbf{b}'\mathbf{x} = .5x_1 + 1.0x_2 + .1x_3 + .2x_4$, whose mean was previously found to be 15.5, would be

$$\mathbf{b}'\mathbf{V}\mathbf{b} = [.5, 1.0, .1, .2] \begin{bmatrix} 25 & 10 & 30 & 50 \\ 10 & 50 & 40 & 30 \\ 30 & 40 & 100 & 60 \\ 50 & 30 & 60 & 125 \end{bmatrix} \begin{bmatrix} .5 \\ 1.0 \\ .1 \\ .2 \end{bmatrix} = 107.65$$

If the distribution of $\mathbf{x} = [x_1, x_2, \ldots, x_p]$ is multivariate normal, then it can be shown that $\mathbf{b}'\mathbf{x}$ is normally distributed with mean, $\mathbf{b}'\mu$, and variance, $\mathbf{b}'\mathbf{V}\mathbf{b}$. A useful application of these vector and matrix expressions for the mean and variance of a linear composite is in the field of psychometrics. Since in many instances the total test score is the sum of correct items, the mean and variance of a test can be expressed as $\mathbf{1}'\mathbf{p}$ and $\mathbf{1}'\mathbf{P}\mathbf{1}$, respectively, where $\mathbf{1}$ is a column vector of 1s, $\mathbf{p}$ is a vector whose elements are the proportion of correct responses for the respective test items, and $\mathbf{P}$ is the covariance matrix of the test items. For example, suppose that we have a reading test made up of five test items with the item means and covariance matrix given in Table 3.2. The elements of $\mathbf{p}$ are the proportions correct for each of the five test items and $\mathbf{P}$ is the covariance matrix for the five test items. For example, .16 is the variance for item 1 and the element in row 1 and column 2 (.10) is the covariance of item 1 with item 2. These variances and covariances can be computed by the standard formulas, but for binary data (that is, 0 = incorrect, 1 = correct) the variances and covariances simplify to $\sigma_i = p_i(1 - p_i)$ and $\sigma_{ij} = p_{ij} - p_i p_j$, respectively, where p_{ij} is the proportion of times that both items i and j are answered correctly. The mean of the test is

$$\mathbf{1'p}\ [1,\ 1,\ 1,\ 1,\ 1] \begin{bmatrix} .20 \\ .40 \\ .30 \\ .60 \\ .70 \end{bmatrix} = .20 + .40 + .30 + .60 + .70 = 2.20,$$

and the variance is

$$\mathbf{1'P1}\ [1,\ 1,\ 1,\ 1,\ 1] \begin{bmatrix} .16 & .10 & .08 & .12 & .11 \\ .10 & .24 & .15 & .20 & .10 \\ .08 & .15 & .21 & .06 & .08 \\ .12 & .20 & .06 & .24 & .12 \\ .11 & .10 & .08 & .12 & .21 \end{bmatrix} \begin{bmatrix} 1 \\ 1 \\ 1 \\ 1 \\ 1 \end{bmatrix} = 3.30$$

The standard deviation is equal to $\sqrt{3.30}$, or 1.82. This method of computing the mean and standard deviation of the test yields the same values as those that would be obtained if each individual's total test score was first computed and the mean and standard deviation then calculated on the basis of total test scores. The advantage of examining the mean and variance of the test score as was done above is that the effects on the mean and variance of the test from the deletion or addition of test items can be quickly determined by the above expressions for the mean and variance of a test. The tests do not have to be rescored.

3.3 COVARIANCE AND CORRELATION BETWEEN LINEAR COMPOSITES

The covariance of two linear composites can be derived in a manner similar to the method shown earlier for the derivation of the variance of a linear composite. If we had two linear composites, each comprising two variables, then the covariance between $b_1x_1 + b_2x_2$ and $b_3x_3 + b_4x_4$ can be defined as

$$E[b_1x_1 + b_2x_2 - (b_1\mu_1 + b_2\mu_2)]\,[b_3x_3 + b_4x_4 - (b_3\mu_3 + b_4\mu_4)]$$

where $b_1\mu_1 + b_2\mu_2$ is the mean of the composite $b_1x_1 + b_2x_2$ and $b_3\mu_3 + b_4\mu_4$ is the mean of the composite $b_3x_3 + b_4x_4$. Furthermore,

$$\begin{aligned} &E[b_1x_1 + b_2x_2 - (b_1\mu_1 + b_2\mu_2)][b_3x_3 + b_4x_4 - (b_3\mu_3 + b_4\mu_4)] \\ &\quad = E[b_1(x_1 - \mu_1) + b_2(x_2 - \mu_2)][b_3(x_3 - \mu_3) + b_4(x_4 - \mu_4)] \\ &\quad = E[b_1b_3(x_1 - \mu_1)(x_3 - \mu_3)] + E[b_1b_4(x_1 - \mu_1)(x_4 - \mu_4)] \\ &\qquad + E[b_2b_3(x_2 - \mu_2)(x_3 - \mu_3)] + E[b_2b_4(x_2 - \mu_2)(x_4 - \mu_4)] \\ &\quad = b_1b_3E(x_1 - \mu_1)(x_3 - \mu_3) + b_1b_4E(x_1 - \mu_1)(x_4 - \mu_4) \\ &\qquad + b_2b_3E(x_2 - \mu_2)(x_3 - \mu_3) + b_2b_4E(x_2 - \mu_2)(x_4 - \mu_4) \\ &\quad = b_1b_3\sigma_{13} + b_1b_4\sigma_{14} + b_2b_3\sigma_{23} + b_2b_4\sigma_{24} \end{aligned}$$

where σ_{13} is the covariance between variables 1 and 3, σ_{14} is the covariance between variables 1 and 4, and so on. The above expression for the covariance between the two composites can be written in matrix notation as

$$\mathbf{b}_1'\mathbf{V}_{12}\mathbf{b}_2$$

where $\mathbf{b}_1' = [b_1, b_2]$, $\mathbf{V}_{12} = \begin{bmatrix} \sigma_{13} & \sigma_{14} \\ \sigma_{23} & \sigma_{24} \end{bmatrix}$, and $\mathbf{b}_2 = \begin{bmatrix} b_3 \\ b_4 \end{bmatrix}$

The matrix $\mathbf{V}_{12}$ is composed of the covariances between the two sets of variables. The covariance matrix for the vector $[x_1, x_2, x_3, x_4]$ can be partitioned as

$$\mathbf{V} = \left[\begin{array}{cc|cc} \sigma_1^2 & \sigma_{12} & \sigma_{13} & \sigma_{14} \\ \sigma_{21} & \sigma_2^2 & \sigma_{23} & \sigma_{24} \\ \hline \sigma_{31} & \sigma_{32} & \sigma_3^2 & \sigma_{34} \\ \sigma_{41} & \sigma_{42} & \sigma_{43} & \sigma_4^2 \end{array}\right]$$

The cross covariance matrix, $\mathbf{V}_{12}$, is the 2 x 2 matrix in the upper right of the matrix $\mathbf{V}$. The covariance matrix in the upper left corresponds to the two variables (x_1 and x_2) in the first linear composite and the covariance matrix in the lower right corresponds to the two variables (x_3 and x_4) in the second linear composite. Because $\mathbf{V}$ is symmetric, $\mathbf{V}_{12} = \mathbf{V}_{21}$.

Suppose that a personnel psychologist had a large sample of data available on two tests or measures: x_1–intelligence (IQ); and x_2–interaction orientation (IO). Furthermore, suppose that he also had a large sample of data avail-

TABLE 3.3 Covariance Matrix of Four Variables

		x_1	x_2	x_3	x_4
IQ	x_1	10	4	1	2
IQ	x_2	4	10	3	1
S	x_3	1	3	5	1
P	x_4	2	1	1	5

able on a group of salespersons for two performance ratings (that is, criteria): x_3–amount of sales (S); and x_4–potential for supervisory position (P).

The personnel psychologist believes that amount of sales (x_3) is twice as important as potential for supervisory position (x_4). Consequently, he believes that interaction orientation (x_2) is twice as important as intelligence (x_1) in predicting job success. As a result, he might want to calculate the correlation between the two linear composites $x_1 + 2x_2$ and $2x_3 + x_4$. The first step in calculating the correlation would be to calculate the covariance between $x_1 + 2x_2$ and $2x_3 + x_4$. If the covariance matrix for the four measures was as shown in Table 3.3, then the covariance between $x_1 + 2x_2$ and $2x_3 + x_4$ can be expressed as

$$[1 \quad 2]\begin{bmatrix} 1 & 2 \\ 3 & 1 \end{bmatrix}\begin{bmatrix} 2 \\ 1 \end{bmatrix} = 18$$

More generally, let $\mathbf{x}$ have a multivariate normal distribution and be partitioned into $[\mathbf{x}_1, \mathbf{x}_2]$, then it can be shown that $\mathbf{b}_1'\mathbf{x}_1$ and $\mathbf{b}_2'\mathbf{x}_2$ have a bivariate normal distribution with means $\mathbf{b}_1'\mu_1$ and $\mathbf{b}_2'\mu_2$; variances $\mathbf{b}_1'\mathbf{V}_1\mathbf{b}_1$ and $\mathbf{b}_2'\mathbf{V}_2\mathbf{b}_2$; and covariance $\mathbf{b}_1'\mathbf{V}_{12}\mathbf{b}_2$; where $\mathbf{b}_1$ and $\mathbf{b}_2$ are the weighting vectors for $\mathbf{x}_1$ and $\mathbf{x}_2$, respectively; μ_1 and μ_2 are the means of $\mathbf{x}_1$ and $\mathbf{x}_2$, respectively; $\mathbf{V}_1$ and $\mathbf{V}_2$ are the variance-covariance matrices of $\mathbf{x}_1$ and $\mathbf{x}_2$, respectively; and $\mathbf{V}_{12}$ is the cross-covariance matrix between $\mathbf{x}_1$ and $\mathbf{x}_2$.

In order to find the correlation between these two composites, we need to develop the formula for the correlation between two linear composites each composed of two variables.

The correlation can be expressed as

$$r_{(b_1x_1 + b_2x_2,\, b_3x_3 + b_4x_4)} = \frac{\sigma_{(b_1x_1 + b_2x_2,\, b_3x_3 + b_4x_4)}}{\sqrt{\sigma^2_{(b_1x_1 + b_2x_2)}}\sqrt{\sigma^2_{(b_3x_3 + b_4x_4)}}}$$

where the numerator is the covariance between the composite $b_1x_1 + b_2x_2$ and the composite

$$b_3x_3 + b_4x_4, \sqrt{\sigma^2_{(b_1x_1 + b_2x_2)}}$$

is the standard deviation for the composite $b_1x_1 + b_2x_2$ and

$$\sqrt{\sigma^2_{(b_3x_3 + b_4x_4)}}$$

is the standard deviation for the composite $b_3x_3 + b_4x_4$. Since

$$\sigma_{(b_1x_1 + b_2x_2, b_3x_3 + b_4x_4)} = [b_1, b_2] \begin{bmatrix} \sigma_{13} & \sigma_{14} \\ \sigma_{23} & \sigma_{24} \end{bmatrix} \begin{bmatrix} b_3 \\ b_4 \end{bmatrix} = \mathbf{b}_1'\mathbf{V}_{12}\mathbf{b}_2;$$

$$\sqrt{\sigma^2_{(b_1x_1 + b_2x_2)}} = \sqrt{[b_1, b_2] \begin{bmatrix} \sigma_1^2 & \sigma_{12} \\ \sigma_{21} & \sigma_2^2 \end{bmatrix} \begin{bmatrix} b_1 \\ b_2 \end{bmatrix}} = \sqrt{\mathbf{b}_1'\mathbf{V}_1\mathbf{b}_1};$$

and
$$\sqrt{\sigma^2_{(b_3x_3 + b_4x_4)}} = \sqrt{[b_3, b_4] \begin{bmatrix} \sigma_3^2 & \sigma_{34} \\ \sigma_{43} & \sigma_3^2 \end{bmatrix} \begin{bmatrix} b_3 \\ b_4 \end{bmatrix}} = \sqrt{\mathbf{b}_2'\mathbf{V}_2\mathbf{b}_2}$$

the correlation,

$$r_{(b_1x_1 + b_2x_2, b_3x_3 + b_4x_4)} = r_{\mathbf{b}_1'\mathbf{x}_1, \mathbf{b}_2'\mathbf{x}_2} = \frac{\mathbf{b}_1'\mathbf{V}_{12}\mathbf{b}_2}{\sqrt{\mathbf{b}_1'\mathbf{V}_1\mathbf{b}_1}\sqrt{\mathbf{b}_2'\mathbf{V}_2\mathbf{b}_2}}$$

We can now calculate the correlation between the linear composite of the predictor variables $(x_1 + 2x_2)$ and the linear composite of the criterion variables $(2x_3 + x_4)$ for our hypothetical personnel psychology problem. The correlation is

$$r_{(x_1 + 2x_2, 2x_3 + x_4)} = \frac{[1, 2] \begin{bmatrix} 1 & 2 \\ 3 & 1 \end{bmatrix} \begin{bmatrix} 2 \\ 1 \end{bmatrix}}{\sqrt{[1, 2] \begin{bmatrix} 10 & 4 \\ 4 & 10 \end{bmatrix} \begin{bmatrix} 1 \\ 2 \end{bmatrix}} \sqrt{[2, 1] \begin{bmatrix} 5 & 1 \\ 1 & 5 \end{bmatrix} \begin{bmatrix} 2 \\ 1 \end{bmatrix}}}$$

$$= \frac{18}{\sqrt{66}\,\sqrt{29}} = .41$$

The magnitude of this correlation indicates that the hypothesized relationship is not very large. We will examine a model subsequently where a vector $\mathbf{b}_1$ and a vector $\mathbf{b}_2$ are determined such that the correlation between the composite $\mathbf{b}_1'\mathbf{x}_1$ and $\mathbf{b}_2'\mathbf{x}_2$ is maximal. This technique is known as "canonical correlation analysis."

The above formula for the correlation between two linear composites can be generalized to situations in which each of the two linear composites is composed of an arbitrary number of variables. The correlation between two composites of p_1 and p_2 variables, respectively, is

$$\frac{\mathbf{b}_1'\mathbf{V}_{12}\mathbf{b}_2}{\sqrt{\mathbf{b}_1'\mathbf{V}_1\mathbf{b}_1}\sqrt{\mathbf{b}_2'\mathbf{V}_2\mathbf{b}_2}}$$

where $\mathbf{b}_1$ is a p_1 dimensional vector of weights for the first composite; $\mathbf{b}_2$ is a p_2 dimensional vector of weights for the second composite; $\mathbf{V}_{12}$ is a p_1 by p_2 matrix of the cross-covariances of the variables constituting the first composite with the variables constituting the second composite; $\mathbf{V}_1$ is the variance-covariance matrix for the variables constituting the first composite; and $\mathbf{V}_2$ is the variance-covariance matrix for the variables constituting the second composite. The numbers of variables making up each of the composites do not have to be equal. The matrix expression is completely general. For example, the correlation between x_1 and $x_2 + x_3 + x_4$ is

$$r_{(x_1, x_2+x_3+x_4)} = \frac{(1)[\sigma_{12}, \sigma_{13}, \sigma_{14}]\begin{bmatrix}1\\1\\1\end{bmatrix}}{\sqrt{(1)\sigma_1^2(1)}\sqrt{[1,\ 1,\ 1]\begin{bmatrix}\sigma_2^2 & \sigma_{23} & \sigma_{24}\\ \sigma_{32} & \sigma_3^2 & \sigma_{34}\\ \sigma_{42} & \sigma_{43} & \sigma_4^2\end{bmatrix}\begin{bmatrix}1\\1\\1\end{bmatrix}}}$$

$$= \frac{\sum_{j=2}^{4}\sigma_{1j}}{\sigma_1\sqrt{\sum_{i=2,j=2}^{4}\sigma_{ij}}}$$

In some cases a researcher might want to form more than one composite from the same subset of variables because he or she may feel that one composite does not adequately summarize the information in the original variables of which the composite is composed. For example, if we had a large set of weakly intercorrelated variables, then we might expect that substantial information about this set of variables would be lost if we tried to summarize the information concerning the variables by one linear composite. We shall see in a subsequent chapter that the largest principal component is a linear composite that maximizes the amount of information contained in the original variables. Hence one or more additional principal components, each statistically independent, are needed to represent the data adequately. In order to summarize completely the information residing in p variables, we also need p composite variables. But if k of these composite variables carry little information about the p original variables, then p − k composite variables may be sufficient to represent the information contained in the p original variables.

3.4 LINEAR TRANSFORMATIONS

A linear composite of a set of p random variables can be considered as a linear transformation from a p-dimensional Euclidean space to a one-dimensional space (that is, the real line). It is a mapping of a vector, $[x_1, x_2, \ldots, x_p]$ into a scalar or single number. The linear composite or linear function $y = b_1x_1 + b_2x_2 + \ldots b_px_p$ takes the vector $[x_1, x_2, \ldots, x_p]$ and transforms it into a single number, y. There is no inherent reason we have to be limited to mapping a vector $[x_1, x_2, \ldots, x_p]$ into a single number. We could map this vector into another k-dimensional vector $[y_1, y_2, \ldots, y_k]$. The dimension of k can even be greater than p, but we are usually interested in the situation where k is equal or less than p. We would prefer k to be considerably less than p so that a low-dimensional vector could represent the information in a high-dimensional vector. The linear transformation from a p-dimensional vector to a k-dimensional vector would be expressed as

$$
\begin{aligned}
y_1 &= b_{11}x_1 + b_{12}x_2 + \ldots b_{1p}x_p \\
y_2 &= b_{12}x_1 + b_{22}x_2 + \ldots b_{2p}x_p \\
&\;\;\vdots \\
y_k &= b_{k1}x_1 + b_{k2}x_2 + \ldots b_{kp}x_p
\end{aligned}
$$

This set of linear equations simply shows the rules for obtaining the elements of $[y_1, y_2, \ldots, y_k]$ given the vector $[x_1, x_2, \ldots, x_p]$.

Figure 3.1 portrays geometrically the mapping or transformation of a three-dimensional vector into a two-dimensional vector. We can express the

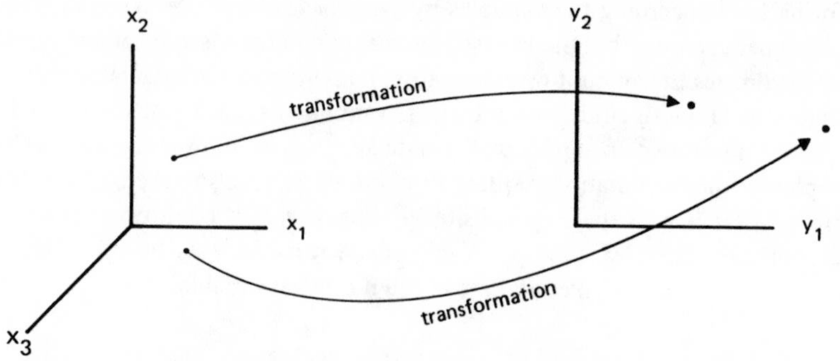

Figure 3.1 Transformation of a Three-Dimensional Vector into a Two-Dimensional Vector

linear transformation of a p-dimensional vector into a k-dimensional vector as $y = \mathbf{B}\mathbf{x}$ where

$$\mathbf{y}' = [y_1, y_2, \ldots, y_k], \mathbf{B} = \begin{bmatrix} b_{11} & b_{12} & \ldots & b_{1p} \\ b_{21} & b_{22} & \ldots & b_{2p} \\ \cdot & \cdot & \ldots & \cdot \\ \cdot & \cdot & \ldots & \cdot \\ b_{k1} & b_{k2} & & b_{kp} \end{bmatrix}$$

and

$$\mathbf{x}' = [x_1, x_2, \ldots, x_p]$$

For the case of linearly transforming a three-dimensional vector into a two-dimensional vector, we would have

$$\mathbf{y} = \begin{bmatrix} y_1 \\ y_2 \end{bmatrix} = \begin{bmatrix} b_{11} & b_{12} & b_{13} \\ b_{21} & b_{22} & b_{23} \end{bmatrix} \begin{bmatrix} x_1 \\ x_2 \\ x_3 \end{bmatrix} = \mathbf{B}\mathbf{x}$$

3.5 COVARIANCE MATRIX OF LINEAR TRANSFORMATIONS

We previously demonstrated that the variance of $y_1 = \mathbf{b}'\mathbf{x}$ where $\mathbf{b}' = [b_1, b_2, \ldots, b_p]$ and $\mathbf{x}' = [x_1, x_2, \ldots, x_p]$ was $\mathbf{b}'\mathbf{V}\mathbf{b}$ where $\mathbf{V}$ is the covariance matrix for the vector $[x_1, x_2, \ldots, x_p]$. We now want to generalize by being able to find the covariance matrix of $\mathbf{y} = \mathbf{Bx}$ where $\mathbf{y}$ is a k-dimensional vector. That is, since we are now constructing two or more composite variables $[y_1, y_2, \ldots, y_k]$ from the original variables, we are interested in finding the covariance matrix $\mathbf{C}$ for our vector of composite variables $[y_1, y_2, \ldots, y_k]$.

Before we consider the general case, let us return to the special case of forming two linear composites from three variables. Since $y_1 = b_{11}x_1 + b_{12}x_2 + b_{13}x_3$, we know that the variance of y_1 equals $\mathbf{b}_1'\mathbf{V}\mathbf{b}_1$ where $\mathbf{b}_1' = [b_{11}, b_{12}, b_{13}]$ and

$$\mathbf{V} = \begin{bmatrix} \sigma_1^2 & \sigma_{12} & \sigma_{13} \\ \sigma_{21} & \sigma_2^2 & \sigma_{23} \\ \sigma_{31} & \sigma_{32} & \sigma_3^2 \end{bmatrix}$$

Similarly, since $y_2 = b_{21}x_1 + b_{22}x_2 + b_{23}x_3$, the variance of y_2 equals $\mathbf{b}_2'\mathbf{V}\mathbf{b}_2$ where $\mathbf{b}_2' = [b_{21}, b_{22}, b_{23}]$ and $\mathbf{V}$ is the same as above.

Since we have found the variance for each of these two composites, all that remains is to find the covariance between them. We previously showed that the covariance between two linear composites of mutually exclusive sets of variables was $\mathbf{b}_1'\mathbf{V}_{12}\mathbf{b}_2$ where $\mathbf{V}_{12}$ was the cross-covariance matrix (that is, the submatrix of $\mathbf{V}$ containing covariances of the variables constituting composite 1 with the variables constituting composite 2). Since each of the two composites is derived from the same three variables, the covariance between the two composites is $\mathbf{b}_1'\mathbf{V}\mathbf{b}_2$. We have now found all of the elements of the 2×2 covariance matrix for the two linear composites. We can now recombine these separate matrix operations into the following single matrix expression:

$$\mathbf{C}_y = \mathbf{B}'\mathbf{V}\mathbf{B}$$

where $\mathbf{C}_y$ is the covariance matrix of the two composite scores, $\begin{bmatrix} \sigma_{y_1}^2 & \sigma_{y_1,y_2} \\ \sigma_{y_2,y_1} & \sigma_{y_2}^2 \end{bmatrix}$

$$\mathbf{B}' = [\mathbf{b}_1, \mathbf{b}_2]' = \begin{bmatrix} b_{11} & b_{12} & b_{13} \\ b_{21} & b_{22} & b_{23} \end{bmatrix} \text{ and } \mathbf{V} = \begin{bmatrix} \sigma_1^2 & \sigma_{12} & \sigma_{13} \\ \sigma_{21} & \sigma_2^2 & \sigma_{23} \\ \sigma_{31}^2 & \sigma_{32} & \sigma_3^2 \end{bmatrix}$$

We can apply this procedure to our personnel psychology problem discussed earlier in this chapter and generate the variance-covariance matrix of the two composites described there directly in one matrix expression as follows: Let $y_1 = x_1 + 2x_2 + 0x_3 + 0x_4$ and $y_2 = 0x_1 + 0x_2 + 2x_3 + 1x_4$; then the covariance matrix of $\mathbf{y}' = [y_1, y_2]$ is

$$\mathbf{C_y} = \begin{bmatrix} \sigma^2_{y_1} & \sigma_{y_1,y_2} \\ \sigma_{y_2,y_1} & \sigma^2_{y_2} \end{bmatrix} = \begin{bmatrix} 1 & 2 & 0 & 0 \\ 0 & 0 & 2 & 1 \end{bmatrix} \begin{bmatrix} 10 & 4 & 1 & 2 \\ 4 & 10 & 3 & 1 \\ 1 & 3 & 5 & 1 \\ 2 & 1 & 1 & 5 \end{bmatrix} \begin{bmatrix} 1 & 0 \\ 2 & 0 \\ 0 & 2 \\ 0 & 1 \end{bmatrix}$$

$$= \begin{bmatrix} 66 & 18 \\ 18 & 29 \end{bmatrix}$$

Next, we might want to convert this covariance matrix into a correlation matrix so that we can easily see the degree of relationship between these two linear functions. If we define $\mathbf{D_y^{-1/2}}$ as a diagonal matrix with the inverse or reciprocal of the standard deviations of the composites y_1 and y_2, respectively, along the principal diagonal, then the correlation matrix for $\mathbf{y}$ is

$$\mathbf{R_y} = \mathbf{D_y^{-1/2} C_y D_y^{-1/2}} = \begin{bmatrix} \frac{1}{\sqrt{66}} & 0 \\ 0 & \frac{1}{\sqrt{29}} \end{bmatrix} \begin{bmatrix} 66 & 18 \\ 18 & 29 \end{bmatrix} \begin{bmatrix} \frac{1}{\sqrt{66}} & 0 \\ 0 & \frac{1}{\sqrt{29}} \end{bmatrix}$$

$$= \begin{bmatrix} 1 & .41 \\ .41 & 1 \end{bmatrix}$$

The above discussion for the case of two composites can be generalized to any number of composites based upon any number of original variables. For example, one might want to summarize the personnel psychologist's data by three linear composites: (1) y_1, an equal weighting of all four variables (that is, $\mathbf{b}_1' = [1, 1, 1, 1]$); (2) y_2, an equal weighting of the two test scores (that is, $\mathbf{b}_2' = [1, 1, 0, 0]$]); and y_3, an equal weighting of the two performance scores (that is, $\mathbf{b}_3' = [0, 0, 1, 1]$). The variance-covariance matrix of these three composites is

$$\mathbf{C_y} = \begin{bmatrix} \sigma^2_{y_1} & \sigma_{y_1,y_2} & \sigma_{y_1,y_3} \\ \sigma_{y_2,y_1} & \sigma^2_{y_2} & \sigma_{y_2,y_3} \\ \sigma_{y_3,y_1} & \sigma_{y_3,y_2} & \sigma^2_{y_3} \end{bmatrix}$$

$$= \begin{bmatrix} 1 & 1 & 1 & 1 \\ 1 & 1 & 0 & 0 \\ 0 & 0 & 1 & 1 \end{bmatrix} \begin{bmatrix} 10 & 4 & 1 & 2 \\ 4 & 10 & 3 & 1 \\ 1 & 3 & 5 & 1 \\ 2 & 1 & 1 & 5 \end{bmatrix} \begin{bmatrix} 1 & 1 & 0 \\ 1 & 1 & 0 \\ 1 & 0 & 1 \\ 1 & 0 & 1 \end{bmatrix}$$

$$= \begin{bmatrix} 54 & 35 & 19 \\ 35 & 28 & 7 \\ 19 & 7 & 12 \end{bmatrix}$$

The correlation matrix is

$$\mathbf{R_y} = \begin{bmatrix} \frac{1}{\sqrt{54}} & 0 & 0 \\ 0 & \frac{1}{\sqrt{28}} & 0 \\ 0 & 0 & \frac{1}{\sqrt{12}} \end{bmatrix} \begin{bmatrix} 54 & 35 & 19 \\ 35 & 28 & 7 \\ 19 & 7 & 12 \end{bmatrix} \begin{bmatrix} \frac{1}{\sqrt{54}} & 0 & 0 \\ 0 & \frac{1}{\sqrt{28}} & 0 \\ 0 & 0 & \frac{1}{\sqrt{12}} \end{bmatrix}$$

$$= \begin{bmatrix} 1 & .90 & .75 \\ .90 & 1 & .38 \\ .75 & .38 & 1 \end{bmatrix}$$

The composite y_1 correlates highly with both y_2 and y_3 because each of the latter two composites has two equally weighted components in common with y_1. On the other hand, y_2 and y_3 have a moderately low correlation because they have no components in common; one is a composite of the test scores and the other is a composite of the performance scores. It should be emphasized again that if $[x_1, x_2, x_3, x_4]$ has a multivariate normal distribution, then so do the linear composites $[y_1, y_2, y_3]$.

The vector of means of the composite variables is $\mu_y = \mathbf{B}'\mu_x$ where

$$\mu_x = \begin{bmatrix} \mu_{x_1} \\ \mu_{x_2} \\ \mu_{x_3} \\ \mu_{x_4} \end{bmatrix} \quad \text{and} \quad \mathbf{B}' = \begin{bmatrix} 1 & 1 & 1 & 1 \\ 1 & 1 & 0 & 0 \\ 0 & 0 & 1 & 1 \end{bmatrix}$$

If the four components of **x** had means of zero, then the three components of **y** would also have means of zero.

3.6 PROBLEMS

(1) Using the sample data in the Appendix, find the means and variances of the following two composites:

$$\sum_{i=1}^{6} x_i, \text{ and } \sum_{i=13}^{16} x_i$$

What is their correlation?

(2) What is the linear transformation matrix associated with transforming the ten variables from problem 1 into the two composites?

(3) From the six ability measures (variables 1 through 6) from problem 1, find the covariance and correlation matrix of the three composites: $x_1 + x_3$; $x_2 + x_4$; and $x_5 + x_6$. What is the associated linear transformation matrix?

(4) Find the means of the three composites.

(5) Kenny (1979) presented some unpublished data on the concerns of 118 terminal cancer patients. Below is a correlation matrix generated from those data.

		X_1	X_2	X_3	X_4
Concern about friends	(x_1)	1.000			
Existential concern	(x_2)	.242	1.000		
Concern about family	(x_3)	.551	.311	1.000	
Concern about self	(x_4)	.577	.416	.719	1.000

(a) What is the correlation between each of the four concern variables and an equally weighted composite of the four variables?

(b) From the pattern of correlations do you think that this linear composite does a pretty good job of summarizing the data?

(c) What is the mean and variance of this linear composite of standardized variables?

(6) In a study conducted by Milburn (1978), data were collected on 140 adult smokers, who were asked to respond on a four-point scale to the following statements about smoking:

x_1: unbearable to run out of cigarettes
x_2: impossible to cut down
x_3: feel more relaxed after smoking

The same three questions were asked one year later; let us label them x_4, x_5, and x_6, respectively. The correlation matrix among the six smoking measures at two time points and the standard deviations are given below.

		x_1	x_2	x_3	x_4	x_5	x_6
Year 1							
unbearable	x_1	1.000					
impossible	x_2	.445	1.000				
relaxed	x_3	.274	.302	1.000			
Year 2							
unbearable	x_4	.601	.268	.340	1.000		
impossible	x_5	.201	.340	.162	.270	1.000	
relaxed	x_6	.222	.249	.484	.268	.293	1.000
Standard deviation		1.053	1.097	.909	.937	1.055	.800

(a) Find the covariance matrix for $x_1 + x_2 + x_3$ and $x_4 + x_5 + x_6$.
(b) What is the correlation between them? Is the composite stable over time?
(c) What is the correlation of each of the six measures with each of the two composites?
(d) Interpret the pattern of correlations in c. Do these two composites make sense conceptually?

4 Multivariate Regression

4.1 INTRODUCTION

In *Introduction to Linear Models*, we spent some time discussing the multiple regression model and some of its extensions. The classical multiple regression model was based upon an $n \times k$ matrix of fixed regressor variables, $\mathbf{X}$, and an associated $n \times 1$ single response vector y. This model can be extended to include any number of response vectors for a given fixed $n \times k$ regressor variable matrix. For example, we might be interested in simultaneously predicting both math (y_1) and reading achievement (y_2) from a particular set of independent variables (for example, socioeconomic status of parents [x_1], ability [x_2], and quality of school [x_3]).

We regress each dependent variable upon the same 3 independent variables. That is,

$$y_1 = \beta_{01} + \sum_{i=1}^{3} \beta_{i1} x_i + \epsilon_1$$

and

$$y_2 = \beta_{02} + \sum_{i=1}^{3} \beta_{i2} x_i + \epsilon_2$$

Each regression equation has the same values for the independent variables, but will in general have different regression weights associated with these variables because the relationships between the single set of independent variables and the dependent variables will differ. For multiple regression, we estimate the regression parameters for only one of the equations and test various hypotheses concerning them. In the present multivariate regression situation we want to estimate two vectors of regression parameters simultaneously and test various joint hypotheses concerning both sets of regression parameters. Let the regression parameter vector of the first equation be

$$\begin{bmatrix} \beta_{01} \\ \beta_{11} \\ \beta_{21} \\ \beta_{31} \end{bmatrix}$$

and the corresponding vector of the second equation be

$$\begin{bmatrix} \beta_{02} \\ \beta_{12} \\ \beta_{22} \\ \beta_{32} \end{bmatrix}$$

One null hypothesis of interest to test statistically is

$$\begin{bmatrix} \beta_{11} \\ \beta_{21} \\ \beta_{31} \end{bmatrix} = \begin{bmatrix} \beta_{12} \\ \beta_{22} \\ \beta_{32} \end{bmatrix} = \begin{bmatrix} 0 \\ 0 \\ 0 \end{bmatrix}$$

This hypothesis states that there are no relationships between the independent and dependent variables in the complete regression system. For convenience we will be considering deviation scores so that the intercept parameters β_{01} and β_{02} drop out of the model, since they are generally of little interest. Let $\mathbf{y}_1$ be the $n \times 1$ vector of deviation responses on the dependent variable for the first model, $\mathbf{y}_2$ the $n \times 1$ vector of deviation responses on the dependent variable for the second model, and $\mathbf{X}$ the common $n \times k$ matrix of deviation scores for the regressor variables. Then the first equation can be expressed as $\mathbf{y}_1 = \mathbf{X}\boldsymbol{\beta}_1 + \boldsymbol{\epsilon}_1$ and the second equation as $\mathbf{y}_2 = \mathbf{X}\boldsymbol{\beta}_2 + \boldsymbol{\epsilon}_2$.

Since we are considering them as a system, let us combine them into one matrix expression $[\mathbf{y}_1, \mathbf{y}_2] = \mathbf{X}[\boldsymbol{\beta}_1, \boldsymbol{\beta}_2] + [\boldsymbol{\epsilon}_1, \boldsymbol{\epsilon}_2]$ or $\mathbf{Y} = \mathbf{X}\boldsymbol{\beta} + \boldsymbol{\epsilon}$, where $\mathbf{Y}$ is an $n \times 2$ response matrix, $\mathbf{X}$ is an $n \times 3$ design matrix, $\boldsymbol{\beta}$ is a 3×2 parameter matrix, and $\boldsymbol{\epsilon}$ is an $n \times 2$ error matrix.

This joint matrix expression is possible because of the common regressor matrix $\mathbf{X}$, and it can be generalized to any number of dependent variables, that is, $[\mathbf{y}_1, \mathbf{y}_2, \ldots, \mathbf{y}_n] = \mathbf{X}[\boldsymbol{\beta}_1, \boldsymbol{\beta}_2, \ldots, \boldsymbol{\beta}_n] + [\boldsymbol{\epsilon}_1, \boldsymbol{\epsilon}_2, \ldots, \boldsymbol{\epsilon}_n]$. In addition, the multivariate regression model, like the multiple regression model, is applicable to the case of a fixed or stochastic $\mathbf{X}$ matrix.

For our example, the system would look like this:

$$
\begin{bmatrix} y_{11} & y_{12} \\ y_{21} & y_{22} \\ y_{31} & y_{32} \\ \cdot & \\ \cdot & \\ \cdot & \\ \cdot & \\ \cdot & \\ \cdot & \\ \cdot & \\ y_{n1} & y_{n2} \end{bmatrix} = \begin{bmatrix} x_{11} & x_{12} & x_{13} \\ x_{21} & x_{22} & x_{23} \\ x_{31} & x_{32} & x_{33} \\ \cdot & \cdot & \cdot \\ \cdot & \cdot & \cdot \\ \cdot & \cdot & \cdot \\ \cdot & \cdot & \cdot \\ \cdot & \cdot & \cdot \\ \cdot & \cdot & \cdot \\ \cdot & \cdot & \cdot \\ x_{n1} & x_{n2} & x_{n3} \end{bmatrix} \begin{bmatrix} \beta_{11} & \beta_{12} \\ \beta_{21} & \beta_{22} \\ \beta_{31} & \beta_{32} \end{bmatrix} + \begin{bmatrix} \epsilon_{11} & \epsilon_{12} \\ \epsilon_{21} & \epsilon_{22} \\ \epsilon_{31} & \epsilon_{32} \\ \cdot & \cdot \\ \cdot & \cdot \\ \cdot & \cdot \\ \cdot & \cdot \\ \cdot & \cdot \\ \cdot & \cdot \\ \cdot & \cdot \\ \epsilon_{n1} & \epsilon_{n2} \end{bmatrix}
$$

where the data are assumed to be in deviation score form.

In the remainder of this chapter we shall examine multivariate regression in detail. We begin by examining the assumptions of the model (section 4.2) and see what these assumptions imply for parameter estimation (section 4.3) and hypothesis testing (section 4.4). We then present a hypothetical example (section 4.5) with three continuous independent variables and two dependent variables, estimate the parameters, and test various hypotheses about them. This discussion is designed to impart greater familiarity with the general nature of the model. The reader will note the similarity to the multiple regression model discussed in *Introduction to Linear Models.*

In section 4.6, a general framework in terms of matrices for expressing any admissible hypotheses concerning the parameters of a multivariate model is presented. This framework is then used to discuss multivariate regression models where the independent variables are categorical. The case of one categorical independent variable is discussed in section 4.7 and generalized to two or more categorical independent variables with balanced data in section 4.8. The more general case of unbalanced designs (that is, correlated independent variables) with two or more categorical independent variables is presented in section 4.9. Section 4.10 discusses general properties and specific aspects of this more general case, including parameter estimation. Hypothesis testing for the general case is discussed in section 4.11. Section 4.12 presents a multivariate growth curve model that is especially appropriate for longitudinal data with many time points. This chapter concludes with a discussion of computer software packages.

4.2 ASSUMPTIONS OF THE MULTIVARIATE REGRESSION MODEL

The assumptions of the multivariate regression model are similar to those of the multiple regression model except for one important difference concerning the correlation of errors across the models. The assumptions are that

$$\mathbf{Y} = \mathbf{X}\beta + \epsilon$$

where

$$E(\epsilon_1) = \mathbf{0},\ E(\epsilon_2) = \mathbf{0} \text{ or equivalently } E(\epsilon) = \mathbf{0};$$

$\mathbf{X}$ is a fixed matrix of rank k (number of regression parameters) so that $\mathbf{X}'\mathbf{X}$ is nonsingular; k is less than the number of sample observations so that error variance may be estimated; and finally

$$E(\epsilon_1 \epsilon_1') = \sigma_{11}^2 \mathbf{I},\quad E(\epsilon_2 \epsilon_2') = \sigma_{22} \mathbf{I},$$

and

$$E(\epsilon_1 \epsilon_2') = \sigma_{12}^2 \mathbf{I} = E(\epsilon_2' \epsilon_1) = \sigma_{21} \mathbf{I}$$

This last assumption concerning the error structure states that the errors within observational units (that is, cases) across the two models are correlated and this correlation gives the multivariate flavor to the model. If $E(\epsilon_1\ \epsilon_2')$ was $\mathbf{0}$, then the two regression systems would be completely independent of one another and hypotheses concerning the regression parameters could be independently tested for each regression equation.

In our example, this assumption means that since math and reading scores are substantially correlated, their residuals based upon the regression model are also likely to be correlated. Note that the assumption $E(\epsilon_1 \epsilon_2') = \sigma_{12} \mathbf{I}$ states that a correlation exists only for residuals observed on the same unit (that is, the same person). That is, the covariance between the reading and math residual score for the ith unit or person is σ_{12}, but the correlation between the reading and math residual scores for the ith and j^{th} persons is zero. Furthermore, the covariances between the two errors are assumed to be identical for all n observations or individuals.

4.3 PARAMETER ESTIMATION

The above model is sometimes expressed in a strung-out fashion as

$$\begin{bmatrix} y_1 \\ y_2 \end{bmatrix} = \begin{bmatrix} \mathbf{X} & 0 \\ 0 & \mathbf{X} \end{bmatrix} \begin{bmatrix} \beta_1 \\ \beta_2 \end{bmatrix} + \begin{bmatrix} \epsilon_1 \\ \epsilon_2 \end{bmatrix}$$

or

$$\mathbf{y}_s = \mathbf{X}_s \boldsymbol{\beta}_s + \boldsymbol{\epsilon}_s$$

where

$$\mathbf{y}_s = \begin{bmatrix} \mathbf{y}_1 \\ \mathbf{y}_2 \end{bmatrix}$$

is now a 2n × 1 response vector,

$$\mathbf{X}_s = \begin{bmatrix} \mathbf{X} & 0 \\ 0 & \mathbf{X} \end{bmatrix}$$

is a 2n × 2k matrix that because of its pattern is sometimes referred to as a block diagonal matrix;

$$\boldsymbol{\beta}_s = \begin{bmatrix} \boldsymbol{\beta}_1 \\ \boldsymbol{\beta}_2 \end{bmatrix}$$

is a 2k × 1 vector of regression parameters; and

$$\boldsymbol{\epsilon}_s = \begin{bmatrix} \boldsymbol{\epsilon}_1 \\ \boldsymbol{\epsilon}_2 \end{bmatrix}$$

is a 2n × 1 vector of errors.

The assumptions concerning the error structure can now be restated as

$$E(\boldsymbol{\epsilon}_s) = \mathbf{0} \text{ and } E(\boldsymbol{\epsilon}_s\boldsymbol{\epsilon}_s') = E\begin{bmatrix} \boldsymbol{\epsilon}_1 \\ \boldsymbol{\epsilon}_1 \end{bmatrix} [\boldsymbol{\epsilon}_1' \ \boldsymbol{\epsilon}_2'] = E\begin{bmatrix} \boldsymbol{\epsilon}_1\boldsymbol{\epsilon}_1' & \boldsymbol{\epsilon}_1\boldsymbol{\epsilon}_2' \\ \boldsymbol{\epsilon}_2\boldsymbol{\epsilon}_1' & \boldsymbol{\epsilon}_2\boldsymbol{\epsilon}_2' \end{bmatrix}$$

$$= \begin{bmatrix} E(\boldsymbol{\epsilon}_1\boldsymbol{\epsilon}_1') & E(\boldsymbol{\epsilon}_1\boldsymbol{\epsilon}_2') \\ E(\boldsymbol{\epsilon}_2\boldsymbol{\epsilon}_1') & E(\boldsymbol{\epsilon}_2\boldsymbol{\epsilon}_2') \end{bmatrix} = \begin{bmatrix} \sigma_{11}\mathbf{I} & \sigma_{12}\mathbf{I} \\ \sigma_{21}\mathbf{I} & \sigma_{22}\mathbf{I} \end{bmatrix}.$$

This last assumption concerning $E(\boldsymbol{\epsilon}_s\boldsymbol{\epsilon}_s')$ in the multivariate regression model is sometimes written as $E(\boldsymbol{\epsilon}_s\boldsymbol{\epsilon}_s') = \boldsymbol{\Omega}_{2\times 2} \otimes \mathbf{I}_{n\times n}$ where $\otimes$ denotes the operation called Kronecker multiplication; $\boldsymbol{\Omega}_{2\times 2}$ is the common 2 × 2 covariance matrix among the residuals of the two independent variables for each observation; and **I** is an n × n identity matrix. The Kronecker product of two matrices **A** of order m × n and **B** of order p × q is defined as

$$\mathbf{A} \otimes \mathbf{B} = \begin{bmatrix} a_{11}\mathbf{B} & a_{12}\mathbf{B} & \cdots & a_{1n}\mathbf{B} \\ a_{21}\mathbf{B} & a_{22}\mathbf{B} & \cdots & a_{2n}\mathbf{B} \\ \cdot & \cdot & \cdot & \cdot \\ \cdot & \cdot & \cdot & \cdot \\ \cdot & \cdot & \cdot & \cdot \\ \cdot & \cdot & \cdot & \cdot \\ a_{m1}\mathbf{B} & a_{m2}\mathbf{B} & \cdots & a_{mn}\mathbf{B} \end{bmatrix}$$

which is of the order mp $\times$ nq.

For our example,

$$\Omega = \begin{bmatrix} \sigma_{11} & \sigma_{12} \\ \sigma_{21} & \sigma_{22} \end{bmatrix},$$

so therefore

$$\Omega \otimes \mathbf{I} = \begin{bmatrix} \sigma_{11} & \sigma_{12} \\ \sigma_{21} & \sigma_{22} \end{bmatrix} \otimes \mathbf{I} = \begin{bmatrix} \sigma_{11}\mathbf{I} & \sigma_{12}\mathbf{I} \\ \sigma_{21}\mathbf{I} & \sigma_{22}\mathbf{I} \end{bmatrix}$$

When the multivariate regression model is expressed in this strung-out fashion, it is in a form equivalent to a single multiple regression analysis. However, since $E(\epsilon_s\epsilon_s') \neq \sigma^2\mathbf{I}_{2n\times 2n}$, but rather equals $\Omega \times \mathbf{I}$, we must use generalized or weighted least squares to estimate β. That is,

$$\hat{\beta}_s = [\mathbf{X}_s'[\Omega \otimes \mathbf{I}]^{-1}\mathbf{X}_s']^{-1}\mathbf{X}_s'[\Omega \otimes \mathbf{I}]^{-1}\mathbf{y}$$

However, after some matrix manipulation, it can be shown that the above expression reduces to

$$\hat{\beta}_s = [\mathbf{X}_s'\mathbf{X}_s]^{-1}\mathbf{X}_s'\mathbf{y}_s$$

the classical least-squares estimator.

Let us examine this solution in more detail. Now,

$$[\mathbf{X}_s'\mathbf{X}_s]^{-1} = \left[\begin{bmatrix} \mathbf{X} & \mathbf{0} \\ \mathbf{0} & \mathbf{X} \end{bmatrix}' \begin{bmatrix} \mathbf{X} & \mathbf{0} \\ \mathbf{0} & \mathbf{X} \end{bmatrix}\right]^{-1} = \begin{bmatrix} \mathbf{X}'\mathbf{X} & \mathbf{0} \\ \mathbf{0} & \mathbf{X}'\mathbf{X} \end{bmatrix}^{-1}$$

$$= \begin{bmatrix} [\mathbf{X}'\mathbf{X}]^{-1} & \mathbf{0} \\ \mathbf{0} & [\mathbf{X}'\mathbf{X}]^{-1} \end{bmatrix}$$

and

$$\mathbf{X}_s'\,\mathbf{y}_s = \begin{bmatrix} \mathbf{X} & \mathbf{0} \\ \mathbf{0} & \mathbf{X} \end{bmatrix}' \begin{bmatrix} \mathbf{y}_1 \\ \mathbf{y}_2 \end{bmatrix} = \begin{bmatrix} \mathbf{X}'\mathbf{y}_1 \\ \mathbf{X}'\mathbf{y}_2 \end{bmatrix}$$

so that

$$\hat{\beta}_s = \begin{bmatrix} \hat{\beta}_1 \\ \hat{\beta}_2 \end{bmatrix} = \begin{bmatrix} [\mathbf{X}'\mathbf{X}]^{-1} & \mathbf{0} \\ \mathbf{0} & [\mathbf{X}'\mathbf{X}]^{-1} \end{bmatrix} \begin{bmatrix} \mathbf{X}'\mathbf{y}_1 \\ \mathbf{X}'\mathbf{y}_2 \end{bmatrix}$$

and consequently

$$\hat{\beta}_1 = [\mathbf{X}'\mathbf{X}]^{-1}\mathbf{X}'\mathbf{y}_1 \text{ and } \hat{\beta}_2 = [\mathbf{X}'\mathbf{X}]^{-1}\mathbf{X}'\mathbf{y}_2$$

But these estimates of β_1 and β_2 are the same as the classical least-squares estimates of the separate multiple regression analyses and so the basic utility of the classical least-squares estimator demonstrates itself once more. In summary, to estimate the regression parameters of a multivariate regression model all we have to do is to conduct a separate multiple regression analysis for each dependent variable. However, because of the nature of the error structure of the residuals, we will see that our hypothesis-testing strategy needs to be modified.

The regression parameters are unbiased since

$$\begin{aligned} E(\hat{\beta}) &= E[[\mathbf{X}'\mathbf{X}]^{-1}\mathbf{X}'\mathbf{Y}] \\ &= E[\beta + [\mathbf{X}'\mathbf{X}]^{-1}\mathbf{X}'\epsilon] \end{aligned}$$

since $\mathbf{Y} = \mathbf{X}\beta + \epsilon$. Continuing,

$$E(\beta + (\mathbf{X}'\mathbf{X})^{-1}\mathbf{X}'\epsilon) = \beta + [\mathbf{X}'\mathbf{X}]^{-1}\mathbf{X}'E(\epsilon) = \beta$$

since $E(\epsilon) = \mathbf{0}$ and $\mathbf{X}$ is a fixed matrix by assumption. The residual covariance matrix, Ω, is also a matrix of parameters that can be estimated. However, a discussion of its estimation seems more natural for the next section.

4.4 HYPOTHESIS TESTING

Let us first discuss the testing of the overall hypothesis that

$$\beta = \begin{bmatrix} \beta_{11} & \beta_{21} \\ \beta_{12} & \beta_{22} \\ \beta_{13} & \beta_{23} \end{bmatrix} = \mathbf{0}$$

In *Introduction to Linear Models*, we saw in the single multiple regression case that the hypothesis

$$\begin{bmatrix} \beta_1 \\ \beta_2 \\ \beta_3 \end{bmatrix} = \mathbf{0}$$

could be tested by appealing to the univariate F statistic whose numerator was the regression sum of squares about the mean divided by its degrees of freedom and the denominator was the error sum of squares divided by its degrees of freedom. That is, assuming all variables are in deviation score form,

$$\frac{\hat{\beta}'\mathbf{X}'y/k}{e'e/n-k-1} \quad \text{or} \quad \frac{(n-k-1)\,\hat{\beta}'\mathbf{X}'y}{k\,e'e}$$

is distributed as F with k and $n - k - 1$ degrees of freedom. From this point on we shall assume deviation scores for both the dependent and independent variables. It was previously shown (in *Introduction to Linear Models*) that the total sum of squares about the mean could be decomposed into a regression sum of squares and an error sum of squares. That is,

$$y'y = \hat{\beta}'\,\mathbf{X}'y + e'e$$

Also, we showed previously that $\hat{\beta}'\mathbf{X}'y = \hat{y}'\hat{y}$ where $\hat{y}$ is the vector of predicted variables scores, so that the above quality can be expressed as

$$y'y = \hat{y}'\hat{y} + e'e$$

We can generalize to the multivariate regression situation by noting that we have the following matrices corresponding to the above vectors:

$$\mathbf{Y} = [y_1, y_2] \text{ or more generally } [y_1, y_2, \ldots, y_p];$$

$$\hat{\mathbf{Y}} = [\hat{y}_1, \hat{y}_2] \text{ or more generally } [\hat{y}_1, \hat{y}_2, \ldots, y_p]; \text{ and}$$

$$\mathbf{E} = [e_1, e_2] \text{ or more generally } [e_1, e_2, \ldots, e_p].$$

The reader can verify that the matrix product $\mathbf{Y}'\mathbf{Y}$ can be decomposed in an analogous manner as

$$\mathbf{Y}'\mathbf{Y} = \hat{\mathbf{Y}}'\hat{\mathbf{Y}} + \mathbf{E}'\mathbf{E}$$

or

$$\begin{bmatrix} y_1' \\ y_2' \end{bmatrix} [y_1, y_2] = \begin{bmatrix} \hat{y}_1' \\ \hat{y}_2' \end{bmatrix} [\hat{y}_1, \hat{y}_2] + \begin{bmatrix} e_1' \\ e_2' \end{bmatrix} [e_1, e_2]$$

which gives

$$\mathbf{Y'Y} = \begin{bmatrix} y_1'y_1 & y_1'y_2 \\ y_2'y_1 & y_2'y_2 \end{bmatrix} = \begin{bmatrix} \hat{y}_1'\hat{y}_1 & \hat{y}_1'\hat{y}_1 \\ \hat{y}_2'\hat{y}_1 & \hat{y}_2'\hat{y}_2 \end{bmatrix} + \begin{bmatrix} e_1'e_1 & e_1'e_2 \\ e_2'e_1 & e_2'e_2 \end{bmatrix}.$$

We can see that the total cross-products matrix $\mathbf{Y'Y}$ is the sum of a cross-products matrix due to regression and a cross-products matrix due to error. It can be easily seen that this is analogous to the univariate decomposition of the total sum of squares about the mean.

We can develop the analogy further into the domain of hypothesis testing. For univariate multiple regression, the test statistic for the hypothesis $\beta_1 = 0$ involved the ratio of the regression sum of squares to the error sum of squares multiplied by a constant. Under the multivariate regression hypothesis that $\beta = [\beta_1, \beta_2] = 0$, it can be shown that certain univariate functions of $[\hat{\mathbf{Y}}'\hat{\mathbf{Y}}]$ $[\mathbf{E'E}]^{-1}$ are distributed in known ways. The matrix due to regression $[\hat{\mathbf{Y}}'\hat{\mathbf{Y}}]$ is conventionally referred to as the matrix due to the hypothesis and denoted as $\mathbf{H}$, while the error matrix $[\mathbf{E'E}]$ is usually referred to as $\mathbf{E}$, so that the test statistic is some function of $\mathbf{HE}^{-1}$.

In the case of two dependent variables, $\mathbf{HE}^{-1}$ is a 2 x 2 matrix but in the more general case of p variables, it would be a p x p matrix. It should also be pointed out that if the elements of $\mathbf{E}$ were divided by the appropriate degrees of freedom, then an unbiased estimate of Ω would result.

Since $\mathbf{HE}^{-1}$ is a matrix, the problem is to reduce this matrix to a single number whose sampling distribution is known under the null hypothesis. For example, the Lawley-Hotelling Trace statistic involves the sampling distribution of the trace of $\mathbf{HE}^{-1}$. Another criterion to be used here is the distribution of the largest characteristic root of $\mathbf{HE}^{-1}$ are defined as the value of λ that satisfy the determinantal equation $|\mathbf{HE}^{-1} - \lambda \mathbf{I}| = 0$.

If we expand the determinant we will find a quadratic equation (for the special case of two dependent variables) in λ. We can then solve for the two values of λ or the roots that satisfy the equation. Upon finding the largest root, λ_1, the statistic

$$\theta_1 = \frac{\lambda}{1 + \lambda_1}$$

can be referred to a chart or table (see Heck, 1960) with parameters:

s = min (k, p) where k is the number of independent variables and p is the number of dependent variables;

$$m = \frac{|k - p| - 1}{2}; \text{ and}$$

$$n = \frac{N - k - p - 2}{2} \quad \text{where N is the number of sample observations.}$$

Let us see how to compute $\mathbf{H} = \hat{\mathbf{Y}}'\hat{\mathbf{Y}}$ and $\mathbf{E} = \mathbf{E}'\mathbf{E}$. Since

$$\hat{\mathbf{Y}} = \mathbf{X}\hat{\beta} \text{ and } \hat{\beta} = [\mathbf{X}'\mathbf{X}]^{-1}\mathbf{X}'\mathbf{Y}, \text{ then}$$

$$\begin{aligned}\mathbf{H} = \hat{\mathbf{Y}}'\hat{\mathbf{Y}} &= [\mathbf{X}\hat{\beta}]'[\mathbf{X}\hat{\beta}] = \hat{\beta}'\mathbf{X}'\mathbf{X}\hat{\beta} \\ &= \mathbf{Y}'\mathbf{X}(\mathbf{X}'\mathbf{X})^{-1}\mathbf{X}'\mathbf{X}(\mathbf{X}'\mathbf{X}]^{-1}\mathbf{X}'\mathbf{Y} \\ &= \mathbf{Y}'\mathbf{X}(\mathbf{X}'\mathbf{X})^{-1}\mathbf{X}'\mathbf{Y}\end{aligned}$$

The matrix **E** can be found by subtracting the matrix **H** from the total sum of squares and sum of cross-products matrix **Y'Y**. Consequently,

$$\mathbf{E} = \mathbf{E}'\mathbf{E} = \mathbf{Y}'\mathbf{Y} - \mathbf{Y}'\mathbf{X}(\mathbf{X}'\mathbf{X})^{-1}\mathbf{X}'\mathbf{Y} = \mathbf{Y}'(\mathbf{I} - \mathbf{X}(\mathbf{X}'\mathbf{X})^{-1}\mathbf{X}')\mathbf{Y}$$

Therefore **H** and **E** can be expressed in terms of the known matrices **X** and **Y**, the sample data.

We can also test other hypotheses concerning β. For example, we could test the hypothesis that

$$[\beta_{13}, \beta_{23}] = \mathbf{0}'$$

which is the hypothesis that the regression parameters associated with the independent variable x_3 are zero. For a univariate multiple regression analysis the numerator for testing the hypothesis that $\beta_3 = 0$ would be obtained by computing the regression sum of squares for the full model and the regression sum of squares for a reduced model excluding variable x_3, taking the difference in the regression sum of squares, and dividing by the difference in the number of parameters between the full and reduced model, which in this case would be 1.

We can do an analogous operation in the multivariate situation by computing the regression sum of squares and cross-products for the full model ($\mathbf{H}_f$) and for the reduced model ($\mathbf{H}_r$) and taking the difference between the two hypothesis matrices,

$$\mathbf{H}_f - \mathbf{H}_r = \mathbf{H}_d$$

Our test statistic would then be based upon the largest root of the determinantal equation

$$|\mathbf{H}_d\mathbf{E}^{-1} - \lambda\mathbf{I}| = 0$$

The error sum of squares and cross-products matrix, **E**, is the same as that used for testing **H**. This situation is again analogous to the multiple regression case. However, in this case the parameters of the distribution of θ_1 need to be revised. In particular, k now becomes the difference in the number of parameters between the full and reduced model. The new **H** matrix becomes

$$\mathbf{H_d} = \mathbf{H_f} - \mathbf{H_r} = \mathbf{Y'X(X'X)^{-1}X'Y} - \mathbf{Y'X_r(X_r'X_r)^{-1}X_r'Y}$$
$$= \mathbf{Y'(X(X'X)^{-1}X'} - \mathbf{X_r(X_r'X_r)^{-1}X_r')Y}$$

where $\mathbf{X_r}$ is the design matrix associated with the reduced model. Let us now demonstrate these procedures with a hypothetical example.

4.5 AN EXAMPLE OF PARAMETER ESTIMATION AND HYPOTHESIS TESTING FOR MULTIVARIATE REGRESSION

Table 4.1 presents a hypothetical correlation matrix for the five variables discussed at the beginning of this chapter. The variables Y_1 and Y_2 will be considered as the dependent variables and X_1, X_2, and X_3 will be the independent variables in the multivariate regression model. Note that the dependent variables Y_1 and Y_2 have a substantial correlation of .45 and that multivariate hypothesis-testing procedures are appropriate. The elements in the correlation matrix summarize the individual relationships between each of the independent variables and the dependent variables as well as the relationships among the independent variables themselves. We can see that each independent variable has a moderate relationship with each dependent variable. For convenience, it is assumed that each of the five variables is scaled so that is has a standard deviation of 1. This, of course, means that the correlation matrix is a covariance matrix for standardized scores. We are working with standardized scores because of the arbitrary nature of the units involved in the original measures of these psychological and sociological variables. The reader should be reminded that since standardization depends upon the variance properties of the specific sample in question, results across samples should be compared only on the basis of nonstandardized scores.

The first thing we want to do is to compute the vector of regression weights for each of the dependent variables. In order to do this we must first calculate the inverse of the cross-product matrix for the three standardized independent variables.

TABLE 4.1 Hypothetical Correlation Matrix: Variables for 200 High School Seniors

		X_1	X_2	X_3	Y_1	Y_2
X_1	socioeconomic status of parents	1.00	.30	.10	.40	.37
X_2	ability		1.00	.30	.40	.43
X_3	quality of school attended			1.00	.29	.35
Y_1	math achievement				1.00	.45
Y_2	reading achievement					1.00

The cross-product matrix is

$$\mathbf{X'X} = 200 \cdot \mathbf{R_x} = 200 \begin{bmatrix} 1.00 & .30 & .10 \\ .30 & 1.00 & .30 \\ .10 & .30 & 1.00 \end{bmatrix}$$

since the correlation matrix, $\mathbf{R_x}$, is the cross-product matrix divided by 200.

The reader can verify that

$$[\mathbf{X'X}]^{-1} = [200 \cdot \mathbf{R_x}]^{-1} = \frac{1}{200} \begin{bmatrix} 1.00 & .30 & .10 \\ .30 & 1.00 & .30 \\ .10 & .30 & 1.00 \end{bmatrix}^{-1}$$

$$= \frac{1}{200} \begin{bmatrix} 1.099034 & -.326087 & -.012077 \\ -.326087 & 1.195652 & -.326087 \\ -.012077 & -.326087 & 1.099034 \end{bmatrix}$$

Next,

$$\mathbf{X'Y} = \mathbf{X'}[\mathbf{y}_1, \mathbf{y}_2] = 200\mathbf{R}_{xy} = 200 \begin{bmatrix} .40 & .37 \\ .40 & .43 \\ .29 & .35 \end{bmatrix}$$

Therefore,

$$(\mathbf{X}'\mathbf{X})^{-1}\mathbf{X}'\mathbf{Y} = \left[\frac{1}{200}\cdot \mathbf{R}_x^{-1}\right][200\cdot \mathbf{R}_{xy}] = \mathbf{R}_x^{-1}\mathbf{R}_{xy}$$

$$= \begin{bmatrix} 1.099034 & -.326087 & -.012077 \\ -.326087 & 1.195652 & -.326087 \\ -.012077 & -.326087 & 1.099034 \end{bmatrix}\begin{bmatrix} .40 & .37 \\ .40 & .43 \\ .29 & .35 \end{bmatrix}$$

$$= \begin{bmatrix} .305676 & .262198 \\ .253261 & .279348 \\ .183454 & .239976 \end{bmatrix} = \hat{\beta} = [\hat{\beta}_1, \hat{\beta}_2] = \begin{bmatrix} \hat{\beta}_{11} & \hat{\beta}_{12} \\ \hat{\beta}_{21} & \hat{\beta}_{22} \\ \hat{\beta}_{31} & \hat{\beta}_{32} \end{bmatrix}$$

Each regression coefficient indicates the average standard unit change of the dependent variable for a standard unit change on the independent variable. Since the scales are in standard deviation units, this means a change of one standard deviation in X_1 results in approximately a change of .31 of a standard deviation in Y_1. It seems that all three independent variables are making some contribution to explaining the variation in each of the two dependent variables. In order to test the hypothesis that

$$\hat{\beta} = \begin{bmatrix} \hat{\beta}_{11} & \hat{\beta}_{12} \\ \hat{\beta}_{21} & \hat{\beta}_{22} \\ \hat{\beta}_{31} & \hat{\beta}_{32} \end{bmatrix} = \mathbf{0}$$

we need to calculate the variance-covariance matrix due to regression, $\hat{\mathbf{Y}}'\hat{\mathbf{Y}}$, and the cross-products matrix due to error, $\mathbf{E}'\mathbf{E}$. The matrix

$$\hat{\mathbf{Y}}'\hat{\mathbf{Y}} = \mathbf{Y}'\mathbf{X}(\mathbf{X}'\mathbf{X})^{-1}\mathbf{X}'\mathbf{Y} = [200\cdot \mathbf{R}_{xy}']\left[\frac{1}{200}\cdot \mathbf{R}_x^{-1}\right][200\cdot \mathbf{R}_{xy}]$$

$$= 200\,\mathbf{R}_{xy}'\mathbf{R}_x^{-1}\mathbf{R}_{xy}$$

$$= 200\begin{bmatrix} .40 & .40 & .29 \\ .37 & .43 & .35 \end{bmatrix}\begin{bmatrix} 1.099034 & -.326087 & -.012077 \\ -.326087 & 1.195652 & -.326087 \\ -.012077 & -.326087 & 1.099034 \end{bmatrix}\begin{bmatrix} .40 & .37 \\ .40 & .43 \\ .29 & .35 \end{bmatrix}$$

$$= 200\begin{bmatrix} .276777 & .286211 \\ .286211 & .301124 \end{bmatrix}$$

The error cross-product matrix is then

$$\mathbf{E}'\mathbf{E} = \mathbf{Y}'\mathbf{Y} - \hat{\mathbf{Y}}'\hat{\mathbf{Y}} = 200\begin{bmatrix} 1.00 & .45 \\ .45 & 1.00 \end{bmatrix} - 200\begin{bmatrix} .276777 & .286211 \\ .286211 & .301124 \end{bmatrix}$$

$$= 200\begin{bmatrix} .723223 & .163789 \\ .163789 & .698876 \end{bmatrix}$$

Letting $\hat{\mathbf{Y}}'\hat{\mathbf{Y}} = \mathbf{H}$ and $\mathbf{E}'\mathbf{E} = \mathbf{E}$, we find

$$\mathbf{HE}^{-1} = \begin{bmatrix} .276777 & .286211 \\ .286211 & .301124 \end{bmatrix} \begin{bmatrix} .723223 & .163789 \\ .163789 & .698876 \end{bmatrix}^{-1}$$

$$= \begin{bmatrix} .276777 & .286211 \\ .286211 & .301124 \end{bmatrix} \begin{bmatrix} 1.460201 & -.342213 \\ -.342213 & 1.511070 \end{bmatrix}$$

$$= \begin{bmatrix} .306205 & .337768 \\ .314877 & .357074 \end{bmatrix}$$

The determinantal equation of this matrix is

$$|\mathbf{HE}^{-1} - \lambda\mathbf{I}| = 0.$$

Let us now substitute into the above equation and expand this determinant. We have

$$\left|\begin{bmatrix} .306205 & .337768 \\ .314877 & .357074 \end{bmatrix} - \lambda\begin{bmatrix} 1 & 0 \\ 0 & 1 \end{bmatrix}\right| = \begin{vmatrix} .306205 - \lambda & .337768 \\ .314877 & .357074 - \lambda \end{vmatrix} = 0$$

A determinant, it will be recalled, involves a set of operations on the elements of a matrix resulting in a single number characterizing the matrix. It is a mapping of the elements of the matrix into a single number. For the case of a 2 × 2 matrix

$$\begin{bmatrix} a_{11} & a_{12} \\ a_{21} & a_{22} \end{bmatrix}$$

the determinant

$$\begin{vmatrix} a_{11} & a_{12} \\ a_{21} & a_{22} \end{vmatrix}$$

is defined as $a_{11}\, a_{22} - a_{21}\, a_{12}$.

The value of the above determinant is therefore

$$(.306205 - \lambda)(.357074 - \lambda) - .314877(.337768)$$
$$= \lambda^2 - .663279\,\lambda + .0029825$$

Setting this quadratic function to zero as required by the determinantal equation, we have the quadratic equation

$$\lambda^2 - .663279\,\lambda + .0029825 = 0$$

There are two roots to this quadratic equation and the test criterion involves the larger of the two roots. The largest root, λ_1, takes the value .65851.[1] Under the null hypothesis $\boldsymbol{\beta} = \mathbf{0}$

$$\theta_1 = \frac{\lambda_1}{1 + \lambda_1} = .397136$$

and we refer this value to a chart of the upper percentage points in the distribution of the largest characteristic root. The distribution is characterized by the parameters

$$s = \min(k, p) = \min(3, 2) = 2$$

$$m = \frac{|k - p| - 1}{2} = \frac{|3 - 2| - 1}{2} = 0$$

and $$n = \frac{N - k - p - 1}{2} = \frac{200 - 3 - 2 - 1}{2} = 97$$

Interpolation on the appropriate chart (Heck, 1960) shows that the value .397136 exceeds the critical value of .095 at the .01 level of significance so that we can reject the hypothesis that $\boldsymbol{\beta} = \mathbf{0}$.

Suppose that we wanted to test the hypothesis that quality of school attended (variable X_3) had no effect on math and reading achievement. In statistical terms this hypothesis would be $[\beta_{31}, \beta_{32}] = 0$. That is, the hypothesis is that coefficients attached to X_3 are zero. In order to test this null hypothesis we must derive a new hypothesis matrix that is the difference between the regression cross-products matrix for the full model (which we already calculated above) and the regression cross-products matrix for the reduced model in which variable X_3 is excluded. The error cross-products matrix remains the same.

The first step in testing this hypothesis is therefore to calculate the regression cross-products matrix for the reduced model

$$\mathbf{Y} = \mathbf{X}_r \boldsymbol{\beta}_r + \epsilon$$

where

$$\mathbf{X}_r = [\mathrm{x}_1, \mathrm{x}_2] \text{ and } \boldsymbol{\beta}_r = \begin{bmatrix} \beta_{11} & \beta_{12} \\ \beta_{21} & \beta_{22} \end{bmatrix}$$

Extracting the appropriate correlation matrices from Table 4.1, the reduced model regression cross-products matrix, $\mathbf{H}_r$, is

$$\mathbf{Y}'\mathbf{X}_r(\mathbf{X}_r'\mathbf{X}_r)^{-1}\mathbf{X}_r'\mathbf{Y}$$

$$= \left[200\begin{bmatrix} .40 & .40 \\ .37 & .43 \end{bmatrix}\right]\left[\frac{1}{200}\begin{bmatrix} 1.00 & .30 \\ .30 & 1.00 \end{bmatrix}^{-1}\right]\left[200\begin{bmatrix} .40 & .37 \\ .40 & .43 \end{bmatrix}\right]$$

which the reader can verify equals

$$200\begin{bmatrix} .246154 & .246154 \\ .246154 & .248725 \end{bmatrix}$$

The appropriate hypothesis matrix for the test of the null hypothesis that $[\beta_{31}, \beta_{32}] = \mathbf{0}$ is

$$\mathbf{H}_f - \mathbf{H}_r = 200\begin{bmatrix} .276777 & .286211 \\ .286211 & .301124 \end{bmatrix} - 200\begin{bmatrix} .246154 & .246154 \\ .246154 & .248725 \end{bmatrix}$$

$$= 200\begin{bmatrix} .030623 & .040057 \\ .040057 & .052399 \end{bmatrix} = \mathbf{H}^*$$

The elements of this hypothesis matrix are the added contribution that variable X_3 makes to the regression sum of squares and regression sum of cross-products. The diagonal elements of $\mathbf{H}_f$ reflect the contribution that all three independent variables make to the regression sum of squares of the dependent variables Y_1 and Y_2, respectively. Since we are dealing with standardized variables, the reader can verify that .276777 and .301124 are the R^2's for predicting Y_1 and Y_2, respectively, from all three independent variables.

Similarly, the diagonal values .246154 and .248725 from the matrix portion representing $\mathbf{H}_r$ are the R^2's for predicting Y_1 and Y_2, respectively, from the independent variables X_1 and X_2. The increments in R^2 due to adding variable X_3 to variables X_1 and X_2 for predicting variables Y_1 and Y_2, respectively, are .030623 and .052399, the diagonal elements of the last matrix, $\mathbf{H}^*$.

The off-diagonal elements in the matrices $\mathbf{H}_f$ and $\mathbf{H}_r$ reflect the covariance between the predicted Y_1 and Y_2 values and hence provide the rationale for the multivariate nature of the hypothesis-testing procedures. If the dependent variables Y_1 and Y_2 were independent, then hypotheses could be tested independently for each regression equation.

Using our new hypothesis matrix $\mathbf{H}^*$ and the same error matrix $\mathbf{E}$, we find

$$\mathbf{H}^*\mathbf{E}^{-1} = \left[200\begin{bmatrix} .030623 & .040057 \\ .040057 & .052399 \end{bmatrix}\right]\left[\frac{1}{200}\begin{bmatrix} 1.460201 & -.342213 \\ -.342213 & 1.511070 \end{bmatrix}\right]$$

$$= \begin{bmatrix} .031008 & .050049 \\ .040559 & .065471 \end{bmatrix}$$

The corresponding determinantal equation is

$$|\mathbf{H}^*\mathbf{E}^{-1} - \lambda\mathbf{I}| = 0$$

Substituting, we have

$$\left|\begin{bmatrix} .031008 & .050049 \\ .040559 & .065471 \end{bmatrix} - \lambda\begin{bmatrix} 1 & 0 \\ 0 & 1 \end{bmatrix}\right| = 0$$

which reduces to the quadratic equation

$$\lambda^2 - .096479\lambda = 0$$

Since

$$\lambda(\lambda - .096479) = 0,$$

the two roots are 0 and .096479.

The matrix is singular and yields only one positive root, so under the null hypothesis that $[\beta_{31}, \beta_{32}] = \mathbf{0}$,

$$\theta_1 = \frac{\lambda_1}{1 + \lambda_1} = \frac{.096479}{1.096479} = .087989$$

Referring this value to a chart of the upper percentage points in the distribution of the largest characteristic root with the parameters

$$s = \min(k_1, p) = \min(1, 2) = 1$$

where k_1 is the difference in the number of independent variables between the full and reduced model;

$$m = \frac{|k_1 - p| - 1}{2} = \frac{|1 - 2| - 1}{2} = 0;$$

and

$$n = \frac{N - k - p - 1}{2} = \frac{200 - 3 - 2 - 1}{2} = 97$$

we find that .087989 exceeds the critical value at the .01 level and we must therefore reject the hypothesis that $[\beta_{31}, \beta_{32}] = \mathbf{0}$. Other hypotheses could be tested, but since the regression weights for all three independent variables are of comparable magnitude for both dependent variables, we would most likely come to the conclusion that all parameters are needed in the model.

4.6 THE GENERAL MULTIVARIATE LINEAR HYPOTHESIS

A linear hypothesis concerning the parameter matrix $\boldsymbol{\beta}$ can be expressed as

$$\mathbf{C}\boldsymbol{\beta}\mathbf{M} = \mathbf{0}$$

where $\mathbf{C}$ is a matrix associated with hypotheses concerning the elements within columns of the parameters matrix $\boldsymbol{\beta}$ and $\mathbf{M}$ is a matrix concerned with hypotheses concerning the elements within rows of $\boldsymbol{\beta}$. The $\mathbf{C}$ matrix reflects hypotheses concerning the overall effects of the independent variables on the dependent variables and $\mathbf{M}$ reflects hypotheses concerning differences among the parameters for the various dependent variables. In many cases, the $\mathbf{M}$

matrix will be an identity matrix of suitable order since our discussions in this chapter will focus largely on hypotheses concerning the overall effects of the independent variables. For categorical independent variables, **C** and **M** must satisfy certain rank conditions to conform with the rank of the design matrix **X**. This will be discussed in more detail later when we turn to multivariate regression analysis with categorical independent variables. For the continuous regression model, the hypothesis matrix **C** is easy to define. Our initial hypothesis that

$$\beta = \begin{bmatrix} \beta_{11} & \beta_{12} \\ \beta_{21} & \beta_{22} \\ \beta_{31} & \beta_{32} \end{bmatrix} = \mathbf{0}$$

can be expressed as

$$\begin{bmatrix} 1 & 0 & 0 \\ 0 & 1 & 0 \\ 0 & 0 & 1 \end{bmatrix} \begin{bmatrix} \beta_{11} & \beta_{12} \\ \beta_{21} & \beta_{22} \\ \beta_{31} & \beta_{32} \end{bmatrix} \begin{bmatrix} 1 & 0 \\ 0 & 1 \end{bmatrix} = \mathbf{0}$$

where $\mathbf{C} = \mathbf{I}_{3\times 3}$ and $\mathbf{M} = \mathbf{I}_{2\times 2}$.

This seems to be a trivial expression, but it turns out that any permissible **C** and **M** matrix, as defined below, can be used in a general matrix expression to derive the hypothesis matrix **H**.

For example, the hypothesis that $[\beta_{31}, \beta_{32}] = \mathbf{0}$ can be expressed as

$$[0,\ 0,\ 1] \begin{bmatrix} \beta_{11} & \beta_{12} \\ \beta_{21} & \beta_{22} \\ \beta_{31} & \beta_{32} \end{bmatrix} \begin{bmatrix} 1 & 0 \\ 0 & 1 \end{bmatrix} = [\beta_{31}, \beta_{32}] = \mathbf{0}'$$

where $\mathbf{C} = [0, 0, 1]$ and $\mathbf{M} = \mathbf{I}_{2\times 2}$.

This matrix expression for hypotheses concerning the multivariate regression parameters can be generalized to a $\boldsymbol{\beta}$ matrix containing any number of rows (that is, independent variables) and any number of columns (dependent variables). The number of columns of **C** must equal the number of rows of β (that is, the number of independent variables), and the number of rows of **C** must be equal to or less than the number of columns of **C**. Also, **C** must be of full row rank. When we are not concerned with hypotheses associated with differences in the equivalent parameters across the various dependent variables, **M** is an identity matrix with order equal to the number of columns of β and therefore can be omitted from the matrix expression for multivariate hypotheses.

Although **M** will usually be an identity matrix in our discussions, it may be instructive to consider what sort of **M** matrices are needed to test various hypotheses. The hypothesis that $\beta_{31} = \beta_{32}$ can be expressed as $\beta_{31} - \beta_{32} = 0$. This hypothesis can be expressed in the general linear hypothesis framework as

$$[0,\ 0,\ 1]\begin{bmatrix}\beta_{11} & \beta_{12}\\ \beta_{21} & \beta_{22}\\ \beta_{31} & \beta_{32}\end{bmatrix}\begin{bmatrix}1\\ -1\end{bmatrix} = \beta_{31} - \beta_{32} = 0$$

where $\mathbf{C} = [0,\ 0,\ 1]$ and $\mathbf{M} = \begin{bmatrix}1\\ -1\end{bmatrix}$.

This is a contrast between the two regression parameters associated with variable X_3. It is a test concerning the equality of the regression parameters associated with X_3 for the two dependent variables.

When expressing hypotheses through the use of **C** and **M** matrices, it can be shown that the hypothesis matrix **H** associated with this hypothesis becomes

$$\mathbf{H} = \mathbf{M}'\mathbf{Y}'\mathbf{X}(\mathbf{X}'\mathbf{X})^{-1}\mathbf{C}'[\mathbf{C}(\mathbf{X}'\mathbf{X})^{-1}\mathbf{C}']^{-1}\mathbf{C}(\mathbf{X}'\mathbf{X})^{-1}\mathbf{X}'\mathbf{Y}\mathbf{M}$$

Since we are not considering contrasts of parameters across dependent variables, **M** is the appropriately sized identity matrix and therefore

$$\mathbf{H} = \mathbf{Y}'\mathbf{X}(\mathbf{X}'\mathbf{X})^{-1}\mathbf{C}'[\mathbf{C}(\mathbf{X}'\mathbf{X})^{-1}\mathbf{C}']^{-1}\mathbf{C}(\mathbf{X}'\mathbf{X})^{-1}\mathbf{X}'\mathbf{Y}$$

Our initial hypothesis, $\beta = \mathbf{0}$, can be expressed using the appropriate identity matrix for **C**. Substituting **I** for **C**, we find that

$$\mathbf{H} = \mathbf{Y}'\mathbf{X}(\mathbf{X}'\mathbf{X})^{-1}[(\mathbf{X}'\mathbf{X})^{-1}]^{-1}(\mathbf{X}'\mathbf{X})^{-1}\mathbf{X}'\mathbf{Y} = \mathbf{Y}'\mathbf{X}(\mathbf{X}'\mathbf{X})^{-1}\mathbf{X}'\mathbf{Y}$$

since $[(\mathbf{X}'\mathbf{X})^{-1}]^{-1} = [\mathbf{X}'\mathbf{X}]$ and $[\mathbf{X}'\mathbf{X}][\mathbf{X}'\mathbf{X}]^{-1} = \mathbf{I}$.

This is equal to the hypothesis matrix we developed earlier in generalizing from the single dependent variable multiple regression model to the multivariate regression model.

The reader should note that the form of **H** is analogous to the form of the regression sum of squares used to test the hypothesis that the vector of multiple regression parameters is **0** in a univariate model. In the multivariate case, we pre- and postmultiply $\mathbf{X}(\mathbf{X}'\mathbf{X})^{-1}\mathbf{X}'$ by the matrices $\mathbf{Y}'$ and $\mathbf{Y}$, respectively, while in the univariate case we pre- and postmultiply by the vectors $\mathbf{y}'$ and $\mathbf{y}$, respectively. In the univariate case, the result is a scalar rather than a matrix.

Using the general matrix expression for **H**, the hypothesis matrix associated with $[\beta_{31}, \beta_{32}] = \mathbf{0}'$ is

$$\mathbf{H} = \mathbf{Y}'\mathbf{X}(\mathbf{X}'\mathbf{X})^{-1}\begin{bmatrix}0\\0\\1\end{bmatrix}\left[[0,\ 0,\ 1]\,[\mathbf{X}'\mathbf{X}]^{-1}\begin{bmatrix}0\\0\\1\end{bmatrix}\right]^{-1}[0\ \ 0\ \ 1]\,(\mathbf{X}'\mathbf{X})^{-1}\mathbf{X}'\mathbf{Y}$$

$$= \begin{bmatrix}\hat\beta_{11} & \hat\beta_{21} & \hat\beta_{31}\\ \hat\beta_{12} & \hat\beta_{22} & \hat\beta_{32}\end{bmatrix}\begin{bmatrix}0\\0\\1\end{bmatrix}[x^{33}]^{-1}[0,\ 0,\ 1]\begin{bmatrix}\hat\beta_{11} & \hat\beta_{12}\\ \hat\beta_{21} & \hat\beta_{22}\\ \hat\beta_{31} & \hat\beta_{32}\end{bmatrix}$$

since $(\mathbf{X}'\mathbf{X})^{-1}\mathbf{X}'\mathbf{Y} = \beta$ and

$$[0,\ 0,\ 1]\,(\mathbf{X}'\mathbf{X})^{-1}\begin{bmatrix}0\\0\\1\end{bmatrix}$$

is the element in the third row and third column of the $(\mathbf{X}'\mathbf{X})^{-1}$, which is denoted as x^{33}. Simplifying the above, we find that

$$\mathbf{H} = \frac{1}{x^{33}}\begin{bmatrix}\hat\beta_{31}^2 & \hat\beta_{31}\hat\beta_{32}\\ \hat\beta_{32}\hat\beta_{31} & \hat\beta_{32}^2\end{bmatrix}$$

The reader is invited to show the equivalence of our original formulation of the hypothesis matrix (which was the difference between the regression sum of squares and cross-products matrix for the full and reduced models) and the present formulation. Note that in this special case where just β_{31} and β_{32} are tested, the hypothesis matrix is simply a function of those parameter estimates and the inverse element associated with the third variable with which these estimated regression parameters are associated. For more complex hypotheses, the hypothesis matrix will, of course, be less simplified.

4.7 MULTIVARIATE ANALYSIS OF VARIANCE FOR A ONE-WAY CLASSIFICATION

The univariate analysis of variance model for a one-way classification is frequently expressed as

$$y_{ij} = \mu + \alpha_i + \epsilon_{ij}$$

where μ is a parameter common to each observation associated with the overall level of the response, α_i is the effect of being in category i of the independent variable, y_{ij} is the jth observation in the ith category, and ϵ_{ij} is the error associated with the jth observation in the ith category. Using a matrix formulation, this model can also be expressed in terms of the regression model.

$$y = \mathbf{X}\beta + \epsilon$$

which, when expanded, is

$$\begin{bmatrix} y_1 \\ y_2 \\ y_3 \\ \cdot \\ \cdot \\ \cdot \\ \cdot \\ \cdot \\ \cdot \\ \cdot \\ \cdot \\ \cdot \\ \cdot \\ \cdot \\ y_n \end{bmatrix} = \begin{bmatrix} 1 & 1 & 0 & 0 & . & . & . & 0 \\ . & . & . & . & . & . & . & . \\ 1 & 1 & 0 & 0 & . & . & . & 0 \\ 1 & 0 & 1 & 0 & . & . & . & 0 \\ . & . & . & . & . & . & . & . \\ 1 & 0 & 1 & 0 & . & . & . & 0 \\ . & . & . & . & . & . & . & . \\ 1 & 0 & 0 & 1 & . & . & . & 0 \\ . & . & . & . & . & . & . & . \\ 1 & 0 & 0 & 1 & . & . & . & 0 \\ . & . & . & . & . & . & . & . \\ 1 & 0 & 0 & 0 & . & . & . & 1 \\ . & . & . & . & . & . & . & . \\ 1 & 0 & 0 & 0 & . & . & . & 1 \end{bmatrix} \begin{bmatrix} u \\ \alpha_1 \\ \alpha_2 \\ \cdot \\ \cdot \\ \cdot \\ \cdot \\ \alpha_k \end{bmatrix} + \begin{bmatrix} \epsilon_1 \\ \epsilon_2 \\ \epsilon_3 \\ \cdot \\ \cdot \\ \cdot \\ \cdot \\ \cdot \\ \cdot \\ \cdot \\ \cdot \\ \cdot \\ \cdot \\ \cdot \\ \epsilon_n \end{bmatrix}$$

We saw in *Introduction to Linear Models* that the design matrix **X** is less than full rank and hence $\mathbf{X}'\mathbf{X}$ is singular and cannot be inverted. This problem can be resolved in three ways. First, we could use the generalized inverse approach that we relied upon consistently in that earlier volume. Second, we could put some constraints on the parameters α_i (for example, $\Sigma\alpha_i = 0$) such that a unique solution for the parameters is possible. Third, we could use the technique of reparameterization to yield a unique solution for the new parameters.

Let us consider reparameterization in the present situation. The null hypothesis of interest in a one-way analysis of variance is

$$\alpha_1 = \alpha_2 = . = . = \alpha_k = 0$$

or that the treatment effects are equal. This hypothesis can also be expressed in terms of parameter contrasts as

$$\alpha_1 - \alpha_2 = \alpha_2 - \alpha_3 = . = . = \alpha_{k-1} - \alpha_k = 0$$

In the case of three mutually exclusive categories for the independent variable, the null hypothesis is

$$\alpha_1 = \alpha_2 = \alpha_3 \text{ or}$$

$$\alpha_1 - \alpha_2 = \alpha_2 - \alpha_3 = 0$$

These contrasts, as we saw in *Introduction to Linear Models*, can be expressed in terms of the matrix expression $\mathbf{K}\beta = \mathbf{0}$, where in the case of three categories of the independent variable

$$\mathbf{K}\beta = \begin{bmatrix} 0 & 1 & -1 & 0 \\ 0 & 0 & 1 & -1 \end{bmatrix} \begin{bmatrix} \mu \\ \alpha_1 \\ \alpha_2 \\ \alpha_3 \end{bmatrix} = \begin{bmatrix} 0 \\ 0 \end{bmatrix}$$

If we reparameterize by setting $\tau_i = \mu + \alpha_i$, then the null hypothesis can be expressed as

$$\tau_1 = \tau_2 = . = . = \tau_k$$

or

$$\tau_1 - \tau_2 = \tau_2 - \tau_3 = . = . = \tau_{k-1} - \tau_k.$$

Any difference among the τ_i's is a function of the α_i's since μ is a constant across all τ_i's. Consequently, the hypotheses are equivalent under the two formulations.

For the three-category case, the null hypothesis can be expressed as

$$\tau_1 = \tau_2 = \tau_3 \text{ or}$$

$$\tau_1 - \tau_2 = \tau_2 - \tau_3 = 0 \text{ or}$$

$$\begin{bmatrix} 1 & -1 & 0 \\ 0 & 1 & -1 \end{bmatrix} \begin{bmatrix} \tau_1 \\ \tau_2 \\ \tau_3 \end{bmatrix} = \begin{bmatrix} 0 \\ 0 \end{bmatrix}$$

But

$$\tau_1 - \tau_2 = (\mu + \alpha_1) - (\mu + \alpha_2) = \alpha_1 - \alpha_2 \text{ and}$$
$$\tau_2 - \tau_3 = (\mu + \alpha_2) - (\mu + \alpha_3) = \alpha_2 - \alpha_3$$

so that the hypotheses are identical under the original formulation of the model and the reparameterization of the model.

The reparameterized model can be written as

$$y_{ij} = \tau_i + \epsilon_{ij}$$

The regression formulation under the reparameterization is now

$$\mathbf{y} = \mathbf{X}^* \beta^* + \epsilon$$

which in the case of three categories of the independent variable is expressed in expanded form as

$$\begin{bmatrix} y_1 \\ y_2 \\ \cdot \\ \cdot \\ \cdot \\ \cdot \\ \cdot \\ \cdot \\ \cdot \\ \cdot \\ \cdot \\ y_n \end{bmatrix} = \begin{bmatrix} 1 & 0 & 0 \\ \cdot & \cdot & \cdot \\ \cdot & \cdot & \cdot \\ 1 & 0 & 0 \\ 0 & 1 & 0 \\ \cdot & \cdot & \cdot \\ \cdot & \cdot & \cdot \\ 0 & 1 & 0 \\ 0 & 0 & 1 \\ \cdot & \cdot & \cdot \\ \cdot & \cdot & \cdot \\ 0 & 0 & 1 \end{bmatrix} \begin{bmatrix} \tau_1 \\ \tau_2 \\ \tau_3 \end{bmatrix} + \begin{bmatrix} \epsilon_1 \\ \epsilon_2 \\ \cdot \\ \cdot \\ \cdot \\ \cdot \\ \cdot \\ \cdot \\ \cdot \\ \cdot \\ \cdot \\ \epsilon_n \end{bmatrix}$$

Cursory examination of the design matrix $\mathbf{X}^*$ reveals that $\mathbf{X}^*$ is full rank and hence $\mathbf{X}^{*\prime}\mathbf{X}^*$ is nonsingular and has a unique inverse; hence a unique estimate of the new parameter vector exists. We saw in *Introduction to Linear Models* that the α_i's were nonestimable, but that the $(\mu + \alpha_i)$ or the τ_i's were estimable. The solution to our reparameterized model directly yields these estimable linear combinations of the original nonestimable parameters.

Let us now extend our univariate dependent variable model into a multivariate analysis of variance model. The approach parallels the multivariate regression approach described in detail earlier in this chapter.

In the case of two dependent variables and three categories of a single independent variable, the model generalizes to

$$\begin{bmatrix} y_{11} & y_{12} \\ y_{21} & y_{22} \\ \cdot & \cdot \\ \cdot & \cdot \\ \cdot & \cdot \\ \cdot & \cdot \\ \cdot & \cdot \\ \cdot & \cdot \\ \cdot & \cdot \\ \cdot & \cdot \\ \cdot & \cdot \\ y_{n1} & y_{n2} \end{bmatrix} = \begin{bmatrix} 1 & 0 & 0 \\ \cdot & \cdot & \cdot \\ \cdot & \cdot & \cdot \\ 1 & 0 & 0 \\ 0 & 1 & 0 \\ \cdot & \cdot & \cdot \\ \cdot & \cdot & \cdot \\ 0 & 1 & 0 \\ 0 & 0 & 1 \\ \cdot & \cdot & \cdot \\ \cdot & \cdot & \cdot \\ 0 & 0 & 1 \end{bmatrix} \begin{bmatrix} \tau_{11} & \tau_{12} \\ \tau_{21} & \tau_{22} \\ \tau_{31} & \tau_{32} \end{bmatrix} + \begin{bmatrix} \epsilon_{11} & \epsilon_{12} \\ \epsilon_{21} & \epsilon_{22} \\ \cdot & \cdot \\ \cdot & \cdot \\ \cdot & \cdot \\ \cdot & \cdot \\ \cdot & \cdot \\ \cdot & \cdot \\ \cdot & \cdot \\ \cdot & \cdot \\ \cdot & \cdot \\ \epsilon_{n1} & \epsilon_{n2} \end{bmatrix}$$

or

$$[y_1, y_2] = \mathbf{X}[\tau_1, \tau_2] + [\epsilon_1, \epsilon_2]$$

or

$$\mathbf{Y} = \mathbf{X}\beta + \epsilon.$$

We can easily generalize to p dependent variables and k categories for the independent variables. The regression model then becomes

$$\mathbf{Y}_{n \times p} = \mathbf{X}_{n \times k}\beta_{k \times p} + \epsilon_{n \times p}.$$

The solution for the estimated parameter matrix is

$$\beta_{k \times p} = (\mathbf{X}'_{k \times n}\mathbf{X}_{n \times k})^{-1}\,\mathbf{X}'_{k \times n}\,\mathbf{Y}_{n \times p}$$

For two dependent variables and three levels of the independent variable, the reader can verify that

$$[\mathbf{X}'\mathbf{X}] = \begin{bmatrix} n_1 & 0 & 0 \\ 0 & n_2 & 0 \\ 0 & 0 & n_3 \end{bmatrix}$$

where n_1, n_2, and n_3 are the numbers of observations in categories 1, 2, and 3 of the dependent variable, respectively, and

$$\mathbf{X'Y} = \begin{bmatrix} \sum_j y_{1j1} & \sum_j y_{1j2} \\ \sum_j y_{2j1} & \sum_j y_{2j2} \\ \sum_j y_{3j1} & \sum_j y_{3j2} \end{bmatrix}$$

where Σy_{1j1} is the sum of the observations falling into category 1 for dependent variable number 1, Σy_{1j2} is the sum of the observations falling into category 1 for dependent variable number 2, and so on. Since

$$(\mathbf{X'X})^{-1} = \begin{bmatrix} \frac{1}{n_1} & 0 & 0 \\ 0 & \frac{1}{n_1} & 0 \\ 0 & 0 & \frac{1}{n_3} \end{bmatrix}$$

therefore

$$\hat{\beta} = \begin{bmatrix} \hat{\tau}_{11} & \hat{\tau}_{12} \\ \hat{\tau}_{21} & \hat{\tau}_{22} \\ \hat{\tau}_{31} & \hat{\tau}_{32} \end{bmatrix} = \begin{bmatrix} \frac{1}{n_1} & 0 & 0 \\ 0 & \frac{1}{n_2} & 0 \\ 0 & 0 & \frac{1}{n_3} \end{bmatrix} \begin{bmatrix} \Sigma y_{1j1} & \Sigma y_{1j2} \\ \Sigma y_{2j1} & \Sigma y_{2j2} \\ \Sigma y_{3j1} & \Sigma y_{3j2} \end{bmatrix}$$

$$= \begin{bmatrix} \frac{\Sigma y_{1j1}}{n_1} & \frac{\Sigma y_{1j2}}{n_1} \\ \frac{\Sigma y_{2j1}}{n_2} & \frac{\Sigma y_{2j2}}{n_2} \\ \frac{\Sigma y_{3j1}}{n_3} & \frac{\Sigma y_{3j2}}{n_3} \end{bmatrix} = \begin{bmatrix} \bar{y}_{11} & \bar{y}_{12} \\ \bar{y}_{21} & \bar{y}_{22} \\ \bar{y}_{31} & \bar{y}_{32} \end{bmatrix}$$

So the parameter estimate $\hat{\tau}_{11}$ is simply the mean of the observations in category 1 for dependent variable y_1; the parameter estimate $\hat{\tau}_{32}$ is the mean of the observations in category 3 for dependent variable y_2; and so on.

The general multivariate linear hypothesis that $\alpha_{11} = \alpha_{21} = \alpha_{31}$ and $\alpha_{12} = \alpha_{22} = \alpha_{32}$ can be restated in reparameterized form as $\tau_{11} - \tau_{21} = \tau_{21} - \tau_{31} = 0$ and $\tau_{12} - \tau_{22} = \tau_{22} - \tau_{32} = 0$. This reparameterized multivariate general linear hypothesis can be expressed in the form $\mathbf{C}\beta = \mathbf{0}$, which, in this particular case, is

$$\begin{bmatrix} 1 & -1 & 0 \\ 0 & 1 & -1 \end{bmatrix} \begin{bmatrix} \tau_{11} & \tau_{12} \\ \tau_{21} & \tau_{22} \\ \tau_{31} & \tau_{32} \end{bmatrix} = \begin{bmatrix} \tau_{11}-\tau_{21} & \tau_{12}-\tau_{22} \\ \tau_{21}-\tau_{31} & \tau_{22}-\tau_{32} \end{bmatrix} = \begin{bmatrix} 0 & 0 \\ 0 & 0 \end{bmatrix}$$

Since

$$\mathbf{C} = \begin{bmatrix} 1 & -1 & 0 \\ 0 & 1 & -1 \end{bmatrix}$$

the hypothesis matrix is

$$\mathbf{H} = \mathbf{Y'X(X'X)^{-1}C'[C(X'X)^{-1}C']^{-1}C(X'X)^{-1}X'Y}$$

$$= \begin{bmatrix} \Sigma y_{1j1} & \Sigma y_{2j1} & \Sigma y_{3j1} \\ \Sigma y_{1j2} & \Sigma y_{2j2} & \Sigma y_{3j2} \end{bmatrix} \begin{bmatrix} \frac{1}{n_1} & 0 & 0 \\ 0 & \frac{1}{n_2} & 0 \\ 0 & 0 & \frac{1}{n_3} \end{bmatrix} \begin{bmatrix} 1 & 0 \\ -1 & 1 \\ 0 & -1 \end{bmatrix}$$

$$\times \left[\begin{bmatrix} 1 & -1 & 0 \\ 0 & 1 & -1 \end{bmatrix} \begin{bmatrix} \frac{1}{n_1} & 0 & 0 \\ 0 & \frac{1}{n_2} & 0 \\ 0 & 0 & \frac{1}{n_3} \end{bmatrix} \begin{bmatrix} 1 & 0 \\ -1 & 1 \\ 0 & -1 \end{bmatrix} \right]$$

$$\times \begin{bmatrix} 1 & -1 & 0 \\ 0 & 1 & -1 \end{bmatrix} \begin{bmatrix} \frac{1}{n_1} & 0 & 0 \\ 0 & \frac{1}{n_2} & 0 \\ 0 & 0 & \frac{1}{n_3} \end{bmatrix} \begin{bmatrix} \Sigma y_{1j1} & \Sigma y_{1j2} \\ \Sigma y_{2j1} & \Sigma y_{2j2} \\ \Sigma y_{3j1} & \Sigma y_{3j2} \end{bmatrix}$$

After multiplying through these matrices and simplifying, we find that

$$\mathbf{H} = \begin{bmatrix} \Sigma n_i \bar{y}_{i1}^2 - N\bar{y}_1^2 & \Sigma n_i \bar{y}_{i1}\bar{y}_{i2} - N\bar{y}_1\bar{y}_2 \\ \Sigma n_i \bar{y}_{i1}\bar{y}_{i2} - N\bar{y}_1\bar{y}_2 & \Sigma n_i \bar{y}_{i2}^2 - N\bar{y}_2^2 \end{bmatrix}$$

where i refers to the category of the independent variable.

But the regression sum of squares and sum of cross-products matrix about the origin, $\hat{\mathbf{Y}}'\hat{\mathbf{Y}}$, is

$$(\mathbf{X}\beta)'(\mathbf{X}\beta) = \beta'\mathbf{X}'\mathbf{X}\beta = \mathbf{Y}'\mathbf{X}(\mathbf{X}'\mathbf{X})^{-1}(\mathbf{X}'\mathbf{X})(\mathbf{X}'\mathbf{X})^{-1}\mathbf{X}'\mathbf{Y}$$
$$= \mathbf{Y}'\mathbf{X}(\mathbf{X}'\mathbf{X})^{-1}\mathbf{X}'\mathbf{Y}$$

Substituting, we find that $\hat{\mathbf{Y}}'\hat{\mathbf{Y}}$ is equal to

$$\begin{bmatrix} \Sigma y_{1j1} & \Sigma y_{2j1} & \Sigma y_{3j1} \\ \Sigma y_{1j2} & \Sigma y_{2j2} & \Sigma y_{3j2} \end{bmatrix} \begin{bmatrix} \frac{1}{n_1} & 0 & 0 \\ 0 & \frac{1}{n_2} & 0 \\ 0 & 0 & \frac{1}{n_3} \end{bmatrix} \begin{bmatrix} \Sigma y_{1j1} & \Sigma y_{1j2} \\ \Sigma y_{2j1} & \Sigma y_{2j2} \\ \Sigma y_{3j1} & \Sigma y_{3j2} \end{bmatrix}$$

$$= \begin{bmatrix} \Sigma n_i \bar{y}_{i1}^2 & \Sigma n_i \bar{y}_{i1}\bar{y}_{i2} \\ \Sigma n_i \bar{y}_{i1}\bar{y}_{i2} & \Sigma n_i \bar{y}_{i2}^2 \end{bmatrix}$$

We have demonstrated that if the elements of the regression sum of squares and cross-products matrix are corrected for the mean, we have the hypothesis matrix for the global hypothesis that the parameters associated with a given dependent variable are equal to one another. The error matrix associated with this hypothesis is

$$\mathbf{E} = \mathbf{Y}'\mathbf{Y} - \mathbf{Y}'\mathbf{X}(\mathbf{X}'\mathbf{X})^{-1}\mathbf{X}'\mathbf{Y}$$

which the reader can verify is equal to

$$\begin{bmatrix} y_1'y_1 - \Sigma n_i \bar{y}_{i1}^2 & y_1'y_2 - \Sigma n_i \bar{y}_{i1}\bar{y}_{i2} \\ y_2'y_1 - \Sigma n_i \bar{y}_{i1}\bar{y}_{i2} & y_2'y_2 - \Sigma n_i \bar{y}_{i2}^2 \end{bmatrix}$$

If we add **H** and **E**, the reader can verify that **H** + **E** = **T** where **T** is the matrix of sum of squares and sum of cross-products about the mean. The parallel between analysis of variance and multivariate analysis of variance is sometimes shown by expressing the above equality as **T** = **B** + **W**, where **T** denotes total sum of squares and cross-products matrix about the mean, **B** (that is, **H**) denotes the between-group sum of squares and cross-products matrix about the mean, and **W** (that is, **E**) denotes the within-group sum of squares and cross-products matrix. Note the analogy to the univariate case, where

$$t = b + w$$

where

$t = \sum_i \sum_j (y_{ij} - \overline{y})^2$ is the total sum of squares about the mean;

$b = \sum_i n_i(\overline{y}_i - \overline{y})^2$ is the between-group sum of squares about the mean; and

$w = \sum_i \sum_j (y_{ij} - \overline{y}_i)^2$ is the within-group sum of squares.

In the multivariate situation, these are the diagonal elements of the **T**, **B**, and **W** matrices, respectively. We can also note the similarity of the statistical test criteria in the univariate and multivariate case. In the univariate case, the test criterion involves the scalar bw^{-1} and in the multivariate case the test criterion involves the matrix $\mathbf{BW}^{-1}$.

4.8 EXTENSIONS OF MULTIVARIATE ANALYSIS OF VARIANCE (ORTHOGONAL CASE)

The univariate analysis of variance can be extended to more than one independent variable and to include interactions among the independent variables. For example, a two-factor model with interactions can be represented as

$$y_{ijk} = \mu + \alpha_i + \beta_j + \alpha\beta_{ij} + \epsilon_{ijk}$$

where μ is the overall effect common to all observations; α_i is the effect of the ith level of factor A; β_j is the effect of the jth level of factor B; $\alpha\beta_{ij}$ is the interaction effect of the ith level of factor A and the jth level of factor B; and ϵ_{ijk} is the error associated with the kth observation of level i of factor A and level j of factor B.

If the design matrix is orthogonal (that is, if there is an equal number of observations in each cell or the row [column] n's are proportional), then the total sum of squares about the mean can be partitioned into a sum of squares due to factor A, a sum of squares due to factor B, a sum of squares due to the interaction between factors A and B, and a sum of squares due to error. That is,

$$T_{SS} = SS_A + SS_B + SS_{AB} + SS_E$$

The appropriate statistical test criteria involves $(SS_A)(SS_E)^{-1}$ for testing the effect of factor A, $(SS_B)(SS_E)^{-1}$ for testing the effect of factor B, and $(SS_{AB})(SS_E)^{-1}$ for testing the interaction. The test criteria are, of course, scalar values and, when multiplied by the appropriate ratios of degrees of freedom, are distributed as F with those degrees of freedom.

The extension to the multivariate situation is straightforward. If the design matrix is orthogonal, the matrix of total sum of squares and cross-products about the mean can be partitioned analogously into a sum of squares and cross-products matrix due to factor A, a sum of squares and cross-products matrix due to factor B, a sum of squares and cross-products matrix due to the interaction between factor A and factor B, and an error sum of squares and cross-products matrix. Let the partitioning be expressed as

$$\mathbf{T} = \mathbf{A} + \mathbf{B} + \mathbf{I} + \mathbf{E}$$

Then the statistical test criteria involve the largest characteristic root of $\mathbf{AE}^{-1}$, $\mathbf{BE}^{-1}$, and $\mathbf{IE}^{-1}$ for testing the effects of factor A, factor B, and the interaction between factors A and B, respectively. Note the analogy between this and the univariate case in regard to the test criteria.

The matrices **A**, **B**, and **I** are also the hypothesis matrices generated by $\mathbf{C}_A\beta = \mathbf{0}$, $\mathbf{C}_B\beta = \mathbf{0}$, and $\mathbf{C}_I\beta = \mathbf{0}$ where $\mathbf{C}_A$ is a contrast matrix that reflects the null hypothesis concerning the parameters associated with factor A, $\mathbf{C}_B$ is a contrast matrix that reflects the null hypothesis concerning the parameters associated with factor B, and $\mathbf{C}_I$ is a contrast matrix that reflects the null hypothesis concerning the interaction parameters.

When the design matrix is nonorthogonal (that is, unequal or nonproportional sample sizes across rows [columns]), then the total sum of squares and cross-products matrix cannot be partitioned as above. We must then cast the problem into a regression framework in order to examine the contributions to the regression sum of squares and cross-products matrix that the various factors and their interactions make. We will next describe the general procedure for multivariate analysis of variance with unbalanced data and illustrate with an example.

4.9 MULTIVARIATE ANALYSIS OF VARIANCE (UNBALANCED DATA)

In univariate regression analysis with nonorthogonal variables, we have seen that the contribution a factor makes to the regression sum of squares is measured by the additional or incremental regression sum of squares that the factor contributes beyond the regression sum of squares contributed by all the remaining factors in the model. It can be computed in two ways. First, we can compute the regression sum of squares for the full model and subtract from it the regression sum of squares resulting from a reduced model where the effects to be tested are not included. Second, we can formulate the problem in terms of contrast matrices and the full parameter matrix, which, when combined with some matrix operations, directly yields the adjusted regression sum of squares. This is, as we saw, the hypothesis matrix approach.

Let us examine an unbalanced data set with a hypothetical data set of two dependent variables (two measures of job satisfaction, y_1, and y_2) cross-classified by two factors, A and B. Factor A comprises two types of organizational structure. Factor B comprises three categories of type of industry. The observations are based upon job satisfaction questionnaires administered to blue-collar workers. The hypothetical data base is presented in Table 4.2.

It can be seen from this table that the data are unbalanced. For dependent variable y_1, an observation can be expressed as

$$y_{1ijk} = \mu_1 + \alpha_{1i} + \beta_{1j} + \alpha\beta_{1ij} + \epsilon_{1ijk}$$

where y_{1ijk} is the kth observation on variable y_1 for the ith level of A and the jth level of B; α_{1i} is the effect on variable y_1 for the ith level of A; β_{1j} is the effect on variable y_1 for the jth level of B; $\alpha\beta_{1ij}$ is the interaction effect on variable y_1 associated with the ith level of A and the jth level of B; and ϵ_{1ijk} is the error for the kth observations in the ith level of A and j^{th} level of B. The ϵ_{1ijk} are assumed to be normally distributed with mean 0 and common variance σ^2. Similarly, the dependent variable y_2 can be expressed as

$$y_{2ijk} = \mu_2 + \alpha_{2i} + \beta_{2j} + \alpha\beta_{2ij} + \epsilon_{2ijk}$$

Each equation has the common design matrix **X** (same factors and levels), so that the multivariate model can be expressed as

TABLE 4.2 Scores on Job Satisfaction Measures y_1 and y_2, Cross-Classified by Organizational Structure and Type of Industry

Factor A *Organizational Structure*	*Factor B* *Type of Industry* 1		2		3	
	y_1	y_2	y_1	y_2	y_1	y_2
1	1	1	2	3	3	3
	1	2	3	4	2	4
	3	2	4	3	5	6
			4	5	6	7
			5	5	7	6
					8	7
					7	8
	n = 3		n = 5		n = 7	
2	2	4	3	4	7	7
	3	3	4	3	7	8
	5	4	6	8		
	4	3	7	7		
	5	4	5	6		
	3	1				
	1	2				
	n = 7		n = 5		n = 2	

$$\mathbf{Y} = [y_1, y_2] = \mathbf{X}[\beta_1, \beta_2] + [\epsilon_1, \epsilon_2]$$

where $\mathbf{X}$ is the common design matrix, β_1 is the vector of parameters associated with dependent variable y_1, and β_2 is the vector of parameters associated with dependent variable y_2. It is assumed that the strung-out error vector

$$\begin{bmatrix} \epsilon_1 \\ \epsilon_2 \end{bmatrix}$$

is multivariate normally distributed with a mean of $\mathbf{0}$ and covariance matrix

$$\begin{bmatrix} \sigma_1^2 & \sigma_{12} \\ \sigma_{21} & \sigma_2^2 \end{bmatrix} \otimes \mathbf{I}_{29 \times 29}$$

where σ_1^2 is the common variance of the residuals from the regression model fitted to y_1; σ_2^2 is the common variance of the residuals for y_2; and $\sigma_{12} = \sigma_{21}$ is the common covariance between the residuals from y_1 and the residuals from y_2.

The expected cell values for y_1 can be expressed in the general regression framework as

$$
E\begin{bmatrix} y_{111} \\ y_{112} \\ y_{113} \\ y_{121} \\ y_{122} \\ y_{123} \end{bmatrix} = \overset{\text{Column}}{\underset{}{\begin{matrix} 1 & 2 & 3 & 4 & 5 & 6 & 7 & 8 & 9 & 10 & 11 & 12 \end{matrix}}}
$$

$$
\begin{bmatrix}
1 & 1 & 0 & 1 & 0 & 0 & 1 & 0 & 0 & 0 & 0 & 0 \\
1 & 1 & 0 & 0 & 1 & 0 & 0 & 1 & 0 & 0 & 0 & 0 \\
1 & 1 & 0 & 0 & 0 & 1 & 0 & 0 & 1 & 0 & 0 & 0 \\
1 & 0 & 1 & 1 & 0 & 0 & 0 & 0 & 0 & 1 & 0 & 0 \\
1 & 0 & 1 & 0 & 1 & 0 & 0 & 0 & 0 & 0 & 1 & 0 \\
1 & 0 & 1 & 0 & 0 & 1 & 0 & 0 & 0 & 0 & 0 & 1
\end{bmatrix}
\begin{bmatrix} \mu_1 \\ \alpha_{11} \\ \alpha_{12} \\ \beta_{11} \\ \beta_{12} \\ \alpha\beta_{111} \\ \alpha\beta_{112} \\ \alpha\beta_{113} \\ \alpha\beta_{121} \\ \alpha\beta_{122} \\ \alpha\beta_{123} \end{bmatrix} = \mathbf{X}_B\beta_1
$$

The above matrix is sort of a miniature design matrix. We could easily expand the above matrix into a design matrix for this data set by replicating row 1 three times, row 2 five times, row 3 seven times, row 4 seven times, row 5 five times, and row 6 two times, yielding a 29 x 12 design matrix. That is, each row of the reduced design matrix would be replicated in accordance with the number of observations in the cell corresponding to the expected value. These are the basic rows of the design matrix and this reduced matrix can be used to determine the rank of **X**. But it will be most useful in the present situation for reparameterizing the model, since we know from previous discussions that the design matrix **X** is less than full rank. The expected cell values for y_2 can also be expressed using the basic design matrix, $\mathbf{X}_B$, as $\mathbf{X}_B\beta_2$.

We know from our previous discussions that the rank of **X** or, equivalently, $\mathbf{X}_B$ is 6, so that a reparameterized model can only have a design matrix with 6 linearly independent columns in order for the $\mathbf{X}'\mathbf{X}$ to possess a unique inverse. The parameters associated with the new design matrix will usually be meaningful contrasts among the original parameters.

Let us see what happens if we form a new design matrix by selecting columns of **X** from left to right until we have a basis for the columns space (that is, an independent set of column vectors equal in number to the rank of **X**). We can do this selection on the $\mathbf{X}_B$ matrix that generated the expected values of the cells since it is easier to see the linear dependencies with this basic design matrix. Moving from left to right, we begin our new design matrix with columns 1 and 2. Column 3 must be skipped since column 1 equals column 2 plus column 3 and hence we have linear dependencies. We can add columns 4 and 5 to columns 1 and 2 and still maintain linear independence among the four column vectors. However, column 6 must be skipped because column 1 equals column 4 plus column 5 plus column 6. Continuing, we find that columns 7 and 8 can be added to columns 1, 2, 4, and 5 without creating any linear dependencies. It can be seen that columns 9, 10, 11, or 12 cannot be added to our basic set without creating linear dependencies. Hence our new design matrix, $\mathbf{X}_R$, is composed of columns 1, 2, 4, 5, 7, and 8 from $\mathbf{X}_B$, which is

$$\begin{bmatrix} 1 & 1 & 1 & 0 & 1 & 0 \\ 1 & 1 & 0 & 1 & 0 & 1 \\ 1 & 1 & 0 & 0 & 0 & 0 \\ 1 & 0 & 1 & 0 & 0 & 0 \\ 1 & 0 & 0 & 1 & 0 & 0 \\ 1 & 0 & 0 & 0 & 0 & 0 \end{bmatrix} = \mathbf{X}_R$$

With this new design matrix, the expected cell values for dependent variable y_1 can be expressed as

$$E(y_{1c}) = \begin{bmatrix} 1 & 1 & 1 & 0 & 1 & 0 \\ 1 & 1 & 0 & 1 & 0 & 1 \\ 1 & 1 & 0 & 0 & 0 & 0 \\ 1 & 0 & 1 & 0 & 0 & 0 \\ 1 & 0 & 0 & 1 & 0 & 0 \\ 1 & 0 & 0 & 0 & 0 & 0 \end{bmatrix} \begin{bmatrix} \theta_{11} \\ \theta_{12} \\ \theta_{13} \\ \theta_{14} \\ \theta_{15} \\ \theta_{16} \end{bmatrix} = \mathbf{X}_R \theta_1$$

or, equivalently, as

$$\begin{aligned} E(y_{111}) &= \theta_{11} + \theta_{12} + \theta_{13} + \theta_{15} \\ E(y_{112}) &= \theta_{11} + \theta_{12} + \theta_{14} + \theta_{16} \\ E(y_{113}) &= \theta_{11} + \theta_{12} \\ E(y_{121}) &= \theta_{11} + \theta_{13} \\ E(y_{122}) &= \theta_{11} + \theta_{14} \\ E(y_{123}) &= \theta_{11} \end{aligned}$$

The expected cell values for the dependent variable y_2 can be expressed similarly as $\mathbf{X}_R \theta_2$.

We can determine the meaning of these new parameters by comparing the expected cell values in terms of the old and the new parameters. Let us drop the variable subscript (that is, the first subscript) on both sets of parameters so that the comparisons can be more easily visualized. Table 4.3 presents the expected cell values in terms of the original model and the reparameterized model.

From this table, let us express the new parameters in terms of the original parameters. First, $\theta_1 = \mu + \alpha_2 + \alpha_3 + \alpha\beta_{23}$. Since

$$\theta_1 + \theta_2 = \mu + \alpha_1 + \beta_3 + \alpha\beta_{13} \quad \text{and} \quad \theta_1 = \mu + \alpha_2 + \beta_2 + \alpha\beta_{23}$$

therefore,

$$\begin{aligned}\theta_2 &= (\theta_1 + \theta_2) - \theta_1 = (\mu + \alpha_1 + \beta_1 + \alpha\beta_{13}) - (\mu + \alpha_1 + \beta_3 + \alpha\beta_{23}) \\ &= (\alpha_1 - \alpha_2) + (\alpha\beta_{13} - \alpha\beta_{23})\end{aligned}$$

Likewise,

$$\begin{aligned}\theta_3 &= (\theta_1 + \theta_3) - \theta_1 = (\mu + \alpha_2 + \beta_1 + \alpha\beta_{21}) - (\mu + \alpha_2 + \beta_3 + \alpha\beta_{23}) \\ &= (\beta_1 - \beta_3) + (\alpha\beta_{21} - \alpha\beta_{23});\end{aligned}$$

$$\begin{aligned}\theta_4 &= (\theta_1 + \theta_4) - \theta_1 = (\mu + \alpha_2 + \beta_2 + \alpha\beta_{22}) - (\mu + \alpha_2 + \beta_3 + \alpha\beta_{23}) \\ &= (\beta_2 - \beta_3) + (\alpha\beta_{22} - \alpha\beta_{23}); \text{ and}\end{aligned}$$

$$\begin{aligned}\theta_5 &= (\theta_1 + \theta_2 + \theta_3 + \theta_5) - (\theta_1 + \theta_3) - \theta_2 \\ &= \mu + \alpha_1 + \beta_1 + \alpha\beta_{11} - (\mu + \alpha_2 + \beta_1 + \alpha\beta_{21}) - [(\alpha_1 - \alpha_2) \\ &\qquad + (\alpha\beta_{13} - \alpha\beta_{23})] \\ &= (\alpha\beta_{11} - \alpha\beta_{21}) - (\alpha\beta_{13} - \alpha\beta_{23})\end{aligned}$$

As an exercise, the reader should verify that

$$\theta_6 = (\alpha\beta_{12} - \alpha\beta_{22}) - (\alpha\beta_{13} - \alpha\beta_{23})$$

TABLE 4.3 Expected Cell Values in Terms of the Original and the Reparameterized Models

Factor A Organizational Structure	*Factor B Type of Industry* 1	2	3
1	$E(y_{11})$ $= \mu + \alpha_1 + \beta_1 + \alpha\beta_{11}$ $= \theta_1 + \theta_2 + \theta_3 + \theta_5$	$E(y_{12})$ $= \mu + \alpha_1 + \beta_2 + \alpha\beta_{12}$ $= \theta_1 + \theta_2 + \theta_4 + \theta_6$	$E(y_{13})$ $= \mu + \alpha_1 + \beta_3 + \alpha\beta_{13}$ $= \theta_1 + \theta_2$
2	$E(y_{21})$ $= \mu + \alpha_2 + \beta_1 + \alpha\beta_{21}$ $= \theta_1 + \theta_3$	$E(y_{22})$ $= \mu + \alpha_2 + \beta_2 + \alpha\beta_{22}$ $= \theta_1 + \theta_4$	$E(y_{23})$ $= \mu + \alpha_2 + \beta_3 + \alpha\beta_{23}$ $= \theta_1$

Thus the relationships between the new and old parameters can be summarized as

$$\theta_1 = \mu + \alpha_2 + \beta_3 + \alpha\beta_{23}$$

$$\theta_2 = (\alpha_1 - \alpha_2) + (\alpha\beta_{13} - \alpha\beta_{23})$$

$$\theta_3 = (\beta_1 - \beta_3) + (\alpha\beta_{21} - \alpha\beta_{23})$$

$$\theta_4 = (\beta_2 - \beta_3) + (\alpha\beta_{22} - \alpha\beta_{23})$$

$$\theta_5 = (\alpha\beta_{11} - \alpha\beta_{21}) - (\alpha\beta_{13} - \alpha\beta_{23})$$

$$\theta_6 = (\alpha\beta_{12} - \alpha\beta_{22}) - (\alpha\beta_{13} - \alpha\beta_{23})$$

The new parameter θ_1 is the expected value of the observation in cell 23. It is an arbitrary constant that is present in all the observations on the dependent variable. It is present in every cell of Table 4.3. It plays a role similar to μ in the original formulation of the model and, like μ, is of little interest in itself.

The remaining parameters, however, are of major interest. The second parameter, θ_2, reflects the difference in the effects for the two levels of factor A (that is, $\alpha_1 - \alpha_2$). It also reflects the difference in the two interaction parameters $\alpha\beta_{13}$ and $\alpha\beta_{23}$. If we place the restriction on the model that $\alpha\beta_{13} = \alpha\beta_{23}$, then θ_2 becomes an estimate of $\alpha_1 - \alpha_2$.

The parameters θ_3 and θ_4 reflect two independent contrasts between the parameters associated with factor β. Both of these new parameters also reflect differences in interaction parameters so that once again restrictions must be put on the interaction parameters if we want estimates of $\beta_1 - \beta_3$ and $\beta_2 - \beta_3$. The remaining two parameters θ_5 and θ_6 are contrasts solely concerned with interaction parameters. The parameter θ_5 contrasts the difference in the interaction parameters of column 1 with the difference in the interaction parameters of the last column, column 3, while the parameter θ_6 contrasts the difference in the interaction parameters of column 2 with the difference again in column 3. The differences in columns 1 and 2 are contrasted to the difference in column 3 so that the column 3 difference acts as a standard for evaluating the interaction parameters.

In summary, θ_2 reflects the contributions of factor A, θ_3 and θ_4 jointly reflect the contribution of factor B, and θ_5 and θ_6 jointly reflect the contributions of the interaction between factor A and B.

For ease of interpretation, we might want to apply, as previously discussed, the following restrictions–($\alpha\beta_{21} = \alpha\beta_{23}$), ($\alpha\beta_{22} = \alpha\beta_{23}$), and ($\alpha\beta_{13} = \alpha\beta_{23}$)–so that the mapping between the new and original parameters can be more simply expressed as

$$\theta_1 = \mu + \alpha_1 + \alpha_2 + \alpha\beta_{32}$$
$$\theta_2 = \alpha_1 - \alpha_2$$
$$\theta_3 = \beta_1 - \beta_3$$
$$\theta_4 = \beta_2 - \beta_3$$
$$\theta_5 = \alpha\beta_{11} - \alpha\beta_{21}$$
$$\theta_6 = \alpha\beta_{12} - \alpha\beta_{22}$$

The parameters now unambigously measure either main effects or interaction effects. Notice also that the new parameters are estimable functions of the original parameters, which are themselves not estimable. For example, α_1 and α_2 are not estimable unless restrictions such as $\Sigma\alpha_i = 0$ were put upon the original parameters, but $\alpha_1 - \alpha_2$ is estimable; for the unrestricted model $\alpha_1 + \alpha\beta_{13}$ and $\alpha_2 + \alpha\beta_{23}$ are not estimable but $\alpha_1 - \alpha_2 + (\alpha\beta_{13} - \alpha\beta_{23})$ is estimable.

4.10 ESTIMATION OF PARAMETERS FOR MULTIVARIATE ANALYSIS OF VARIANCE WITH UNBALANCED DATA

For our hypothetical data base presented in Table 4.2, our reparameterized multivariate model

$\mathbf{Y} = \mathbf{X}\theta + \epsilon$ takes the specific form

$$
\begin{array}{l}
\\ \text{cell 11} \\ \\
\\ \\ \text{cell 12} \\ \\ \\
\\ \\ \\ \text{cell 13} \\ \\ \\ \\
\\ \\ \\ \text{cell 21} \\ \\ \\ \\
\\ \\ \text{cell 22} \\ \\ \\
\text{cell 23} \\ \\
\end{array}
\begin{bmatrix}
1 & 1 \\ 1 & 2 \\ 3 & 2 \\ \hline
2 & 3 \\ 3 & 4 \\ 4 & 3 \\ 4 & 5 \\ 5 & 5 \\ \hline
3 & 3 \\ 2 & 4 \\ 5 & 6 \\ 6 & 7 \\ 7 & 6 \\ 8 & 7 \\ 7 & 8 \\ \hline
2 & 4 \\ 3 & 3 \\ 5 & 4 \\ 4 & 3 \\ 5 & 4 \\ 3 & 1 \\ 1 & 2 \\ \hline
3 & 4 \\ 4 & 3 \\ 6 & 8 \\ 7 & 7 \\ 5 & 6 \\ \hline
7 & 7 \\ 7 & 8
\end{bmatrix}
=
\begin{bmatrix}
111010 \\ 111010 \\ 111010 \\ \hline
110101 \\ 110101 \\ 110101 \\ 110101 \\ 110101 \\ \hline
110000 \\ 110000 \\ 110000 \\ 110000 \\ 110000 \\ 110000 \\ 110000 \\ \hline
101000 \\ 101000 \\ 101000 \\ 101000 \\ 101000 \\ 101000 \\ 101000 \\ \hline
100100 \\ 100100 \\ 100100 \\ 100100 \\ 100100 \\ \hline
100000 \\ 100000
\end{bmatrix}
\begin{bmatrix}
\theta_{11} & \theta_{12} \\
\theta_{21} & \theta_{22} \\
\theta_{31} & \theta_{32} \\
\theta_{41} & \theta_{42} \\
\theta_{51} & \theta_{52} \\
\theta_{61} & \theta_{62}
\end{bmatrix}
+
\begin{bmatrix}
\epsilon_{1111} & \epsilon_{2111} \\
\epsilon_{1112} & \epsilon_{2112} \\
\epsilon_{1113} & \epsilon_{2113} \\ \hline
\epsilon_{1121} & \epsilon_{2121} \\
\epsilon_{1122} & \epsilon_{2122} \\
\epsilon_{1123} & \epsilon_{2123} \\
\epsilon_{1124} & \epsilon_{2124} \\
\epsilon_{1125} & \epsilon_{2125} \\ \hline
\epsilon_{1131} & \epsilon_{2131} \\
\epsilon_{1132} & \epsilon_{2132} \\
\epsilon_{1133} & \epsilon_{2133} \\
\epsilon_{1134} & \epsilon_{2134} \\
\epsilon_{1135} & \epsilon_{2135} \\
\epsilon_{1136} & \epsilon_{2136} \\
\epsilon_{1137} & \epsilon_{2137} \\ \hline
\epsilon_{1211} & \epsilon_{2211} \\
\epsilon_{1212} & \epsilon_{2212} \\
\epsilon_{1213} & \epsilon_{2213} \\
\epsilon_{1214} & \epsilon_{2214} \\
\epsilon_{1215} & \epsilon_{2215} \\
\epsilon_{1216} & \epsilon_{2216} \\
\epsilon_{1217} & \epsilon_{2217} \\ \hline
\epsilon_{1221} & \epsilon_{2221} \\
\epsilon_{1222} & \epsilon_{2222} \\
\epsilon_{1223} & \epsilon_{2223} \\
\epsilon_{1224} & \epsilon_{2224} \\
\epsilon_{1225} & \epsilon_{2225} \\ \hline
\epsilon_{1231} & \epsilon_{2231} \\
\epsilon_{1232} & \epsilon_{2232}
\end{bmatrix}
$$

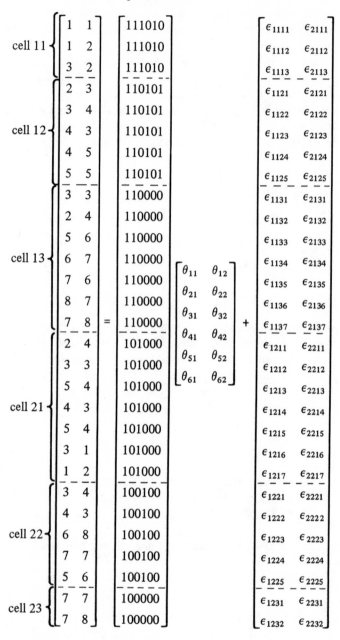

Let us first estimate the parameter matrix $\boldsymbol{\theta}$. We know from our previous discussions that $\hat{\theta} = (\mathbf{X}'\mathbf{X})^{-1}\mathbf{X}'\mathbf{Y}$.

The reader can verify that

$$\mathbf{X}'\mathbf{X} = \begin{bmatrix} 29 & 15 & 10 & 10 & 3 & 5 \\ 15 & 15 & 3 & 5 & 3 & 5 \\ 10 & 3 & 10 & 0 & 3 & 0 \\ 10 & 5 & 0 & 10 & 0 & 5 \\ 3 & 3 & 3 & 0 & 3 & 0 \\ 5 & 5 & 0 & 5 & 0 & 5 \end{bmatrix} \quad \text{and its inverse}$$

$$(\mathbf{X}'\mathbf{X})^{-1} = \begin{bmatrix} .5 & -.5 & -.5 & -.5 & .5 & .5 \\ -.5 & .642857 & .5 & .5 & -.642857 & -.642857 \\ -.5 & .5 & .642857 & .5 & -.642857 & -.5 \\ -.5 & .5 & .5 & .7 & -.5 & -.7 \\ .5 & -.642857 & -.642857 & -.5 & 1.119048 & .642857 \\ .5 & -.642857 & -.5 & -.7 & .642857 & 1.042857 \end{bmatrix}$$

and since

$$\mathbf{X}'\mathbf{Y} = \begin{bmatrix} 123 & 130 \\ 61 & 66 \\ 28 & 26 \\ 43 & 48 \\ 5 & 5 \\ 18 & 20 \end{bmatrix}$$

therefore

$$\hat{\theta} = \begin{bmatrix} .5 & -.5 & -.5 & -.5 & .5 & .5 \\ -.5 & .642857 & .5 & .5 & -.642857 & -.624857 \\ -.5 & .5 & .652857 & .5 & -.642857 & -.5 \\ -.5 & .5 & .5 & .7 & -.5 & -.7 \\ .5 & -.642857 & -.642857 & -.5 & 1.119048 & .642857 \\ .5 & -.642857 & -.5 & -.7 & .642857 & 1.042857 \end{bmatrix} \begin{bmatrix} 123 & 130 \\ 61 & 66 \\ 28 & 26 \\ 43 & 48 \\ 5 & 5 \\ 18 & 20 \end{bmatrix}$$

$$= \begin{bmatrix} 7 & 7.5 \\ -1.571 & -1.642 \\ -3.714 & -4.500 \\ -2 & -1.9 \\ -.047 & .309 \\ .171 & .042 \end{bmatrix} = \begin{bmatrix} \hat{\theta}_{11} & \hat{\theta}_{12} \\ \hat{\theta}_{21} & \hat{\theta}_{22} \\ \hat{\theta}_{31} & \hat{\theta}_{32} \\ \hat{\theta}_{41} & \hat{\theta}_{42} \\ \hat{\theta}_{51} & \hat{\theta}_{52} \\ \hat{\theta}_{61} & \hat{\theta}_{62} \end{bmatrix}$$

The first column of the parameter matrix contains the six parameters associated with the first dependent variable y_1, while the second column contains the six parameters associated with the second dependent variable y_2.

The parameter estimate $\hat{\theta}_{11}$, which in terms of the old parameters, is the mean of cell 23 (that is, $\hat{\theta}_{11} = \widehat{\mu_1 + \alpha_{21} + \beta_{31} + \alpha\beta_{231}}$), is equal to 7, which the reader can verify is the mean of dependent variable y_1 for the cell 23. For the restricted model, $\hat{\theta}_{21}$ is the difference in the effects of the two levels of Factor A. Since $\hat{\theta}_{21} = \widehat{\alpha_{11} - \alpha_{21}} = 1.571434$, the second level of Factor A or second type of organizational structure. Similarly, the third level of Factor B or third type of industry had a larger effect than the first type of industry on job satisfaction variable y_1 and since $\hat{\theta}_{31} = \widehat{\beta_{11} - \beta_{31}} = -3.714289$. The third type of industry also had a larger effect than the second type of industry since $\hat{\theta}_{41} = \beta_{21} - \beta_{31} = -2$. Since $\widehat{\beta_{11} - \beta_{21}} = \hat{\theta}_{31} - \hat{\theta}_{41} = -3.714289 - (-2) = -1.714289$, the second type of industry is more beneficial than the first in reference to job satisfaction measure y_1. The last two parameters in the first column reflect the interaction effects of Factors A and B on dependent variable y_1. The first interaction parameter, $\hat{\theta}_{51}$, reflects the differential effects of Factor A at the first level of Factor B as contrasted with the third level of Factor B. Similarly, the second interaction parameter, $\hat{\theta}_{61}$, reflects the differential effects of Factor A at the second level of Factor B as contrasted with the third level of Factor B. Both of these interaction parameters are quite small when compared with the main effect parameters. The first hypothesis that we will test subsequently will be the hypothesis that the interaction parameters are zero.

The second column of the parameter matrix contains the equivalent parameters associated with the second measure of job satisfaction. It can be seen that the magnitudes and signs of these parameters are similar to the counterparts in the first column. In both cases the parameters reflecting main effect contrasts are large while the parameters reflecting interaction parameter contrasts are quite small. The similarity of the two parameter vectors no doubt reflects a high correlation between the two job satisfaction measures.

The reader can verify that any cell mean in Table 4.2 for either dependent variable can be exactly reconstructed as a linear combination of the appropriate parameters. For example, the mean of cell 11 for dependent variable

y_1 is 1.666, which, in terms of the model parameters, can be represented as $\hat{\theta}_{11} + \hat{\theta}_{21} + \hat{\theta}_{31} + \hat{\theta}_{51}$, which for our example equals

$$7 + (-1.571434) + (-3.714289) + (-.047607) \text{ or } 1.666$$

A basic inference problem is to determine if all twelve parameters are needed to explain the variation in the dependent variables. For example, the model would certainly be simplified if we could infer that all four interaction parameters were zero. Then we would be dealing with a main effects model where the effects of each factor were the same across the levels of the other factor. We also would not need to put restrictions on the interaction parameters (since they were inferred to be zero) in order to obtain main effect contrasts uncontaminated by interaction parameters.

4.11 HYPOTHESIS TESTING

Before moving to tests of specific hypotheses concerning the interaction parameters or main effect parameters, the researcher might want to test the overall hypothesis

$$\begin{bmatrix} 0 & 1 & 0 & 0 & 0 & 0 \\ 0 & 0 & 1 & 0 & 0 & 0 \\ 0 & 0 & 0 & 1 & 0 & 0 \\ 0 & 0 & 0 & 0 & 1 & 0 \\ 0 & 0 & 0 & 0 & 0 & 1 \end{bmatrix} \begin{bmatrix} \theta_{11} & \theta_{12} \\ \theta_{21} & \theta_{22} \\ \theta_{31} & \theta_{32} \\ \theta_{41} & \theta_{42} \\ \theta_{51} & \theta_{52} \\ \theta_{61} & \theta_{62} \end{bmatrix} = \begin{bmatrix} \theta_{21} & \theta_{22} \\ \theta_{31} & \theta_{32} \\ \theta_{41} & \theta_{42} \\ \theta_{51} & \theta_{52} \\ \theta_{61} & \theta_{62} \end{bmatrix} = \mathbf{0}$$

Note that we are not really interested in testing hypotheses concerning θ_{11} and θ_{12} for these parameters, which, like μ, reflect the overall level of the responses of the first and second dependent variables, respectively. In particular, θ_{11} is the expected value of the first dependent variable in cell 23. It is also a component of the expected value of y_1 for each of the 6 cells and hence does not provide any information concerning the effects of Factors A, B, or their interaction. We are most interested in the remaining parameters that reflect main effect and interaction contrasts for Factors A and B.

If the above null hypothesis is not rejected, then the last five parameters for each dependent variable can be removed from the model and the model simplifies to

$$\mathbf{y}_1 = \mathbf{1}\theta_{11} + \epsilon_1 \text{ and}$$

$$\mathbf{y}_2 = \mathbf{1}\theta_{21} + \epsilon_2$$

where **1** is a column vector of 29 ones for the present example.

This of course means that the expected value of each cell is equal to θ_{11} for y_1 and θ_{21} for y_2. Furthermore, if all cell means are equal, then they in turn must equal the overall mean μ. The model, therefore, is equivalent to

$$\mathbf{y}_1 = \mathbf{1}\mu_1 + \epsilon_1 \quad \text{and}$$

$$\mathbf{y}_2 = \mathbf{1}\mu_2 + \epsilon_2$$

To test the hypothesis that

$$\begin{bmatrix} \theta_{21} & \theta_{22} \\ \theta_{31} & \theta_{32} \\ \theta_{41} & \theta_{42} \\ \theta_{51} & \theta_{52} \\ \theta_{61} & \theta_{62} \end{bmatrix} = \mathbf{0}$$

we could estimate the regression sum of squares and cross-products matrix for the full model, $\mathbf{H}_f$, and subtract from this the regression sum of squares and cross-products matrix for the reduced model, $\mathbf{H}_r$, where each observation can be explained by the overall mean plus an error component. For the reduced model, the regression sum of squares and cross-products matrix for $\mathbf{H}_r$ is simply

$$\hat{\mathbf{Y}}'\hat{\mathbf{Y}} = (\mathbf{X}\hat{\beta})'(\mathbf{X}\hat{\beta}) = [\mathbf{1}(\hat{\theta}_{11}, \hat{\theta}_{12})]'[\mathbf{1}(\hat{\theta}_{11}, \hat{\theta}_{12})]$$

Since $\hat{\theta}_{11} = \overline{y}_1$ and $\hat{\theta}_{12} = \overline{y}_2$, we have

$$[\mathbf{1}(\overline{y}_1, \overline{y}_2)]'[\mathbf{1}(\overline{y}_1, \overline{y}_2)] = \begin{bmatrix} \overline{y}_1 \\ \overline{y}_2 \end{bmatrix} \mathbf{1}'\mathbf{1}[\overline{y}_1, \overline{y}_2] = N \begin{bmatrix} \overline{y}_1^2 & \overline{y}_1\,\overline{y}_2 \\ \overline{y}_2\,\overline{y}_1 & \overline{y}_2^2 \end{bmatrix}$$

$$= \begin{bmatrix} N\overline{y}_1^2 & N\overline{y}_1\,\overline{y}_2 \\ N\overline{y}_2\,\overline{y}_1 & N\overline{y}_2^2 \end{bmatrix}$$

$$= \begin{bmatrix} 29(4.241)^2 & 29(4.241)(4.482) \\ 29(4.482)(4.241) & 29(4.482)^2 \end{bmatrix}$$

$$= \begin{bmatrix} 521.689 & 551.379 \\ 551.379 & 582.758 \end{bmatrix}$$

This is simply the matrix to be used to subtract out from the regression sum of squares and cross-products matrix for the full model that portion of the regression sum of squares and cross-products that is due to the mean. It adjusts the regression sum of squares and cross-products matrix for the full model so that the elements reflect regression sums of squares and cross-products about the mean rather than about zero.

The regression sum of squares and cross-products matrix for the full model is

$$\mathbf{H}_f = \hat{\mathbf{Y}}'\hat{\mathbf{Y}} = \hat{\beta}'\mathbf{X}'\mathbf{X}\hat{\beta}.$$

Substituting the previously estimated parameter matrix and the corresponding $\mathbf{X}'\mathbf{X}$, we find

$$\mathbf{H}_f = \begin{bmatrix} 7 & -1.57 & -3.71 & -2 & -.05 & .17 \\ 7.5 & -1.64 & -4.50 & -1.9 & .31 & .04 \end{bmatrix} \begin{bmatrix} 29 & 15 & 10 & 10 & 3 & 5 \\ 15 & 15 & 3 & 5 & 3 & 5 \\ 10 & 3 & 10 & 0 & 3 & 0 \\ 10 & 5 & 0 & 10 & 0 & 5 \\ 3 & 3 & 3 & 0 & 3 & 0 \\ 5 & 5 & 0 & 5 & 0 & 5 \end{bmatrix}$$

$$\times \begin{bmatrix} 7.00 & 7.50 \\ -1.57 & -1.64 \\ -3.71 & -4.50 \\ -2.00 & -1.90 \\ -.05 & .31 \\ .17 & .04 \end{bmatrix} = \begin{bmatrix} 577.990 & 616.904 \\ 616.904 & 660.774 \end{bmatrix}$$

The hypothesis matrix for testing $\begin{bmatrix} \theta_{21} & \theta_{22} \\ \theta_{31} & \theta_{32} \\ \theta_{41} & \theta_{42} \\ \theta_{51} & \theta_{52} \\ \theta_{61} & \theta_{62} \end{bmatrix} = \mathbf{0}$ is

$$\mathbf{H} = \mathbf{H}_f - \mathbf{H}_r = \begin{bmatrix} 577.990 & 616.904 \\ 616.904 & 660.775 \end{bmatrix} - \begin{bmatrix} 521.689 & 551.379 \\ 551.379 & 582.758 \end{bmatrix}$$

$$= \begin{bmatrix} 56.300 & 65.525 \\ 65.525 & 78.017 \end{bmatrix}$$

The appropriate error sum of squares and cross-products matrix, $\mathbf{E}$, can be expressed as $\mathbf{Y}'\mathbf{Y} - \hat{\mathbf{Y}}'\hat{\mathbf{Y}}$, where $\mathbf{Y}'\mathbf{Y}$ is the total sum of squares and cross-products about the origin and $\hat{\mathbf{Y}}'\hat{\mathbf{Y}}$ is the regression sum of squares and cross-products about the origin, which we previously computed as $\mathbf{H}_f$. For our hypothetical data set

$$\mathbf{Y}'\mathbf{Y} = \begin{bmatrix} 639 & 657 \\ 657 & 710 \end{bmatrix}, \text{ so that}$$

$$\mathbf{E} = \begin{bmatrix} 639 & 657 \\ 657 & 710 \end{bmatrix} - \begin{bmatrix} 577.990 & 616.904 \\ 616.904 & 660.775 \end{bmatrix} = \begin{bmatrix} 61.009 & 40.095 \\ 40.095 & 49.224 \end{bmatrix}$$

The inverse of $\mathbf{E}$ is

$$\mathbf{E}^{-1} = \begin{bmatrix} 61.009 & 40.095 \\ 40.095 & 49.224 \end{bmatrix}^{-1} = \begin{bmatrix} .035273 & -.028732 \\ -.028732 & .043719 \end{bmatrix}$$

and

$$\mathbf{HE}^{-1} = \begin{bmatrix} 56.30066 & 65.52519 \\ 65.52519 & 78.01719 \end{bmatrix} \begin{bmatrix} .035273 & -.028732 \\ -.028732 & .043719 \end{bmatrix}$$

$$= \begin{bmatrix} .103223 & 1.247065 \\ .069680 & 1.528163 \end{bmatrix}$$

The next step in our hypothesis-testing procedure is to find the largest root of the characteristic equation

$$|\mathbf{HE}^{-1} - \lambda\mathbf{I}| = 0.$$

Substituting, we find

$$\begin{vmatrix} .103223 - \lambda & 1.247065 \\ .069680 & 1.528163 - \lambda \end{vmatrix} = 0$$

and upon evaluating the determinant and simplifying we obtain the quadratic equation

$$\lambda^2 - 1.631386\lambda + .070847 = 0.$$

Using the formula for finding the roots of a quadratic equation, we find the two roots $\lambda_1 = 1.5867$ and $\lambda_2 = .045149$. The value of the test statistic is therefore

$$\theta_1 = \frac{\lambda_1}{1 + \lambda_1} = \frac{1.5867}{1 + 1.5867} = .6134$$

The parameters of the distribution of this test statistic under the null hypothesis are

$s = 2$ (number of dependent variables in this case)

$m = \dfrac{|q - u| - 1}{2} = 1$ where q is equal to the number of independent variables (5) and u is the rank of $\mathbf{M}$ in $\mathbf{C}\beta\mathbf{M}$, and, since $\mathbf{M} = \mathbf{I}_{2\times 2}$, $u = 2$,

and

$$n = \frac{N - r - u - 1}{2} = \frac{29 - 5 - 2 - 1}{2} = 10\frac{1}{2}$$

where r is equal to the number of nonnull column vectors of **C**, which is 5.

Referring to the appropriate chart (Heck, 1960) and interpolating on the appropriate curve, we find that .6134 exceeds the critical value needed to be significant at the .01 level and, hence, we reject the hypothesis that

$$\begin{bmatrix} \theta_{21} & \theta_{22} \\ \theta_{31} & \theta_{32} \\ \theta_{41} & \theta_{42} \\ \theta_{51} & \theta_{52} \\ \theta_{61} & \theta_{62} \end{bmatrix} = \mathbf{0}$$

The rejection of the above hypothesis, however, gives us no indication if the significance is due to the effects of Factor A, Factor B, or their interactions. For example, it could be that the parameters associated with Factor B are the major contributors to the variation in the two dependent variables. Or it could be that Factor A alone would explain essentially as much variation as the full model. Finally, maybe just the parameters reflecting the contributions of Factor A and Factor B jointly are needed and the interaction parameters can be discarded from the model.

There are a number of approaches we could take to test further hypotheses that might simplify our model. For example, we could generate a hypothesis matrix based upon the difference in the regression sum of squares and cross-products for the full model and the model that contains only the parameters reflecting Factor B. This is equivalent to testing the hypothesis

$$\mathbf{C}\beta = \begin{bmatrix} 0 & 1 & 0 & 0 & 0 & 0 \\ 0 & 0 & 0 & 0 & 1 & 0 \\ 0 & 0 & 0 & 0 & 0 & 1 \end{bmatrix} \begin{bmatrix} \theta_{11} & \theta_{12} \\ \theta_{21} & \theta_{22} \\ \theta_{31} & \theta_{32} \\ \theta_{41} & \theta_{42} \\ \theta_{51} & \theta_{52} \\ \theta_{61} & \theta_{62} \end{bmatrix} = \begin{bmatrix} \theta_{21} & \theta_{22} \\ \theta_{51} & \theta_{52} \\ \theta_{61} & \theta_{62} \end{bmatrix} = \mathbf{0}$$

The appropriate **H** matrix can be generated directly from the general matrix expression that we discussed earlier for deriving the hypothesis matrix or can be derived by subtracting the hypothesis matrix for the reduced model from the hypothesis matrix for the full model. Similarly, we could test for the significance of the single parameter associated with Factor A.

The basic idea is to obtain the most parsimonious model for explaining the variation in the two dependent variables. That is, if two models explain essentially the same amount of variation in the dependent variable, then the simplest one should be chosen if there is no evidence to indicate otherwise. This parsimony comes about by testing various hypotheses concerning the parameters of the model and excluding parameters from the final model that have been accepted as zero on the basis of hypothesis testing.

First, let us test if Factor B alone is sufficient to explain the variation in the two dependent variables. This, as we saw above, means that we are hypothesizing that

$$\begin{bmatrix} \theta_{21} & \theta_{22} \\ \theta_{51} & \theta_{52} \\ \theta_{61} & \theta_{62} \end{bmatrix} = \mathbf{0}$$

These, of course, are the parameters associated with Factor A and the interaction between Factors A and B. The appropriate hypothesis matrix can be obtained from substituting into the general matrix expression

$$\mathbf{H} = \mathbf{Y}'\mathbf{X}(\mathbf{X}'\mathbf{X})^{-1}\mathbf{C}'[\mathbf{C}(\mathbf{X}'\mathbf{X})^{-1}\mathbf{C}']^{-1}\mathbf{C}(\mathbf{X}'\mathbf{X})^{-1}\mathbf{X}'\mathbf{Y}$$

where

$$\mathbf{C} = \begin{bmatrix} 0 & 1 & 0 & 0 & 0 & 0 \\ 0 & 0 & 0 & 0 & 1 & 0 \\ 0 & 0 & 0 & 0 & 0 & 1 \end{bmatrix}$$

and where $(\mathbf{X}'\mathbf{X})^{-1}$ and $\mathbf{X}'\mathbf{Y}$ have previously been computed. Let us now proceed to test this hypothesis. (The reader may wish to demonstrate the numerical equivalence between this method and the method whereby the two models are separately fitted and the differences in their hypothesis matrices are taken.) Continuing, we find that

$\mathbf{Y}'\mathbf{X}(\mathbf{X}'\mathbf{X})^{-1}\mathbf{C}'$

$$= \begin{bmatrix} 123 & 61 & 28 & 43 & 5 & 18 \\ 130 & 66 & 26 & 48 & 5 & 20 \end{bmatrix}$$

$$\times \begin{bmatrix} .5 & -.5 & -.5 & -.5 & .5 & .5 \\ -.5 & -.642857 & .5 & .5 & -.642857 & -.642857 \\ -.5 & .5 & .642857 & .5 & -.642857 & -.5 \\ -.5 & .5 & .5 & .7 & -.5 & -.7 \\ .5 & -.642857 & -.642857 & -.5 & 1.118048 & .642857 \\ .5 & -.642857 & -.5 & -.7 & .642857 & 1.042857 \end{bmatrix} \begin{bmatrix} 0 & 0 & 0 \\ 1 & 0 & 0 \\ 0 & 0 & 0 \\ 0 & 0 & 0 \\ 0 & 1 & 0 \\ 0 & 0 & 1 \end{bmatrix}$$

$$= \begin{bmatrix} -1.571434 & -.047607 & .171434 \\ -1.642863 & .309536 & .042863 \end{bmatrix}$$

and since

$$\mathbf{C}(\mathbf{X}'\mathbf{X})^{-1}\mathbf{X}'\mathbf{Y} = [\mathbf{Y}'\mathbf{X}(\mathbf{X}'\mathbf{X})^{-1}\mathbf{C}']',$$

therefore

$$\mathbf{C}(\mathbf{X}'\mathbf{X})^{-1}\mathbf{X}'\mathbf{Y} = \begin{bmatrix} -1.571434 & -1.642863 \\ -.047607 & .309536 \\ .171434 & .042863 \end{bmatrix}$$

The last expression we need to calculate is $[\mathbf{C}(\mathbf{X}'\mathbf{X})^{-1}\mathbf{C}']^{-1}$, which the reader can verify takes the value

$$\begin{bmatrix} 6.155554 & 2.099997 & 2.5 \\ 2.099997 & 2.099997 & 0 \\ 2.5 & 0 & 2.5 \end{bmatrix}$$

Substituting these three matrix expressions into the formula for **H**, we find

$$\mathbf{H} = \begin{bmatrix} -1.571434 & -.047607 & .171434 \\ -1.642863 & .309536 & .042863 \end{bmatrix}$$

$$\times \begin{bmatrix} 6.155554 & 2.099997 & 2.5 \\ 2.099997 & 2.099997 & 0 \\ 2.5 & 0 & 2.5 \end{bmatrix} \begin{bmatrix} -1.571434 & -1.642863 \\ -.047607 & .309536 \\ .171434 & .042863 \end{bmatrix}$$

$$= \begin{bmatrix} 14.246008 & 14.149190 \\ 14.149190 & 14.331172 \end{bmatrix}$$

Next, we find the largest root of the characteristic equation

$$|\mathbf{HE}^{-1} - \lambda\mathbf{I}| = 0.$$

Substituting, we have

$$\begin{vmatrix} .095965 - \lambda & .209272 \\ .087321 & .220010 - \lambda \end{vmatrix} = 0$$

and upon evaluating the determinant and simplifying we obtain the quadratic equation

$$\lambda^2 - .315975\lambda + .002839 = 0$$

The two roots are $\lambda_1 = .306719$ and $\lambda_2 = .009256$ and the test statistic is

$$\theta_2 = \frac{.306719}{1.306719} = .2347$$

Referring this value to the appropriate table or chart with s = 2, m = 0, and n = $11\frac{1}{2}$, we find that we must retain the null hypothesis that

$$\begin{bmatrix} \theta_{21} & \theta_{22} \\ \theta_{51} & \theta_{52} \\ \theta_{61} & \theta_{62} \end{bmatrix} = \mathbf{0}$$

Consequently, our model can be simplified to include only parameters reflecting main effect contrasts among the levels of Factor B. The expected cell values become

$$\begin{bmatrix} y_{111} & y_{211} \\ y_{112} & y_{212} \\ y_{113} & y_{213} \\ y_{121} & y_{221} \\ y_{122} & y_{222} \\ y_{123} & y_{223} \end{bmatrix} = \begin{bmatrix} 1 & 1 & 0 \\ 1 & 0 & 1 \\ 1 & 0 & 0 \\ 1 & 1 & 0 \\ 1 & 0 & 1 \\ 1 & 0 & 0 \end{bmatrix} \begin{bmatrix} \theta_{11} & \theta_{12} \\ \theta_{31} & \theta_{32} \\ \theta_{41} & \theta_{42} \end{bmatrix}$$

This is simply the model for a one-way multivariate analysis of variance. The above was just an example of testing a particular hypothesis. We could test any hypothesis in this manner. Actually, we might want to begin by testing the hypothesis that the interaction parameters were zero. If this hypothesis was not rejected, then the model would be simplified considerably. Next, we would test whether or not both factors were needed in the model.

4.12 GROWTH CURVE ANALYSIS FOR LONGITUDINAL DATA

In many instances, the dependent variables will be measured at one point in time; this is what is known as a cross-sectional analysis. In other instances, we could have repeated measures of the same variable over successive points in time. For example, in a child development study, one might measure weight, height, or intelligence at yearly intervals over a long time span. This type of study is referred to as "longitudinal." The general multivariate regression model is applicable in both situations, but in this case of a longitudinal repeated measures design, it could be more meaningful to summarize the p measurements in terms of a smaller number of parameters from individual growth curves. We can then compare different groups in terms of the average characteristics of the growth curves within each group. For example, we could compare groups in terms of the relative height of the average growth curve, relative rate of change, relative acceleration in growth, and so on. In many instances this is conceptually more appealing than contrasting regression parameters based upon the original repeated measures, especially if the individual growth curves can be adequately characterized by considerably fewer parameters than the number of repeated measures, p.

For example, suppose there are six repeated measures of some developmental variable for three different groups of children as plotted in Figure 4.1. Cursory examination of this figure suggests that the mean curve for each of the three groups could be adequately summarized by a straight line, a + bt, with two parameters a and b and where t takes the values 1 through 6. The parameter a, the intercept, reflects the height of the growth curve and b the slope or rate of change of the developmental measure through time. In this instance, we have summarized the six repeated measures in each group by two growth curve parameters, a and b. In some cases, if the growth curve is not linear, higher-order polynomials such as $a + bt + ct^2 + dt^3$ might be needed to provide an adequate fit. By defining $x_1 = t$, $x_2 = t^2$, and $x_3 = t^3$, we can use ordinary least squares to fit individual curves and arrive at the parameters, a, b, c, and d for a particular individual. The first step is to determine the order of the polynomial that is needed to give an adequate fit for each group's mean growth curve. We can test the hypothesis that the three growth curves are linear by testing the hypothesis

$$\begin{bmatrix} 1 & -2 & 1 & 0 & 0 & 0 \\ 0 & 1 & -2 & 1 & 0 & 0 \\ 0 & 0 & 1 & -2 & 1 & 0 \\ 0 & 0 & 0 & 1 & -2 & 1 \end{bmatrix} \begin{bmatrix} \mu_{11} & \mu_{12} & \mu_{13} \\ \mu_{21} & \mu_{22} & \mu_{23} \\ \mu_{31} & \mu_{32} & \mu_{33} \\ \mu_{41} & \mu_{42} & \mu_{43} \\ \mu_{51} & \mu_{52} & \mu_{53} \\ \mu_{61} & \mu_{62} & \mu_{63} \end{bmatrix} = \mathbf{0}$$

where the first matrix is postmultiplied by the matrix of the means of the six repeated measures for each group. If the population means fall on a line, then the linear combinations of the means given by the matrix expression will all be zero. For example, if the six means for group 1 fall on a line, then from the above matrix expression we can see that the following restrictions must hold for the means of group 1:

$$\mu_{11} - 2\mu_{21} + \mu_{31} = 0$$

$$\mu_{21} - 2\mu_{31} + \mu_{41} = 0$$

$$\mu_{31} - 2\mu_{41} + \mu_{51} = 0$$

$$\mu_{41} - 2\mu_{51} + \mu_{61} = 0$$

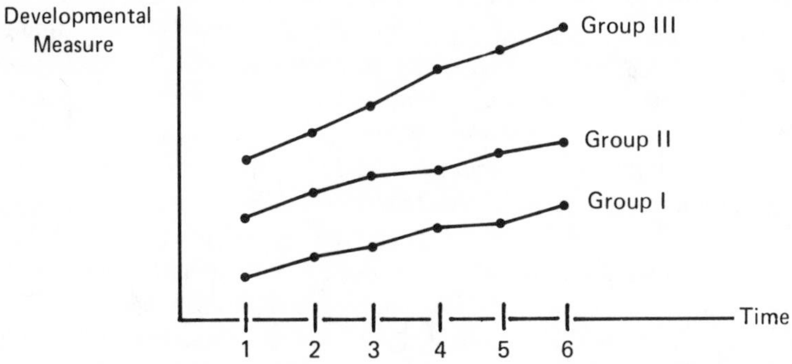

Figure 4.1 Mean Development of Three Groups of Children over Six Years

The first restriction for group 1 holds because if the means fall on a straight line then $(\mu_{11} - \mu_{21}) - (\mu_{21} - \mu_{31}) = \mu_{11} - 2\mu_{21} + \mu_{31} = 0$. The reader can verify that the remaining three restrictions must also follow. We can test the above hypothesis using the methods discussed earlier in this chapter. If the linear hypothesis is rejected, we can test whether a quadratic growth curve, $a + bt + ct^2$, fits the means of each group. (Note that the parameters of the growth curves across the groups are not tested for equality, but the functional form of the growth curve is tested for sameness.) The test of whether or not a quadratic growth curve fits all three groups corresponds to the hypothesis that

$$\begin{bmatrix} 1 & -3 & 3 & -1 & 0 & 0 \\ 0 & 1 & -3 & 3 & -1 & 0 \\ 0 & 0 & 1 & -3 & 3 & -1 \end{bmatrix} \begin{bmatrix} \mu_{11} & \mu_{12} & \mu_{13} \\ \mu_{21} & \mu_{22} & \mu_{23} \\ \mu_{31} & \mu_{32} & \mu_{33} \\ \mu_{41} & \mu_{42} & \mu_{43} \\ \mu_{51} & \mu_{52} & \mu_{53} \\ \mu_{61} & \mu_{62} & \mu_{63} \end{bmatrix} = \mathbf{0}$$

The matrix associated with the quadratic hypothesis may simply be obtained from the matrix associated with the linear hypothesis by subtracting each successive row from its previous row. If the population means can be summarized by a quadratic growth curve, then the following restrictions must hold for each group.

$$\mu_{1i} - 3\mu_{2i} + 3\mu_{3i} - \mu_{4i} = 0$$

$$\mu_{2i} - 3\mu_{3i} + 3\mu_{4i} - \mu_{5i} = 0$$

$$\mu_{3i} - 3\mu_{4i} + 3\mu_{5i} - \mu_{6i} = 0$$

The rationale behind these restrictions is that the acceleration or rate of change of growth rate is constant for a quadratic curve. If this is true, then $(\mu_{1i} - \mu_{2i}) - (\mu_{2i} - \mu_{3i}) = (\mu_{2i} - \mu_{3i}) - (\mu_{3i} - \mu_{4i})$. Simplifying, we find $\mu_{1i} - 3\mu_{2i} + 3\mu_{3i} - \mu_{4i} = 0$, the first of the above restrictions. The other restrictions follow. For a cubic equation, that is, $a + bt + ct^2 + dt^3$, the change in acceleration is constant. This leads to two restrictions on the means, which the reader can derive as an exercise. Hypothesis such as these can be tested to find the appropriate polynomial growth curve.

The next step is to estimate the parameters of the growth curve and test various hypotheses about them. Let us assume that the hypothesis that the means for all three groups of children fall on a straight line is accepted. Then, for each child, we can fit a straight line to the six measures and determine the individual growth curve parameters. The linear model for the six measurements on the ith child is

$$\begin{bmatrix} y_{1i} \\ y_{2i} \\ y_{3i} \\ y_{4i} \\ y_{5i} \\ y_{6i} \end{bmatrix} = \begin{bmatrix} 1 & t_1 \\ 1 & t_2 \\ 1 & t_3 \\ 1 & t_4 \\ 1 & t_5 \\ 1 & t_6 \end{bmatrix} \begin{bmatrix} \beta_{0i} \\ \beta_{1i} \end{bmatrix} + \begin{bmatrix} \epsilon_{1i} \\ \epsilon_{2i} \\ \epsilon_{3i} \\ \epsilon_{4i} \\ \epsilon_{5i} \\ \epsilon_{6i} \end{bmatrix}$$

An error vector is necessary since a line will not fit each child's six repeated measures perfectly. If we assume the errors are independent, then we can use ordinary least squares to solve for the growth curve parameters (β_{0i} and β_{1i}) for the ith child. The solution is

$$\hat{\beta}_i = (\mathbf{T}'\mathbf{T})^{-1}\mathbf{T}'\mathbf{y}_i$$

where

$$\hat{\beta}_i = \begin{bmatrix} \hat{\beta}_{0i} \\ \hat{\beta}_{1i} \end{bmatrix}, \quad \mathbf{T} = \begin{bmatrix} 1 & t_1 \\ 1 & t_2 \\ 1 & t_3 \\ 1 & t_4 \\ 1 & t_5 \\ 1 & t_6 \end{bmatrix}; \text{ and } \mathbf{y}_i = \begin{bmatrix} y_{1i} \\ y_{2i} \\ y_{3i} \\ y_{4i} \\ y_{5i} \\ y_{6i} \end{bmatrix}$$

The 2 by N matrix of growth curve parameters for the total sample of children can now be easily expressed as $\hat{\beta} = (\mathbf{T}'\mathbf{T})^{-1}\mathbf{T}'\mathbf{Y}$, where β is a 2 by N matrix of growth curve parameters and **Y** is a 6 by N matrix of measures on the six repeated measures for each child. That is,

$$\beta = \begin{bmatrix} \beta_{01} & \beta_{02} & \cdots & \beta_{0N} \\ \beta_{11} & \beta_{12} & \cdots & \beta_{1N} \end{bmatrix} \quad \text{and} \quad \mathbf{Y} = \begin{bmatrix} y_{11} & y_{12} & \cdots & y_{1N} \\ y_{21} & y_{22} & \cdots & y_{2N} \\ y_{31} & y_{32} & \cdots & y_{3N} \\ y_{41} & y_{42} & \cdots & y_{4N} \\ y_{51} & y_{52} & \cdots & y_{5N} \\ y_{61} & y_{62} & \cdots & y_{6N} \end{bmatrix}$$

We have transformed the six dependent measures for each child into two growth curve parameters by the transformation matrix $(\mathbf{T}'\mathbf{T})^{-1}\mathbf{T}'$. We can then consider β as a matrix of dependent variables and, by selecting the appropriate design matrix, develop a multivariate regression model for these parameters. For our example, we have only children classified into three groups and so with no other information available we can consider only a one-way multivariate analysis of variance. If we adopt the design matrix

$$\mathbf{X} = \begin{bmatrix} 1 & 0 & 0 \\ 1 & 0 & 0 \\ \cdot & \cdot & \cdot \\ \cdot & \cdot & \cdot \\ \cdot & \cdot & \cdot \\ 1 & 0 & 0 \\ 0 & 1 & 0 \\ 0 & 1 & 0 \\ \cdot & \cdot & \cdot \\ \cdot & \cdot & \cdot \\ \cdot & \cdot & \cdot \\ 0 & 1 & 0 \\ 0 & 0 & 1 \\ 0 & 0 & 1 \\ \cdot & \cdot & \cdot \\ \cdot & \cdot & \cdot \\ \cdot & \cdot & \cdot \\ 0 & 0 & 1 \end{bmatrix}$$

to represent the mutually exclusive membership of each child in one of the three groups, then we can construct the following multivariate model for explaining the individual growth curve parameters:

$$\beta' = \mathbf{X}\begin{bmatrix} {}_1\beta_0 & {}_1\beta_1 \\ {}_2\beta_0 & {}_2\beta_1 \\ {}_3\beta_0 & {}_3\beta_1 \end{bmatrix} + \mathbf{E}$$

where the parameter matrix represents the population means of the two growth curve parameters for each of the three groups. For example, ${}_1\beta_0$ is the population mean of the intercept parameter for group 1. The error matrix **E** has the same dimension (N by 2) as β' with an individual error corresponding to each of the two parameters for all N children. It is assumed that the two growth parameters within an individual are correlated so that the error covariance matrix takes the form

$$\begin{bmatrix} \Sigma & 0 & 0 & 0 & . & . & . \\ 0 & \Sigma & 0 & 0 & . & . & . \\ 0 & 0 & \Sigma & 0 & . & . & . \\ 0 & 0 & 0 & \Sigma & . & . & . \\ . & . & . & . & . & . & . \\ . & . & . & . & . & . & \Sigma \end{bmatrix}$$

where Σ is the 2×2 common covariance between the errors associated with the two growth curve parameters within individuals. This gives the model its multivariate nature. From our previous study of multivariate regression, we can see that the parameter matrix is estimated as

$$\hat{\beta}_p = \begin{bmatrix} {}_1\hat{\beta}_0 & {}_1\beta_1 \\ {}_2\beta_0 & {}_2\beta_1 \\ {}_3\beta_0 & {}_3\beta_1 \end{bmatrix} = [\mathbf{X}'\mathbf{X}]^{-1}\mathbf{X}'\beta'$$

By using the appropriate matrices **C** and **M** we may test hypotheses of the form $\mathbf{C}\beta_p\mathbf{M} = \mathbf{0}$ as demonstrated earlier in this chapter. For example, the hypothesis that the slope parameters across the three groups are equal, that is, ${}_1\beta_2 = {}_2\beta_1 = {}_3\beta_1 = 0$, can be expressed in the above framework as

$$\begin{bmatrix} 1 & -1 & 0 \\ 0 & 1 & -1 \end{bmatrix} \begin{bmatrix} {}_1\beta_0 & {}_1\beta_1 \\ {}_2\beta_0 & {}_2\beta_1 \\ {}_3\beta_0 & {}_3\beta_1 \end{bmatrix} \begin{bmatrix} 0 \\ 1 \end{bmatrix} = \begin{bmatrix} {}_1\beta_1 - {}_2\beta_1 \\ {}_2\beta_1 - {}_3\beta_1 \end{bmatrix} = \begin{bmatrix} 0 \\ 0 \end{bmatrix}$$

This hypothesis can be tested using the procedures discussed earlier in this chapter. The growth curve model can be extended to any design whatsoever. We can cross-classify individuals on any number of factors and model the individual growth curve parameter accordingly, just as we would any other vector of dependent variables.

The growth curve model reduced the number of parameters that needed to be considered from eighteen to six. If the original vector of six dependent variables was modeled, then differences between the groups would have to be tested by a large number of awkward contrasts that would be difficult to interpret and summarize. The reader interested in the further study of growth curve analysis is referred to Grizzle and Allen (1969) and Kleinbaum (1973).

4.13 COMPUTER CONSIDERATIONS

There are a number of computer software packages that do multivariate regression analysis. SAS is particularly useful for this purpose and the following discussion will focus on it. If some or all of the independent variables are categorical, then SAS allows us to specify a reparameterization of the model (as we did in our MANOVA example) so that estimable functions of the regression parameters are being estimated. (A more extensive discussion of reparameterization can be found in *Introduction to Linear Models*.) SAS, then, allows us to specify as many tests of hypotheses concerning the regression parameters as desired. For example, we could test the hypothesis that a certain set of parameters are zero for all dependent variables. (These are hypotheses corresponding to the **C** matrix in $\mathbf{C}\beta\mathbf{M}$.) On the other hand, we could test the hypothesis that a certain set of parameters is the same for all dependent variables. (These are hypotheses corresponding to the **M** matrix in $\mathbf{C}\beta\mathbf{M}$.)

The program prints out a separate regression analysis for each dependent variable. Included in each analysis are the estimates of the regression parameters in the case of continuous variables and estimable functions of the parameters in the case of categorical variables. The associated standard errors and tests of significance are also presented. Then, multivariate tests are presented for each hypothesis specified by the user. Four different multivariate tests are presented for each hypothesis, including the greatest root test discussed earlier. The **H** and **E** matrix associated with each hypothesis can also be printed out. For example, in a two-way MANOVA, the hypotheses matrices for the row effects ($\mathbf{H}_r$), the column effects ($\mathbf{H}_c$), and the interaction effects ($\mathbf{H}_{r \times c}$) could be printed out.

4.14 PROBLEMS

(1) Using the sample data in the Appendix, consider variables 1, 3, and 5 (ability measures) as the vector of dependent variables and race and SES as independent variables. Analyze the data and discuss your findings.

(2) Test the hypothesis that the effects of race and SES are equal across the six dependent variables. (Hint: Use an **M** matrix.)

(3) Below are some correlations taken from Hauser (1973):

		x_1	x_2	x_3	y_1	y_2
Father's education	x_1	1.000				
Father's occupation	x_2	.494	1.000			
Family income	x_3	.389	.523	1.000		
Mental ability	y_1	.244	.212	.203	1.000	
High school grades	y_2	.151	.127	.116	.586	1.000

The independent variables are X_1, X_2, and X_3; the dependent variables are Y_1 and Y_2.

(a) Test the hypothesis that the three independent variables have no effect on the two dependent variables (use .01 level).

(b) If the above hypothesis is rejected, test the hypothesis that X_3 has no effect on the dependent variables (use .01 level).

(c) Does it make sense to test the hypothesis that the effect of X_3 is equal for both dependent variables? Why?

(4) A classic data set that was originally used by Fisher (1939) to demonstrate the application of linear discriminant function analysis is partially presented below. The data involved three species of flowers from which four measurements were taken.

Iris Species	Mean Measure: Sepal Length	Sepal Width	Petal Length	Petal Width	Sample Sizes
Virginica	6.588	2.974	5.552	2.026	50
Versicolor	5.936	2.770	4.260	1.326	50
Setosa	5.006	3.428	1.462	.246	50

$$\text{Error Matrix } (\mathbf{E}) = \begin{bmatrix} 38.96 & 13.63 & 24.62 & 6.64 \\ & 16.96 & 8.12 & 4.81 \\ & & 27.22 & 6.27 \\ & & & 6.16 \end{bmatrix}$$

(a) Conduct a one-way multivariate analysis of variance and test the hypothesis that the flower means are equal for each of the four measurements (use .01 level of significance).
(b) If this hypothesis is rejected, test the hypothesis that the Virginica and Versicolor means are equal for each of the four measurements at the .01 level of significance.
(c) Find a **C** and an **M** matrix such that $\mathbf{C}\beta\mathbf{M} = 0$ (where β is the regression parameter matrix) such that the hypothesis that the three species profiles on the four measurements are parallel to one another is being tested. Test this hypothesis.

(5) Conduct a multivariate analysis of variance on the hypothetical data set presented below and interpret the results.

Sex	Drug A y_1	A y_2	B y_1	B y_2	C y_1	C y_2
Male	5	6	7	6	20	15
	5	4	6	6	14	10
	8	8	9	11	17	11
	6	5	5	7	12	10
Female	7	10	10	12	15	11
	5	6	7	6	14	9
	9	7	6	5	13	8
	8	11	7	9	9	4

(6) See the data set above. Suppose the data for the first male subject in treatment A and the last female subject in treatment B were lost. Conduct a multivariate analysis of variance on this unbalanced data set.

NOTE

1. The formula for determining the two roots of a quadratic equation in the form of

$$a\lambda^2 + b\lambda + c = 0$$

is $\lambda_1, \lambda_2 = \dfrac{-b \pm (b^2 - 4ac)^{\frac{1}{2}}}{2a}$

Substituting into the above formula, we obtain

$$\lambda_1, \lambda_2 = \frac{-(.663279) \pm \left[(-.663279)^2 - 4(1)(.002983)\right]^{\frac{1}{2}}}{2(1)}$$

$$= .658751, .004527$$

5 Classification Procedures and Discriminant Analysis

5.1 INTRODUCTION

A problem that arises frequently in the social and behavioral sciences as well as in the biological sciences is that of classifying an object into one of a number of possible categories. For example, a botanist might want to determine if a new plant fits into one of a large possible number of plant categories; an archaeologist might want to classify the skeletal remains from an excavation site into one of a number of possible anthropomorphic categories; a clinical psychologist might want to classify a patient into one of a number of possible neurotic or psychotic categories; and a school psychologist might want to classify a child in regard to whether he or she has a remedial reading need. These can all be referred to as classification problems. In the case of a clinical psychologist classifying a patient into one of a number of psychiatric classifications, the psychologist might have a vector of psychological test scores upon which to base his or her decision. The classification problem involves the development of techniques to classify objects optimally into one of a number of possible known categories.

Section 5.2 begins with the simplest classification situation, classifying a person or object into one or two groups on the basis of one measure or variable. These simple classification rules are then modified to consider additional information: prior probabilities of group membership (section 5.3) and the costs of misclassification (section 5.4). In section 5.5 univariate classification is extended to three populations or groups. The reader will see that the univariate classification rules can be extended easily to k populations. The classification model is then extended in section 5.6 to the general case of p variables and k populations. Up to this point the classification procedures involve quadratic (that is, nonlinear) classification equations. In section 5.7 the quadratic equations are transformed into linear classification equations. The advantages of linear classification equations are that they simplify the classification rules and yield more insight concerning the relative importance of the variables in discriminating among populations. The efficiency of any classification procedure can be judged by how well it predicts group membership. Efficiency is discussed in section 5.8.

Linear discriminant function analysis (section 5.9) is a related approach for examining between-group differences on a set of measures. However, this approach focuses more on understanding between-group differences than on developing rules to classify units into one population or another. The procedure involves transforming the original variable into new variables, discriminant functions, which describe group differences on the basis of a few fundamental dimensions. Section 5.10 shows the close relationship of linear discriminant function analysis to the one-way multivariate analysis of variance discussed in the previous chapter. The computational procedures for estimating linear discriminant functions are developed and illustrated in section 5.11. Various properties of linear discriminant functions are discussed in section 5.12. The distance function is defined for the discriminant function space and compared with the distance function in the original variable space (section 5.13). Section 5.14 presents an interesting real-life application of linear discriminant function analysis. The final section briefly discusses computer software.

5.2 CLASSIFICATION WITH ONE VARIABLE AND TWO CATEGORIES

Before discussing the multivariate situation, let us discuss a hypothetical univariate situation in which two possible categories are involved and one measure is available on the object to be classified. Let us assume that a clinical psychologist has collected from various sources a large amount of data on this single characteristic (for example, a psychomotor test) from a population of normal children and a population of brain-damaged children. The means and standard deviations of the normal and brain-damaged children on the psychomotor test are shown in Table 5.1.

Since the sample size (n) for each group is based upon a large random sample, the means and standard deviations are rather precise estimates of the corresponding population means. For example, the standard error of the mean of the normal child is $5/\sqrt{9{,}000}$ or .05, and the standard error of the mean of the brain-damaged children is $5/\sqrt{1{,}000}$, or .15. This example assumes that the standard deviation of the psychomotor test for both groups is equal to 5 and the ratio of normal to brain-damaged children is 9 to 1.

In many applied situations we will not know the proportion of people in each of the categories. In our hypothetical example, we have assumed that we have drawn a random sample of children of 10,000 children to be tested and that 9,000 of these children were classified as normal and 1,000 of these children were classified as brain damaged on the basis of a comprehensive series

TABLE 5.1 Means, Standard Deviations, and Sample Sizes of Normal and Brain-Damaged Children on Psychomotor Test

	$\overline{X}$	S.D.	n
Normal	30	5	9,000
Brain damaged	20	5	1,000

of psychological and physiological tests independent of the one currently being used for diagnosis. It is furthermore assumed that the full battery of psychological and physiological tests is too expensive for initial screening and that we want to see how well we can do with a single psychomotor test.

If we assume that these two populations are normally distributed on the psychomotor test, we can portray the situation as in Figure 5.1. From Figure 5.1 we can see that there is overlap in the two distributions and that any rule we use for classifying a child into one of these two categories on the basis of the psychomotor test score will generate classification errors. The optimal classification rule in this situation is to categorize a child as brain damaged if his or her score is less than 25 and as normal if his or her score is greater than 25.[1] This is where the densities of the test scores for the two subpopulations of children are equal. This rule is optimal in that the proportion of misclassified children using this rule is smaller compared to any other rule. This classification rule assumes that the costs of misclassification are equal and that the proportions of children in both subpopulations or categories are equal. In other words, it is assumed that the cost of misclassifying a normal child as brain damaged is equal to the cost of misclassifying a brain-damaged child as normal. This might not be a reasonable assumption, for in classifying a brain-damaged child as normal we are denying him or her proper medical and psychological attention, which may have irreversible consequences and high economic and emotional costs for the child and his or her family. We also know from the empirical data that the incidence of brain damage is quite different from that of normality. For the time being we will treat the oversimplified situation; later, possible modifications of the decision rules to incorporate the additional information of costs and population proportions will be discussed.

The reason for choosing 25 as the decision point is that it is the score that has the same relative frequency for each of the two populations. Let $f_1(25)$ be the sample density (relative frequency) of the score 25 for the brain-damaged children (BD) and $f_2(25)$ be the sample density (relative frequency) of the score 25 for the normal children (N), then $f_1(25) = f_2(25)$. This can easily be shown by noting that

$$f_1(25) = \frac{1}{\sqrt{2\pi}(5)} e^{-\frac{1}{2}\frac{(25-20)^2}{25}} = \frac{1}{\sqrt{2\pi}(5)} e^{-\frac{1}{2}}$$

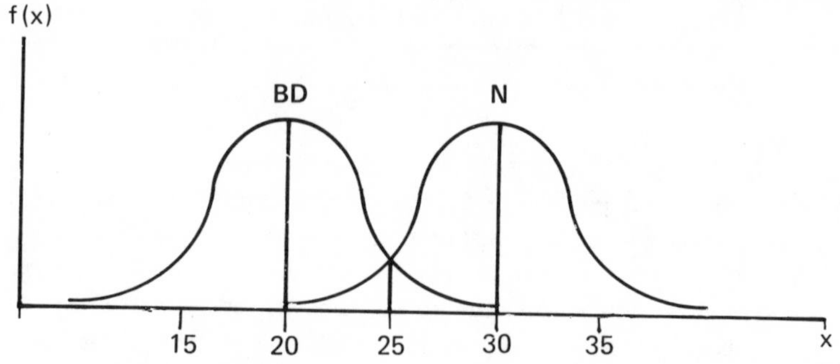

Figure 5.1 Empirical Frequency Distributions for a Group of Normal and Brain-Damaged Children

and

$$f_2(25) = \frac{1}{\sqrt{2\pi}(5)} e^{-\frac{1}{2}\frac{(25-30)^2}{25}} = \frac{1}{\sqrt{2\pi}(5)} e^{-\frac{1}{2}}$$

and that consequently $f_1(25) = f_2(25)$. Since the relative frequency of 25 is the same for both populations, we could flip a coin to determine to which of two populations a child with a score of 25 should be assigned. Using similar logic and referring to Figure 5.2, we would classify a child with a score of less than 25 as brain damaged since the relative frequency of any score less than 25 is greater for the brain-damaged group than for the normal group. Similarly, we would classify a child with a score of greater than 25 as normal since the relative frequency of any score greater than 25 is greater for the normal than for the brain-damaged group. For example, if a child had a score of 20, then

$$f_1(20) = \frac{1}{\sqrt{2\pi}(5)} e^{-\frac{1}{2}\frac{(20-20)^2}{25}} = \frac{1}{\sqrt{2\pi}(5)} \quad \text{and}$$

$$f_2(20) = \frac{1}{\sqrt{2\pi}(5)} e^{-\frac{1}{2}\frac{(20-30)^2}{25}} = \frac{1}{\sqrt{2\pi}(5)} e^{-2};$$

$$\frac{1}{\sqrt{2\pi}(5)} \text{ is greater than } \frac{1}{\sqrt{2\pi}(5)} e^{-2};$$

hence $f_1(20) > f_2(20)$ and we would assign a child with a score of 20 to the brain-damaged category.

To summarize, our decision rule is to classify a child as belonging to the normal group if $f_2(x) > f_1(x)$, classify a child as brain damaged if $f_2(x) < f_1(x)$, and classify him into either group if $f_2(x) = f_1(x)$. It will be convenient in further discussions always to assign a child to one of the two populations in

TABLE 5.2 Percentages of Correct and Incorrect Classifications

Actual Population	*Predicted Population* N	BD
N	84	16
BD	16	84

the situation where $f_1(x) = f_2(x)$ so that our simplified decision rule could be as follows: If $f_2(x) \geqslant f_1(x)$, assign to population N; if $f_2(x) < f_1(x)$, assign to population BD.

If the clinical psychologist applied this decision rule continuously for a large number of children, he or she would be classifying a normal child as brain damaged about 16 percent of the time and likewise would be classifying a brain-damaged child as normal about 16 percent of the time. The 16 percent misclassification for each of the two groups is derived by noting that brain-damaged children scoring above one standard deviation (5 points) from their own mean (20) will be classified as normal since for all scores equal or greater than ($\geqslant$) 25, the relative frequency is greater for the normal population than for the brain-damaged population (that is, $f_2(x) \geqslant f_1(x)$ for $x \geqslant 25$). Referring to a z table for the normal distribution, one can see that approximately 16 percent of the scores of the BD group fall at or above one standard deviation (that is, have a z score $\geqslant 1$) above the mean. The reader is asked to use the same logic to verify that 16 percent of the normal children would be classified as brain damaged. The percentages of correct and incorrect classification are summarized in Table 5.2.

It can be seen that the average percentage of correct classifications is 84 and the average percentage of incorrect classifications is 16. We would expect to be wrong about 50 percent of the time if we based our classification decision on the flip of a coin—that is, on chance alone.

5.3 INCORPORATING A PRIORI PROBABILITIES OF GROUP MEMBERSHIP

Let us now include some further information to be used in our decision rule—the a priori probability of a child being a member of one or the other of the two populations. We have estimated from Table 5.1 that the ratio of normal to brain-damaged children is 9 to 1, so that the a priori probability of a child being normal is .90 and the a priori probability of being brain damaged is .10.

From Bayes's theorem, it can be shown that

$$\rho(\text{BD}|x) \propto \rho\,(\text{BD})(\ell(x|\text{BD}))$$

and

$$\rho(\text{N}|x) \propto \rho(\text{N})(\ell(x|\text{N}))$$

where $\rho(BD|x)$ is the probability of being brain damaged given a score x on the psychomotor test, $\rho(BD)$ is the a priori probability of being brain damaged (.10), and $\ell(x|BD)$ is the likelihood function representing the likelihood of the score x given that the child is brain damaged, and $\propto$ is a notational symbol meaning proportional. The terms in $\rho(N|x) \propto \rho(N)(\ell(x|N))$ are interpreted analogously. The likelihood function is simply the density function of the scores for that group.

In other words, the a priori information is represented by $\rho(BD)$, the information lying in the sample (the density of a particular test score) is represented by $\ell(x|BD)$, and the posterior information concerning the probability of group membership given a certain test score, x, is represented by $\rho(BD|x)$ and reflects both priori information ($\rho(BD)$) and test data ($\ell(x|BD)$). The nature of these terms will become clearer in the examples that follow.

A decision maker would want to classify a child as BD if $\rho(BD|x) \geqslant \rho(N|x)$ or equivalently if $\rho(BD)(\ell(x|BD)) \geqslant \rho(N)(\ell(x|N)$. In other words, if combining a priori information with test information indicates a higher posterior probability of being in BD than N, then the child would be classified as BD. The optimal rule would be to assign a child to the BD group if for a particular score x:

$$\rho(BD)(\ell(x|BD)) \geqslant \rho(N)(\ell(x|N)$$

and to assign the child to the normal group if for this same particular score

$$\rho(BD)(\ell(x|BD)) < \rho(N)(\ell(x|N))$$

In Figure 5.1, $\ell(x|BD)$ represents the curve on the left and $\ell(x|N)$ represents the curve on the right (since $\ell(x|BD)$ and $\ell(x|N)$ can be considered density functions). If we then plotted $\rho(BD)(\ell(x|BD) = .10(\ell(x|BD)$ and $\rho(N)(\ell(x|N) = .90(\ell(x|N))$ we would have the situation portrayed in Figure 5.2.

Figure 5.2 indicates that for scores below approximately 20 we would classify the child as brain damaged. It turns out that for scores less than 19.53 we would classify the child as brain damaged and for scores equal to or greater than 19.53 we would classify the child as normal. In applied situations we would, of course, have to assign an integer decision point (such as 20) since most tests yield integer scores. The value of 19.53 was determined by noting that we want to find an x such that $\rho(BD)(\ell(x|BD)) = \rho(N)(\ell(x|N))$, which for our data results in the equality

$$(.10)\frac{1}{\sqrt{2\pi}(5)}e^{-\frac{1}{2}\frac{(x-20)^2}{25}} = (.90)\frac{1}{\sqrt{2\pi}(5)}e^{-\frac{1}{2}\frac{(x-30)^2}{25}}$$

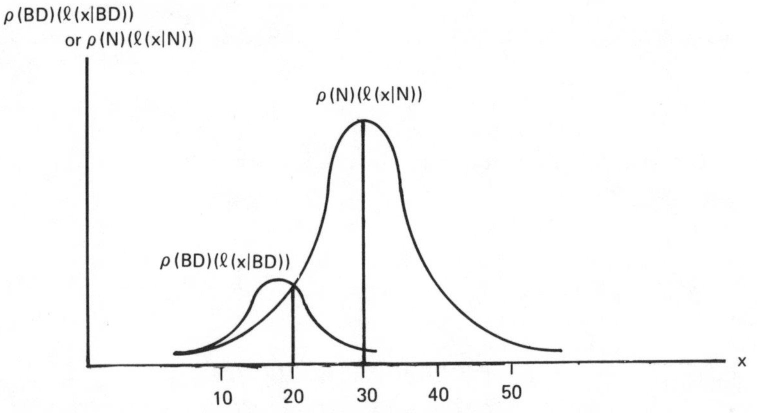

Figure 5.2 ρ(BD) (ℓ(x|BD)) and ρ(N) (ℓ(x|N)) as a Function of X

Simplifying the equality, we find that

$$e^{-\frac{1}{2}\frac{(x-20)^2}{25}} = 9e^{-\frac{1}{2}\frac{(x-30)^2}{25}}$$

and

$$\log_e e^{-\frac{(x-20)^2}{50}} = \log_e\left(9e^{-\frac{(x-30)^2}{50}}\right)$$

and

$$-\frac{(x-20)^2}{50} = \log_e 9 - \frac{(x-30)^2}{50}$$

and

$$-(x-20)^2 = 50 \log_e 9 - (x-30)^2$$

from which x can be found to be 19.53.

Notice how the inclusion of prior information altered the decision rule. Without the prior information our decision rule would have been to classify a child as brain damaged if he or she scored below 25. With the prior information that brain-damaged children are relatively rare compared to normal children, our cutpoint has been moved down more than 5 points, or approximately one standard deviation. Intuitively, the decision rule is telling us that since the incidence of brain damage is rare one should not classify a child as

TABLE 5.3 Classification Cost

Actual Population	*Predicted Population* N	BD
N	0	1
BD	3	0

brain damaged unless he or she scores roughly near the mean of the brain-damaged population.

5.4 INCORPORATING COSTS OF MISCLASSIFICATION

We will now examine the decision rules in classification analysis when costs of misclassification are considered. Earlier in our discussion, it was mentioned that the costs of misclassifying a brain-damaged child as normal are probably greater than the costs of misclassifying a normal child as brain damaged. Further examination will reveal the misdiagnosed normal child to be normal, but the misclassified brain-damaged child may not undergo any further diagnostic testing. It is extremely difficult to derive misclassification costs in decision problems such as this regarding human and social welfare. What cost does one assign to misclassifying a patient with a brain tumor as normal? Let us assume for our example that the costs of correct classification are 0, that the act of misclassifying a normal child as brain damaged has 1 unit of cost associated with it, and that the act of misclassifying a brain-damaged child as normal has 3 units of cost associated with it. These costs could be in terms of money or in terms of psychological and physical discomfort. They are represented in Table 5.3.

If the costs of misclassification are known and incorporated into our model, then it can be shown that an optimal decision rule that minimizes expected costs is to classify a child as brain damaged if

$$C_{(N|BD)}\rho(BD)\ell(x|BD) \geqslant C_{(BD|N)}\rho(N)\ell(x|N)$$

and to classify a child as normal if

$$C_{(N|BD)}\rho(BD)\ell(x|BD) < C_{(BD|N)}\rho(N)\ell(x|N)$$

where $C_{(BD|N)}$ is the cost of misclassifying a normal child as brain damaged and $C_{(N|BD)}$ is the cost of misclassifying a brain-damaged child as normal. We can rewrite these two decision rules as follows:

Classify as brain damaged if

$$\frac{\ell(x|BD)}{\ell(x|N)} \geqslant \frac{C_{(BD|N)}\rho(N)}{C_{(N|BD)}\rho(BD)}$$

and classify as normal if

$$\frac{\ell(x|BD)}{\ell(x|N)} < \frac{C_{(BD|N)}\rho(N)}{C_{(N|BD)}\rho(BD)}$$

We can derive some interesting conclusions upon examining the above decision rules. First, if the two costs and the two prior probabilities are equal to each other, then the decision rule simplifies to classify as brain damaged if

$$\frac{\ell(x|BD)}{\ell(x|N)} \geqslant 1$$

and classify as normal if

$$\frac{\ell(x|BD)}{\ell(x|N)} < 1$$

These decision rules are identical to those previously discussed where neither costs nor prior probabilities are known.

Second, if the costs of misclassification are equal but the prior probabilities are known and unequal, then the decision rule simplifies to classify as brain damaged if

$$\frac{\ell(x|BD)}{\ell(x|N)} \geqslant \frac{\rho(N)}{\rho(BD)}$$

and classify as normal if

$$\frac{\ell(x|BD)}{\ell(x|N)} < \frac{\rho(N)}{\rho(BD)}$$

This rule is equivalent to the rule previously discussed where the costs were assumed to be equal but prior probabilities unequal. Since the probability of being from a brain-damaged population in our example is only .10, our decision rule tells us that the likelihood or, equivalently, the density of x for the brain-damaged population must be nine times greater than the density of x for the normal population before a child is classified as brain damaged. That is,

$$\frac{\ell(x|BD)}{\ell(x|N)} \geqslant 9$$

In other words, the prior probability of being in the brain-damaged population is so small that the brain-damaged likelihood has to be many times greater than the normal likelihood before we would be willing to classify a child as brain damaged.

If, on the other hand, the cost of misclassifying a brain-damaged child as normal ($C_{(N|BD)}$) is 3 units and the cost of misclassifying a normal child as brain damaged ($C_{(BD|N)}$) is 1 unit, then our decision rule would be modified such that we would classify a child as brain damaged if

$$\frac{\ell(x|BD)}{\ell(x|N)} \geqslant \frac{1}{3}\left(\frac{.90}{.10}\right) = 3$$

We can see that since the cost of misclassifying a child as normal is higher than misclassifying a child as brain damaged, the above modified decision rule is more lenient in classifying a child as brain damaged than a decision rule assuming equal misclassification costs. In the latter case the ratio of the likelihoods or densities has to be 9, while in the former case it only has to be 3. In order to be classified as brain damaged a child would have to make a score of 22.25 or less on the psychomotor test. This cutpoint can be determined in a manner similar to that used earlier to determine the cutpoint or decision point for the decision rule:

$$\frac{\ell(x|BD)}{\ell(x|N)} \geqslant 9$$

We can derive the cutpoint by noting that solving for x in the equation

$$\frac{e^{-\frac{1}{2}\frac{(x-20)^2}{25}}}{e^{-\frac{1}{2}\frac{(x-30)^2}{25}}} = 3$$

will yield the correct solution. Taking the natural logarithm of both sides of this equation, we find that

$$\log_e \frac{e^{-\frac{(x-20)^2}{50}}}{e^{-\frac{(x-30)^2}{50}}} = \log_e 3$$

or

$$-\frac{(x-20)^2}{50} + \frac{(x-30)^2}{25} = 1.0986$$

The solution x can be easily found to be 22.25. This cutpoint is between the cutpoint of 25, which would be used if no information were available on either costs or prior probabilities, and the cutpoint of 19.53, which would be used if information were available on prior probabilities but not on costs.

5.5 UNIVARIATE NORMAL CLASSIFICATION FOR THREE POPULATIONS

In this section, we will examine univariate normal classification procedures for three populations that can easily be generalized to k populations. In order to shorten the exposition, we will no longer consider costs of misclassification in our decision models. However, the reader should be able to generalize to the k population situation on the basis of our previous discussion of the two-group cost decision model. Suppose that we know or have estimated from a large sample the density function of a preschool reading readiness test for each of the following populations: poor readers, average readers, and good readers in grade 1. This problem is to predict which reading performance category a child will be in when he or she enters grade 1 on the basis of the child's score on a preschool reading readiness test taken when the child was 5 years old. The hypothetical means and standard deviations for these three groups are presented in Table 5.4. These three distributions are also plotted in Figure 5.3.

TABLE 5.4 Means, Standard Deviations, and Prior Probabilities for Each of Three Reading Populations

First-Grade Reading Level	$\overline{X}$	*S.D.*	*Prior Probability*
Poor	20	10	.20
Average	40	10	.60
Good	50	10	.20

If neither prior probabilities nor costs are included in the decision model, then the optimum decision regions are as follows:

R_1: classify as poor reader if $x \leq 30$

R_2: classify as average reader if $30 < x \leq 45$

R_3: classify as good reader if $x > 45$

The cutpoints and regions are indicated in Figure 5.3. Scores in R_1 are more likely to be generated by children coming from the poor reading population; scores in R_2 are more likely to be generated by children coming from the average reading population; and scores in R_3 are more likely to be generated by children coming from the good reading population. The decision rule that yielded these three regions of classification is as follows:

(1) Classify as poor reader if

$$\rho(x|PR) \geqslant \rho(x|AR) \text{ and } \rho(x|PR) \geqslant \rho(x|GR)$$

(2) Classify as average reader if

$$\rho(x|AR) \geqslant \rho(x|PR) \text{ and } \rho(x|AR) \geqslant \rho(x|GR)$$

(3) Classify as good reader if

$$\rho(x|GR) \geqslant \rho(x|PR) \text{ and } \rho(x|GR) \geqslant \rho(x|AR)$$

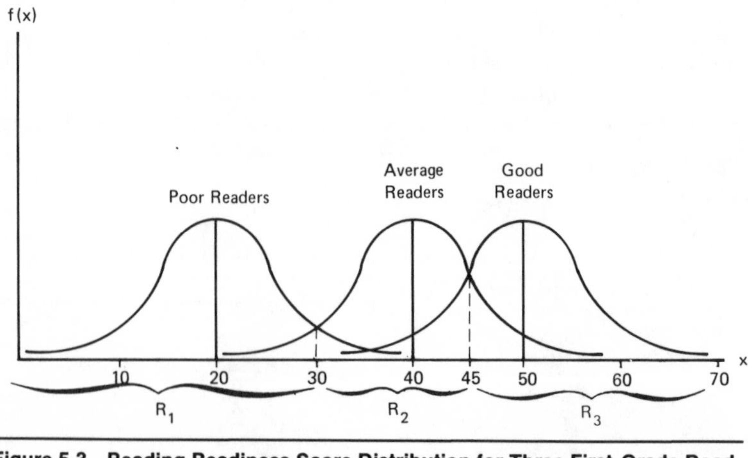

Figure 5.3 Reading Readiness Score Distribution for Three First-Grade Reading Populations

where $\rho(x|PR)$ is the density of x or likelihood of x for the poor reader population (that is,

$$\rho(x|PR) = \frac{1}{\sqrt{2\pi}(10)} e^{-\frac{1}{2}\frac{(x-20)^2}{100}}\Bigg),$$

$\rho(x|AR)$ is the density of x for the average reader population, and $\rho(x|GR)$ is the density of x for the good reader population. As an exercise, the reader should verify these cutpoints and classification regions by using methods similar to those discussed earlier regarding the two-group classification problem.

We will now examine this three-population case when prior probabilities are considered in the decision rule. The decision rule in this case is to com- for a given observation x, $\rho(PR)\rho(x|PR)$, $\rho(AR)\rho(x|AR)$, and $\rho(GR)\rho(x|GR)$, and classify the child into that group for which the appropriate index, which is proportional to the posterior probability, has the largest value. For example, if a child had an observed score of 50, we would make the following calculations:

$$\rho(PR|50) \propto \rho(PR)\rho(50|PR) \propto .20e^{-\frac{1}{2}\frac{(50-20)^2}{100}} = .20(.01110899) = .0022$$

and

$$\rho(AR|50) \propto \rho(AR)\rho(50|AR) \propto .60e^{-\frac{1}{2}\frac{(50-40)^2}{100}} = .60(.606530) = .3639$$

and

$$\rho(GR|50) \propto \rho(GR)\rho(50|GR) \propto .20e^{-\frac{1}{2}\frac{(50-50)^2}{100}} = .20(1) = .2000$$

If we normalize these numbers by dividing each by the sum of the numbers, then we have the posterior probabilities of a child with a score of 50 belonging to each of the three reading categories:

Poor readers

$$\rho(PR|50) = \frac{.0022}{.5661} = .003$$

Average Readers

$$\rho(\text{AR}|50) = \frac{.3639}{.5661} = .642$$

Good Readers

$$\rho(\text{GR}|50) = \frac{.2000}{.5661} = .353$$

It can be seen that the posterior probability of coming from the average reader group is highest (.642) and, consequently, we would classify the child with a score of 50 as being an average reader in grade 1. For every possible test score, there is a posterior probability distribution. As an exercise, the reader should calculate the posterior probabilities of being members of the three populations for the scores of 75 and 55. The decision rules can be summarized as follows:

Classify as a poor reader if

$$\rho(\text{PR})\rho(\text{x}|\text{PR}) \geqslant \rho(\text{AR})\rho(\text{x}|\text{AR}) \text{ and } \rho(\text{PR})\rho(\text{x}|\text{PR}) \geqslant \rho(\text{GR})\rho(\text{x}|\text{GR})$$

Classify as an average reader if

$$\rho(\text{AR})\rho(\text{x}|\text{AR}) \geqslant \rho(\text{PR})\rho(\text{x}|\text{PR}) \text{ and } \rho(\text{AR})\rho(\text{x}|\text{AR}) \geqslant \rho(\text{GR})\rho(\text{x}|\text{GR})$$

Classify as a good reader if

$$\rho(\text{GR})\rho(\text{x}|\text{GR}) \geqslant \rho(\text{AR})\rho(\text{x}|\text{AR}) \text{ and } \rho(\text{GR})\rho(\text{x}|\text{GR}) \geqslant \rho(\text{PR})\rho(\text{x}|\text{PR})$$

We can write still another set of equivalent decision rules:

Classify as a poor reader if

$$\frac{\rho(\text{x}|\text{PR})}{\rho(\text{x}|\text{AR})} \geqslant \frac{\rho(\text{AR})}{\rho(\text{PR})} \text{ and } \frac{\rho(\text{x}|\text{PR})}{\rho(\text{x}|\text{GR})} \geqslant \frac{\rho(\text{GR})}{\rho(\text{PR})}$$

Classify as an average reader if

$$\frac{\rho(\text{x}|\text{AR})}{\rho(\text{x}|\text{PR})} \geqslant \frac{\rho(\text{PR})}{\rho(\text{AR})} \text{ and } \frac{\rho(\text{x}|\text{AR})}{\rho(\text{x}|\text{GR})} \geqslant \frac{\rho(\text{GR})}{\rho(\text{AR})}$$

Classify as a good reader if

$$\frac{\rho(x|GR)}{\rho(x|AR)} \geqslant \frac{\rho(AR)}{\rho(GR)} \text{ and } \frac{\rho(x|GR)}{\rho(x|PR)} \geqslant \frac{\rho(PR)}{\rho(GR)}$$

For our example, the first decision rule of the latter set can be written as

$$\frac{e^{-\frac{1}{2}\frac{(x-20)^2}{100}}}{e^{-\frac{1}{2}\frac{(x-40)^2}{100}}} \geqslant \frac{.60}{.20}$$

and

$$\frac{e^{-\frac{1}{2}\frac{(x-40)^2}{100}}}{e^{-\frac{1}{2}\frac{(x-50)^2}{100}}} \geqslant \frac{.20}{.20}$$

Since $\log_e$ is a monotonic function, these two inequalities are equivalent, respectively, to

$$\log_e \frac{e^{-\frac{1}{2}\frac{(x-20)^2}{100}}}{e^{-\frac{1}{2}\frac{(x-40)^2}{100}}} \geqslant \log_e 3$$

and

$$\log_e \frac{e^{-\frac{1}{2}\frac{(x-40)^2}{100}}}{e^{-\frac{1}{2}\frac{(x-50)^2}{100}}} \geqslant \log_e 1$$

Furthermore,

$$\log_e \frac{e^{-\frac{1}{2}\frac{(x-20)^2}{100}}}{e^{-\frac{1}{2}\frac{(x-40)^2}{100}}} = \frac{-1}{200}[(x-20)^2 - (x-40)^2]$$

and

$$\log_e 3 = 1.098$$

and

$$\log_e \frac{e^{-\frac{1}{2}\frac{(x-40)^2}{100}}}{e^{-\frac{1}{2}\frac{(x-40)^2}{100}}} = \frac{-1}{200}[(x-40)^2 - (x-50)^2]$$

and

$$\log_e 1 = 0$$

Consequently, we would classify a child as a poor reader if his score, x, satisfied the following two inequalities

$$\frac{-1}{200}[(x-20)^2 - (x-40)^2] \geqslant 1.098$$

and

$$\frac{-1}{200}[(x-40)^2 - (x-50)^2] \geqslant 0$$

For example, a child scoring 10 on the reading readiness test would be predicted to be a poor reader in grade 1 since

$$\frac{-1}{200}[(10-20)^2 - (10-40)^2] = 4.50, \text{ which is} \geqslant 1.098$$

and

$$\frac{-1}{200}[(10-40)^2 - (10-50)^2] = 3.50, \text{ which is} \geqslant 0$$

If the child's score did not satisfy both of these inequalities, then the child would be classified into one or the other of the remaining two groups, whose decision rules can be derived similarly.

5.6 MULTIVARIATE NORMAL CLASSIFICATION

We went into some detail concerning classification procedures for the univariate case so that we could more easily generalize to the multivariate normal situation. Costs of misclassification will not be considered. The posterior probability of a p-dimensional multivariate normally distributed vector, **x**, coming from each of n populations can be expressed as

$$\rho(\mathrm{i}|\mathbf{x}) = \frac{\rho(\mathrm{i})\rho(\mathbf{x}|\mathrm{i})}{\sum_{\mathrm{i}} \rho(\mathrm{i})\rho(\mathbf{x}|\mathrm{i})}$$

where $\rho(\mathrm{i})$ is the a priori probability of coming from population i and $\rho(\mathbf{x}|\mathrm{i})$ is the density of the p-dimensional vector x for population i. Since

$$\frac{1}{\sum_{\mathrm{i}} \rho(\mathrm{i})\rho(\mathbf{x}|\mathrm{i})}$$

is simply a normalizing constant that is equal for each of the i equations, the posterior probability of **x** coming from population i is proportional to $\rho(\mathrm{i})\rho(\mathbf{x}|\mathrm{i})$. Noting that $\log_e \rho(\mathrm{i})\rho(\mathbf{x}|\mathrm{i}) = \log_e \rho(\mathrm{i}) + \log_e \rho(\mathbf{x}|\mathrm{i})$ is monotonically related to $\rho(\mathrm{i})\rho(\mathbf{x}|\mathrm{i})$, we see that classification on the basis of posterior probabilities is equivalent to classification on the basis of the following classification equations:

$$C(\mathrm{i}) = \log_e \rho(\mathrm{i}) + \log_e \rho(\mathbf{x}|\mathrm{i}) \text{ for population i}$$

Substituting the multivariate normal density function in the above, the classification equations would become

$$C(\mathrm{i}) = \log_e \rho(\mathrm{i}) + \log_e \frac{1}{(2\pi)^{p/2}|\mathbf{V}|^{1/2}} e^{-\frac{1}{2}(\mathbf{x}-\boldsymbol{\mu}_\mathrm{i})'\mathbf{V}^{-1}(\mathbf{x}-\boldsymbol{\mu}_\mathrm{i})}$$

which, in turn, equals

$$\log_e \rho(\mathrm{i}) + \log_e \frac{1}{(2\pi)^{p/2}|\mathbf{V}|^{1/2}} - \frac{1}{2}(\mathbf{x}-\boldsymbol{\mu}_\mathrm{i})'\mathbf{V}^{-1}(\mathbf{x}-\boldsymbol{\mu}_\mathrm{i})$$

Here we have assumed that each population has a common dispersion matrix **V** so that the second term in each classification equation is constant. The classification equations thus simplify to $\log_e \rho(\mathrm{i}) - \frac{1}{2}(\mathbf{x}-\boldsymbol{\mu}_\mathrm{i})'\mathbf{V}^{-1}(\mathbf{x}-\boldsymbol{\mu}_\mathrm{i})$, where $\rho(i)$ is the a priori probability of coming from population i, $\mathbf{V}^{-1}$ is the inverse of the common p × p variance-covariance for the random p dimensional vector $\mathbf{x}$, and μ_i is the p dimensional vector of population means corresponding to the p components of $\mathbf{x}$ for population i. In many instances the assumption of equal variance-covariance matrices is appropriate. If it is not, then the term

$$\log_e \frac{1}{(2\pi)^{p/2}\,|\mathbf{V}|^{1/2}}$$

must be retained in all of the classification equations.

For a given observed vector $\mathbf{x}$, we compute the value of C(i) for each of the n populations and then classify the person or object associated with the vector $\mathbf{x}$ into the population that yields the largest numerical value for C(i).

As an example, let us suppose that we want to classify a psychiatric patient into one of three groups: neurotic, psychotic, or organic brain damaged. On the basis of past experience with a large number of previous patients, the researcher also has rather precise estimates of the mean scores on three psychological tests for each of these three patient populations. In addition, let us assume that the researcher has a precise estimate of the common variance-covariance matrix for these three test scores. The needed hypothetical information is presented in Tables 5.5 and 5.6, respectively.

The classification equation for neurotics would be

$$C(\text{neurotic}) = \log_e .60 - \frac{1}{2}[x_1 - 10,\ x_2 - 5,\ x_3 - 15]\begin{bmatrix} 100 & 30 & 40 \\ 30 & 50 & 20 \\ 40 & 20 & 80 \end{bmatrix}^{-1}\begin{bmatrix} x_1 - 10 \\ x_2 - 5 \\ x_3 - 15 \end{bmatrix}$$

$$= -.5108 - \frac{1}{2}[x_1 - 10,\ x_2 - 5,\ x_3 - 15]\begin{bmatrix} .01406 & -.00625 & -.00547 \\ -.00625 & .02500 & -.00313 \\ -.00547 & -.00313 & .01602 \end{bmatrix}\begin{bmatrix} x_1 - 10 \\ x_2 - 5 \\ x_3 - 15 \end{bmatrix}$$

The remaining two quadratic classification equations can easily be seen to be

$$C(\text{psychotic}) = -1.2040 - \frac{1}{2}[x_1 - 20,\ x_2 - 10,\ x_3 - 10]\begin{bmatrix} .01406 & -.00625 & -.00547 \\ -.00625 & .02500 & -.00313 \\ -.00547 & -.00313 & .01602 \end{bmatrix}\begin{bmatrix} x_1 - 20 \\ x_2 - 10 \\ x_3 - 10 \end{bmatrix}$$

and

$$C(\text{brain damaged}) = -2.30258 - \frac{1}{2}[x_1 - 15,\ x_2 - 15,\ x_3 - 15]\begin{bmatrix} .01406 & -.00625 & -.00547 \\ -.00625 & .02500 & -.00313 \\ -.00547 & -.00313 & .01602 \end{bmatrix}\begin{bmatrix} x_1 - 15 \\ x_2 - 15 \\ x_3 - 15 \end{bmatrix}$$

Our strategy for classifying a new patient would be to obtain his or her vector of text scores $[x_1, x_2, x_3]$, substitute this vector into each of the three classification equations, and then assign the patient to that population whose corresponding classification equation yields the highest numerical value.

For illustrative purposes, let us assume that a tested patient's vector of scores

$$\begin{bmatrix} x_1 \\ x_2 \\ x_3 \end{bmatrix} \text{ for the three tests was } \begin{bmatrix} 5 \\ 10 \\ 15 \end{bmatrix}$$

If we substituted this vector of scores in each of the three classification equations, we would find that

$$C(\text{neurotic}) = -.5108 - \frac{1}{2}[-5,\ 5,\ 0] \begin{bmatrix} .01406 & -.00625 & -.00547 \\ -.00625 & .02500 & -.00313 \\ -.00547 & -.00313 & .01602 \end{bmatrix} \begin{bmatrix} -5 \\ 5 \\ 0 \end{bmatrix} = -1.1555$$

$$C(\text{psychotic}) = -1.2040 - \frac{1}{2}[-15,\ 0,\ 5] \begin{bmatrix} .01406 & -.00625 & -.00547 \\ -.00625 & .02500 & -.00313 \\ -.00547 & -.00313 & .01602 \end{bmatrix} \begin{bmatrix} -15 \\ 0 \\ 5 \end{bmatrix} = -3.3967$$

and

$$C(\text{brain damaged}) = -2.3058 - \frac{1}{2}[-10,\ -5,\ 0] \begin{bmatrix} .01406 & -.00625 & -.00547 \\ -.00625 & .02500 & -.00313 \\ -.00547 & -.00313 & .01602 \end{bmatrix} \begin{bmatrix} -10 \\ -5 \\ 0 \end{bmatrix} = -1.6028$$

Consequently, we would assign a patient with the vector of scores

$$\begin{bmatrix} 5 \\ 10 \\ 15 \end{bmatrix}$$

to the neurotic group. As an exercise, the reader can classify a patient with the vector of scores

$$\begin{bmatrix} 20 \\ 5 \\ 10 \end{bmatrix}$$

TABLE 5.5 Prior Probabilities and Means for Neurotic, Psychotic, and Brain-Damaged Patients

	Means			*Prior*
Patient Category	*Test 1*	*Test 2*	*Test 3*	*Probabilities*
Neurotic	10	5	15	.60
Psychotic	20	10	10	.30
Brain damaged	15	15	15	.10

TABLE 5.6 Variance-Covariance Matrix for Tests 1, 2, and 3

	Test		
Test	1	2	3
1	100	30	40
2	30	50	20
3	40	20	80

5.7 LINEAR CLASSIFICATION EQUATIONS

The above classification equations are quadratic (that is, $(\mathbf{x}-\mu_i)'\mathbf{V}^{-1}(\mathbf{x}-\mu_i)$) in form. We could obtain a set of linear functions of

$$\begin{bmatrix} x_1 \\ x_2 \\ x_3 \end{bmatrix}$$

to be used for classifying patients. They are referred to in the literature as "discriminant functions." There are two major advantages in using linear functions of the observations. First, their numerical values for a particular vector of scores are easier to calculate than the more cumbersome quadratic equations. Second, the weights corresponding to particular scores or components of the vector give some indication of the relative importance of the scores or components of the vector in discriminating between any two populations. These discriminant functions will result in the exact same classification of vectors as the quadratic equations. With the above two advantages in mind, we will now derive a set of decision rules using discriminant functions.

We first note that in order for an individual to be classified as a neurotic two conditions must hold. They are

$$\begin{aligned} C_{N,P} = \log_e \rho(N) - \tfrac{1}{2}(\mathbf{x}-\mu_N)'\mathbf{V}^{-1}(\mathbf{x}-\mu_N) \\ -[\log_e \rho(P) - \tfrac{1}{2}(\mathbf{x}-\mu_P)'\mathbf{V}^{-1}(\mathbf{x}-\mu_P)] \geqslant 0 \end{aligned}$$

and

$$C_{N,BD} = \log_e \rho(N) - \frac{1}{2}(x - \mu_N)'V^{-1}(x - \mu_N)$$
$$- [\log_e \rho(BD) - \frac{1}{2}(x - \mu_{BD})'V^{-1}(x - \mu_{BD})] \geqslant 0$$

where N symbolizes neurotic, P symbolizes psychotic, and BD symbolizes brain damaged. The former equation, $C_{N,P}$, can be reduced to

$$x'V^{-1}(\mu_n - \mu_P) - \frac{1}{2}(\mu_N + \mu_P)'V^{-1}(\mu_N - \mu_P) + \log_e \frac{\rho(N)}{\rho(P)} \geqslant 0$$

by noting that

$$-\frac{1}{2}[(x - \mu_N)'V^{-1}(x - \mu_N) - (x - \mu_P)'V^{-1}(x - \mu_P)]$$
$$= -\frac{1}{2}[x'V^{-1}x - x'V^{-1}\mu_N - \mu_N'V^{-1}x + \mu_N'V^{-1}\mu_N - x'V^{-1}x$$
$$+ x'V^{-1}\mu_P + \mu_P'V^{-1}x - \mu_P'V^{-1}\mu_P]$$
$$= x'V^{-1}(\mu_N - \mu_p) - \frac{1}{2}(\mu_N + \mu_p)'V^{-1}(\mu_N - \mu_p)$$

and that

$$\log_e \rho(N) - \log_e \rho(P) = \log_e \frac{\rho(N)}{\rho(P)}$$

The $C_{N,BD}$ equation can likewise be reduced to

$$x'V^{-1}(\mu_N - \mu_{BD}) - \frac{1}{2}(\mu_N + \mu_{BD})'V^{-1}(\mu_N - \mu_{BD}) + \log_e \frac{\rho(N)}{\rho(BD)} \geqslant 0$$

If the value of $C_{N,P}$ and $C_{N,BD}$ are both $\geqslant 0$ for a vector of the observed scores, then we would classify the patient into the neurotic group. A positive value of $C_{N,P}$ indicates that the posterior probability of coming from group N is larger than the posterior probability of coming from group P. Likewise, a positive value of $C_{N,BD}$ indicates that the posterior probability of coming from group N is larger than the posterior probability of coming from group P. These two equations are both linear functions of **x** because

$$-\frac{1}{2}(\mu_N + \mu_P)'V^{-1}(\mu_N - \mu_p) + \log_e \frac{\rho(N)}{\rho(P)}$$

and

$$-\frac{1}{2}(\mu_N + \mu_{BD})'V^{-1}(\mu_N - \mu_{BD}) + \log_e \frac{\rho(N)}{\rho(BD)}$$

are both scalars or constants in their respective equations, $C_{N,P}$ and $C_{N,BD}$. On the other hand $x'V^{-1}(\mu_N - \mu_p)$ and $x'V^{-1}(\mu_N - \mu_{BD})$ are each linear functions of x in their respective equations, $C_{N,P}$ and $C_{N,BD}$. This is because $V^{-1}(\mu_N - \mu_p)$ and $V^{-1}(\mu_N - \mu_{BD})$ are each known vectors of weights. Notice that the weights for the components of x (that is, scores) for each of the equations are a function of the structure of the variance-covariance matrix V and the differences of the means for the two populations under consideration.

Using the above logic, the reader is urged to verify that a patient would be classified as psychotic if the following two conditions hold.

$$C_{P,N} = x'V^{-1}(\mu_P - \mu_N) - \frac{1}{2}(\mu_P + \mu_N)'V^{-1}(\mu_P - \mu_N) + \log_e \frac{\rho(P)}{\rho(N)} \geqslant 0$$

$$C_{P,BD} = x'V^{-1}(\mu_P - \mu_{BD}) - \frac{1}{2}(\mu_P + \mu_{BD})'V^{-1}(\mu_P - \mu_{BD}) + \log_e \frac{\rho(P)}{\rho(BD)} \geqslant 0$$

The reader can verify that $C_{P,N} = -C_{N,P}$ and that consequently we do not have to compute $C_{P,N}$, but just change the sign for the value of $C_{N,P}$. Continuing, the patient would be classified as brain damaged if

$$C_{BD,N} = -C_{N,BD} \geqslant 0$$

and

$$C_{BD,P} = -C_{P,BD} \geqslant 0$$

To summarize, we have three populations, and six discriminant functions. We would classify a patient as neurotic if $C_{N,P} \geqslant 0$ and $C_{N,BD} \geqslant 0$; as psychotic if $C_{P,N} \geqslant 0$ and $C_{P,BD} \geqslant 0$; and as brain damaged if $C_{BD,N} \geqslant 0$ and $C_{BD,P} \geqslant 0$.

Since only three of these discriminant functions are unique up to a sign change, we need only derive three discriminant functions. For our example, we will derive the discriminant functions for $C_{N,P}$, $C_{N,BD}$, and $C_{P,BD}$. The remaining three discriminant functions will then be $C_{P,N} = -C_{N,P}$, $C_{BD,N} = -C_{N,BD}$, and $C_{BD,P} = -C_{P,BD}$. Thus

$$C_{N,P} = x'V^{-1}(\mu_N - \mu_P) - \frac{1}{2}(\mu_N + \mu_P)'V^{-1}(\mu_N - \mu_P) + \log_e \frac{\rho(N)}{\rho(P)}$$

$$= [x_1, x_2, x_3] \begin{bmatrix} .01406 & -.00625 & -.00547 \\ -.00625 & .02500 & -.00313 \\ -.00547 & -.00313 & .01602 \end{bmatrix} \begin{bmatrix} -10 \\ -5 \\ 5 \end{bmatrix}$$

$$-\frac{1}{2}[30, 15, 25] \begin{bmatrix} .01406 & -.00625 & -.00547 \\ -.00625 & .02500 & -.00313 \\ -.00547 & -.00313 & .01602 \end{bmatrix} \begin{bmatrix} -10 \\ -5 \\ 5 \end{bmatrix} + \log_e 2$$

$$= -.1367x_1 - .07815x_2 + .15045x_3 + 1.4491$$

Notice that the weight for x_3 is largest in absolute value and that the weight for x_2 is smallest in absolute value. Even though the mean difference between the neurotic and psychotic populations is relatively small for test score 3, the nature of the variance-covariance structure along with the mean differences yields the largest weight for test score 3.

It is interesting to note at this point that if the variance-covariance matrix had the form

$$\sigma^2 \mathbf{I}_{3\times 3} = \begin{bmatrix} \sigma^2 & 0 & 0 \\ 0 & \sigma^2 & 0 \\ 0 & 0 & \sigma^2 \end{bmatrix}$$

then the weight vector would be

$$\begin{bmatrix} \sigma^2 & 0 & 0 \\ 0 & \sigma^2 & 0 \\ 0 & 0 & \sigma^2 \end{bmatrix}^{-1} \begin{bmatrix} -10 \\ -5 \\ 5 \end{bmatrix}$$

which is equal to

$$\frac{1}{\sigma^2}[-10, -5, 5]'$$

The vector of discriminant function weights under the condition of independence among the variables would then be proportional to the vector of respective mean differences. If the variance-covariance matrix had the following form

$$\begin{bmatrix} \sigma_1^2 & 0 & 0 \\ 0 & \sigma_2^2 & 0 \\ 0 & 0 & \sigma_3^2 \end{bmatrix}$$

then the weight vector would be

$$\begin{bmatrix} \frac{1}{\sigma_1^2} & 0 & 0 \\ 0 & \frac{1}{\sigma_2^2} & 0 \\ 0 & 0 & \frac{1}{\sigma_3^2} \end{bmatrix} \begin{bmatrix} -10 \\ -5 \\ 5 \end{bmatrix}$$

which is equal to

$$\left[\frac{-10}{\sigma_1^2}, \frac{-5}{\sigma_2^2}, \frac{5}{\sigma_3^2}\right]'$$

In this situation, the weights are the corresponding mean differences divided by their respective variances. Variables with large variances relative to their mean differences would have small weights and, conversely, variables with small variances relative to their mean differences would have large weights. In any event, if the variance-covariance matrix is diagonal in form the computation and interpretation of the discriminant functions becomes much simplified. Each variable makes a contribution in the discriminant function independent of the behavior of the remaining variables since the variables are independent of one another.

Continuing, the reader can verify that

$$C_{N,BD} = -.00780x_1 - .21875x_2 + .05865x_3 + 3.05638$$

and

$$C_{P,BD} = .12890x_1 - .14060x_2 - .09180x_3 + 1.74786$$

Since the other three possible equations are each the opposite of one of the above three equations, the six discriminant functions are as follows:

$$C_{N,P} = -.13570x_1 - .07815x_2 + .15045x_3 + 1.44910$$

$$C_{N,BD} = -.00780x_1 - .21875x_2 + .05865x_3 + 3.05638$$

$$C^*_{P,N} = .13670x_1 + .07815x_2 - .15045x_3 - 1.44910$$

$$C_{P,BD} = .12890x_1 - .14060x_2 - .09180x_3 + 1.74786$$

$$C^*_{BD,N} = .00780x_1 + .22875x_2 - .05865x_3 - 3.05638$$

$$C^*_{BD,P} = -.12890x_1 + .14060x_2 - .09180x_3 + 1.74786$$

The above equations with asterisks were derived by multiplying the corresponding originally derived equations by −1. There are apparently only three independent discriminant functions. However, the fourth discriminant function, $C_{P,BD}$, is equal to $C_{N,BD} - C_{N,P}$, so that there are actually only two linearly independent discriminant functions. The remaining four discriminant functions can easily be derived from those two. The implications of this fact are that all the information needed to discriminate among three groups is contained in two linearly independent discriminant functions. If the number of variables (p) is at least as large as the number of groups (k), then the number of linearly independent discriminant functions needed to discriminate among the groups is $k - 1$. We shall say more about this later. The reader can verify that the classification of an observation, **x**, on the basis of these discriminant functions is equivalent to using the three quadratic functions discussed earlier.

When we look at the above set of discriminant functions, their advantage over quadratic equations from an interpretation viewpoint becomes clear. For example, it can easily be seen that test score x_3 play a minor role in discriminating between the neurotic and brain-damaged populations. Its absolute weight is only .05865, which might be expected since the population means for these two groups are identical. It is interesting to note, however, that its weight is not zero because $\mathbf{V}^{-1}$ plays a role in determining the weights and the off-diagonal elements of $\mathbf{V}^{-1}$ are nonzero. If the test scores were independent (that is, if the off-diagonal elements of $\mathbf{V}^{-1}$ were zero), then test score x_3 would have a zero weight. Similarly, x_1 plays a minor role in discriminating between the neurotic and brain-damaged populations even though there is a five-point mean difference on x_1 for these two populations.

If the a priori probabilities of being a member of each of the populations are assumed to be equal, then $\log_e p$ would be a constant for each of the quadratic classification equations and consequently the form of the quadratic classification equation would simplify to

$$C(i) = -\tfrac{1}{2}(\mathbf{x} - \mu_i)'\mathbf{V}_i^{-1}(\mathbf{x} - \mu_i).$$

The above classification procedures have assumed a common variance-covariance matrix, **V**, for each of the populations under consideration. However, if this is not a realistic assumption, we can modify our procedure by using the $\mathbf{V}_i$ matrix or its estimate corresponding to the population of interest. The quadratic classification equations then take the form

$$C(i) = \log_e(p_i) - \frac{1}{2}(x - \mu_i)'V_i^{-1}(x - \mu_i).$$

This is identical in form to previously discussed quadratic classification equations except that the appropriate $\mathbf{V}_i$ has been substituted for the common variance-covariance matrix, **V**. When this situation occurs we can no longer derive linear discriminant functions. The decision boundaries are no longer linear surfaces, but rather curved surfaces.

We have assumed that our observations were generated from multivariate normally distributed populations for two main reasons. First, real-life data approximate this situation. Second, statistical theory, especially multivariate distribution theory, is most highly developed for the multivariate normal situation. These are cases, however, when other multivariate distributions should be considered.

5.8 ESTIMATING THE EFFICIENCY OF A CLASSIFICATION PROCEDURE

If we know the population parameters for each of the multivariate normal distributions of interest, then it is a straightforward matter to derive the expected proportions of correct and incorrect classifications for the populations of interest. However, in many applied research situations, the population parameters are not known but are estimated from sample data. With luck, the sample is large enough to yield rather stable estimates of the population parameters. If we have estimated the discriminant functions from sample data and have then used these discriminant functions to classify a relatively large number of additional observations, then we can estimate the efficiency of our classification system by forming the matrix presented in Table 5.7.

The rows of this matrix correspond to the true populations from which the observations were generated; the columns correspond to the populations to which the observations were classified by the discriminant functions; and the cell entries are the proportions of observations predicted to come from particular populations given that they in fact belong to given true populations. The rows are conditional probability distributions and so $\Sigma_j p_{ij} = 1$ for all i. For example, p_{11} is the probability of correctly classifying an observation from population 1 into population 1 and p_{12} is the probability of incorrectly classifying an observation from population 1 into population 2. Ideally, we would like all of the diagonal entries or the probabilities of correct classification to be 1 and all of the off-diagonal entries to be 0. This situation, of course, would be relatively rare. But, in any event, we would like the diagonal entries to be large relative to the off-diagonal entries. If the classification efficiency matrix for our hypothetical psychological diagnosis problem turned out to be as shown in Table 5.8, then a researcher would be satisfied that his or her screening tests were doing a good job.

TABLE 5.7 Classification Efficiency Matrix

True Population	Predicted Population 1	2	3		k
1	p_{11}	p_{12}	p_{13}	. . .	p_{1k}
2	p_{21}	p_{22}	p_{23}	. . .	p_{2k}
3	p_{31}	p_{32}	p_{33}	. . .	p_{3k}
.	.	.	.	. . .	.
.	.	.	.	. . .	.
.	.	.	.	. . .	.
k	p_{k1}	p_{k2}	p_{k3}	. . .	p_{kk}

TABLE 5.8 Classification Efficiency Matrix for Patient Populations

	Predicted Population		
True Population	*Neurotic*	*Psychotic*	*Brain Damaged*
Neurotic	.91	.03	.06
Psychotic	.08	.89	.03
Brain damaged	.04	.02	.94

5.9 LINEAR DISCRIMINANT FUNCTION ANALYSIS

The discriminant analysis technique previously discussed that results in a classification equation (that is, a linear function of the original variables) is a useful tool for the mechanistic assignment of observations from unknown groups or populations to one of two or more mutually exclusive groups or populations. However, it is not as useful as a descriptive tool that captures the nature of the differences among the groups in terms of the dimensions of discrimination and the magnitude of the differences among the groups.

The related technique of linear discriminant function analysis involves finding one or more linear combinations of the original variables that maximize the between-group differences relative to within-group differences. If there are more than two groups or more than two variables, then more than one discriminant function may be necessary to characterize group differences completely. Each discriminant function is orthogonal to all others. In general, the number of discriminant functions necessary to characterize between-group differences completely is equal to the number of groups minus one $(g - 1)$ or the number of variables (p), whichever is smaller (that is, the number of discriminant functions is $\min \{g - 1, p\}$).

For two groups, then, there will be one discriminant function that will exhaust all between-group differences regardless of the number of variables. This can be seen from a geometric perspective since two centroids in the space of the original variables (p space) can be projected upon a single line and thus their differences can be characterized by a single dimension or discriminant function. For more than two groups but only two variables, the group centroids lie in two space or the real plane and hence can be characterized by two coordinate axes or two linear discriminant functions. Likewise, the differences among three centroids in a variable space greater than three dimensions can be characterized by two coordinate axes or two linear discriminant functions (that is, a plane can be passed through three points). As the number of groups and variables multiply, the number of discriminant functions needed to represent group differences increases.

The objective of linear discriminant function analysis is to derive linear functions of the original variables that maximize between-group variation relative to within-group variation. Each successive discriminant function is orthogonal to the preceding ones and each successive discriminant function accounts for less between-group variation relative to within-group variation. This technique involves finding the characteristic roots and their associated characteristic vectors for certain characteristic equations.

5.10 RELATIONSHIP TO ONE-WAY MULTIVARIATE ANALYSIS OF VARIANCE

For a one-way MANOVA, we saw earlier that the total sum of squares and cross-products matrix about the mean (**T**) could be decomposed or partitioned into a between-group sum of squares and cross-products matrix (**B**) and an error sum of squares and cross-products matrix (**W**). That is, $\mathbf{T} = \mathbf{B} + \mathbf{W}$.

We saw that the test criterion for the null hypothesis that the mean vectors of the dependent variables are equal across the k groups (that is, $\mathbf{u}_1 = \mathbf{u}_2 = . = . = \mathbf{u}_k$) involved the largest characteristic root of $\mathbf{BW}^{-1}$. It turns out that the value of this root is the ratio of the between-group to within-group variation for the linear discriminant function with maximum between-group variation relative to within-group variation. The characteristic vector associated with this root is the weight vector to apply to the original variables to obtain the linear discriminant function with maximal between-group variation relative to within-group variation. The number of positive characteristic roots of $\mathbf{BW}^{-1}$ is equal to the rank of $\mathbf{BW}^{-1}$. The rank of $\mathbf{BW}^{-1}$ will be equal to the minimum of the number of groups minus one $(g - 1)$ or the number of variables (p). In our discriminant analysis example, we had three groups and three variables, so that the rank of $\mathbf{BW}^{-1}$ in this case would be two. Consequently, there would be two positive characteristic roots, each having an associated characteristic vector. The characteristic vectors would be orthogonal, as would the two linear discriminant functions.

Let us sketch an informal proof that the ratio of between-group variation to within-group variation of each linear discriminant function is a characteristic root of $\mathbf{BW}^{-1}$ and that the weighting vector of each discriminant function is the associated characteristic vector. The variance of a linear composite can be expressed as $\mathbf{a}'\mathbf{Ca}$ where $\mathbf{a}$ is the column vector of weights and $\mathbf{C}$ is the covariance matrix for the variables. Thus the between-group sum of squares for an arbitrary vector of weights, $\mathbf{a}$, can be expressed as $\mathbf{a}'\mathbf{Ba}$, where $\mathbf{B}$ is the between-group sum of squares and cross-products matrix. For our discriminant analysis example with three variables, $\mathbf{B}$ would be a 3×3 matrix and $\mathbf{a}$ would be a column vector with three elements or weights. But we want to find a weighting vector that maximizes the between-group sum of squares relative to the within-group sum of squares. So what we want to maximize is the ratio

$$\frac{\mathbf{a}'\mathbf{Ba}}{\mathbf{a}'\mathbf{Wa}}$$

In order to do this, we need to appeal to differential calculus. If we partially differentiate

$$\frac{\mathbf{a}'\mathbf{Ba}}{\mathbf{a}'\mathbf{Wa}}$$

with respect to $\mathbf{a}$ and set the partial derivatives equal to zero, it can be shown that we end up with the characteristic equation

$$(\mathbf{W}^{-1}\mathbf{B} - \lambda\mathbf{I})\mathbf{a} = \mathbf{0}$$

This matrix equation can also be written as

$$\mathbf{W}^{-1}\mathbf{Ba} = \lambda\mathbf{a}$$

where λ is a characteristic root associated with the matrix $\mathbf{W}^{-1}\mathbf{B}$ and $\mathbf{a}$ is its associated characteristic vector.

Since $\mathbf{W}^{-1}\mathbf{B}$ is known, the problem is to find a λ and a vector $\mathbf{a}$ that satisfy this equation. There is an iterative procedure that will be discussed in relation to principal components analysis whereby the roots and characteristic vectors can be solved for. We will use another method to solve for the characteristic roots and associated vectors of $\mathbf{W}^{-1}\mathbf{B}$ in order to gain an understanding of characteristic roots and vectors from another perspective. For large matrices, we would, of course, use electronic computer algorithms, but for smaller problems algebraic solutions are convenient.

5.11 ESTIMATING LINEAR DISCRIMINANT FUNCTIONS

Let us perform a linear discriminant function analysis on the hypothetical test data used to discriminate among the three psychiatric patient categories. The first step is to compute the matrices **B** and **W**. Discriminant analysis, like MANOVA, assumes that the dispersion matrices within groups, $\mathbf{W}_i$, come from a common population covariance matrix so that the estimate of **W** is a pooled estimate based upon a weighted sum of the $\mathbf{W}_i$ matrices where the weights are the sample sizes of the respective groups.

Let us assume that there are 100 observations for each of the three groups. The between-group sum of squares and cross-products matrix, **B**, is then

$$100 \sum_{i=1}^{3} (\overline{y}_i - \overline{y})(y_i - \overline{y})'$$

where i is a subscript denoting the group, $\overline{y}_i$ is the vector of the three test means for group i, and $\overline{y}$ is the vector of the three test means for the total sample. The sum of squares and cross-products about the mean contributed by group 1 is

$$(\overline{y}_1 - \overline{y})(\overline{y}_1 - \overline{y})' = \begin{bmatrix} \overline{y}_{11} - \overline{y}_1 \\ \overline{y}_{12} - \overline{y}_2 \\ \overline{y}_{13} - \overline{y}_3 \end{bmatrix} [\overline{y}_{11} - \overline{y}_1, \overline{y}_{12} - \overline{y}_2, \overline{y}_{13} - \overline{y}_3]$$

where $\overline{y}_{11}$ is the mean of variable 1 for group 1 and $\overline{y}_1$ is the total sample mean for variable 1 and so on. Calculating the total means, which are averages of the group means since the group sizes are equal, we have

$$(\overline{y}_1 - \overline{y})(\overline{y}_1 - \overline{y})' = \begin{bmatrix} 10 - 15 \\ 5 - 10 \\ 15 - 13.3333 \end{bmatrix} [10 - 15, 5 - 10, 15 - 13.3333]$$

$$= \begin{bmatrix} -5 \\ -5 \\ 1.6666 \end{bmatrix} [-5 \;\; -5 \;\; 1.6666]$$

$$= \begin{bmatrix} 25 & 25 & -8.3333 \\ 25 & 25 & -8.3333 \\ -8.3333 & -8.3333 & 2.7777 \end{bmatrix}$$

The reader can verify that

$$(\bar{y}_2 - \bar{y})(\bar{y}_2 - \bar{y})' = \begin{bmatrix} 25 & 0 & -16.6666 \\ 0 & 0 & 0 \\ -16.6666 & 0 & 11.1111 \end{bmatrix}$$

and that

$$(\bar{y}_3 - \bar{y})(\bar{y}_3 - \bar{y})' = \begin{bmatrix} 0 & 0 & 0 \\ 0 & 25 & 8.3333 \\ 0 & 8.3333 & 2.7777 \end{bmatrix}$$

so that

$$\mathbf{B} = 100 \sum_{i=1}^{3} (\bar{y}_i - \bar{y})(\bar{y}_i - \bar{y})' = \begin{bmatrix} 5{,}000 & 2{,}500 & -2{,}500 \\ 2{,}500 & 5{,}000 & 0 \\ -2{,}500 & 0 & 1{,}666.666 \end{bmatrix}$$

The within-group variance-covariance matrix or dispersion matrix was assumed to be

$$\begin{bmatrix} 100 & 30 & 40 \\ 30 & 50 & 20 \\ 40 & 20 & 80 \end{bmatrix}$$

for each of the three patient groups. Each of the three within-group dispersion matrices was based upon 99 degrees of freedom. The error sum of squares and cross-products matrix, $\mathbf{W}_i$, for each group is thus

$$99 \begin{bmatrix} 100 & 30 & 40 \\ 30 & 50 & 20 \\ 40 & 20 & 80 \end{bmatrix}$$

The total error sum of squares and cross-products matrix, **W**, is the sum of these three identical matrices for each of the three groups or

$$\mathbf{W} = 297 \begin{bmatrix} 100 & 30 & 40 \\ 30 & 50 & 20 \\ 40 & 20 & 80 \end{bmatrix}$$

Since the inverse of the common dispersion matrix was found to be

$$\begin{bmatrix} .014063 & -.006250 & -.005469 \\ -.006250 & .025000 & -.003125 \\ -.005469 & -.003125 & .016016 \end{bmatrix}$$

$$\mathbf{W}^{-1} = \frac{1}{297}\begin{bmatrix} .014063 & -.006250 & -.005469 \\ -.006250 & .025000 & -.003125 \\ -.005469 & -.003125 & .016016 \end{bmatrix}$$

$$= \begin{bmatrix} .0000473 & -.0000210 & -.0000184 \\ -.0000210 & .0000841 & -.0000105 \\ -.0000184 & -.0000105 & .0000539 \end{bmatrix}$$

Therefore,

$$\mathbf{W}^{-1}\mathbf{B} = \begin{bmatrix} .230166 & .013152 & -.149060 \\ .131523 & .368266 & .035073 \\ -.253183 & -.098642 & .135907 \end{bmatrix}$$

The next step is to find the two positive roots of $\mathbf{W}^{-1}\mathbf{B}$. The roots of $\mathbf{W}^{-1}\mathbf{B}$ are those values of λ that satisfy the determinantal equation

$$|\mathbf{W}^{-1}\mathbf{B} - \lambda\mathbf{I}| = 0$$

since if $(\mathbf{W}^{-1}\mathbf{B} - \lambda\mathbf{I})\mathbf{a} = \mathbf{0}$, for a nonnull $\mathbf{a}$, then the matrix $(\mathbf{W}^{-1}\mathbf{B} - \lambda\mathbf{I})$ must be singular and hence its determinant must vanish.

Since this is the determinant of a 3 × 3 matrix, substituting $\mathbf{W}^{-1}\mathbf{B}$ in the above determinantal equation will result in a cubic equation. That is, the equation will take the form

$$\lambda^3 + a\lambda^2 + b\lambda + c = 0$$

By expanding the determinant, it can be shown that the coefficient a is equal to the negative of the trace of $\mathbf{W}^{-1}\mathbf{B}$, b is equal to the sum of the principal minor determinants[2] of $\mathbf{W}^{-1}\mathbf{B}$ and c is equal to the negative of the determinant of $\mathbf{W}^{-1}\mathbf{B}$. The trace of $\mathbf{W}^{-1}\mathbf{B}$ or the sum of its diagonal elements is .73434, so that a = −.73434. The three principal minor determinants of $\mathbf{W}^{-1}\mathbf{B}$ are

$$\begin{vmatrix} .368266 & .035073 \\ -.098642 & .135907 \end{vmatrix} = .053509$$

$$\begin{vmatrix} .230166 & -.149060 \\ -.253183 & .135907 \end{vmatrix} = -.006458$$

and

$$\begin{vmatrix} .230166 & .013152 \\ .131523 & .368266 \end{vmatrix} = .083032$$

so that b = .053509 − .006458 + .083032 = .130094.

The reader can verify that $|\mathbf{W}^{-1}\mathbf{B}| = 0$ so that c = 0 and the cubic equation becomes

$$\lambda^3 - .734339\lambda^2 + .130084\lambda = 0$$

Factoring, we find

$$\lambda(\lambda^2 - .734339\lambda + .130084) = 0$$

so that one root is zero. The remaining two roots can be found by solving the quadratic in the parentheses using the quadratic formula. The resulting roots are $\lambda_1 = .435940$ and $\lambda_2 = .298399$. Both of these roots are relatively large so that, perhaps, two linear discriminant functions are needed to characterize the differences among the three patient groups. Let us now find the characteristic vector associated with each of these characteristic roots. The characteristic vector, $\mathbf{a}_1$, associated with λ_1 must satisfy

$$\mathbf{W}^{-1}\mathbf{B}\mathbf{a}_1 - \lambda_1\mathbf{a}_1 = \mathbf{0}$$

Substituting $\lambda_1 = .435940$ into the above equation, we find

$$\begin{bmatrix} .230166 & .013152 & -.149060 \\ .131523 & .368266 & .035073 \\ -.253183 & -.098642 & .135907 \end{bmatrix} \begin{bmatrix} a_{11} \\ a_{21} \\ a_{31} \end{bmatrix} - .435940 \begin{bmatrix} a_{11} \\ a_{21} \\ a_{31} \end{bmatrix} = \begin{bmatrix} 0 \\ 0 \\ 0 \end{bmatrix}$$

or

$$\begin{aligned} -.205774\, a_{11} + .013152\, a_{21} - .149060\, a_{31} &= 0 \\ .131523\, a_{11} - .067674\, a_{21} + .035073\, a_{31} &= 0 \\ -.253183\, a_{11} - .09864\ \ a_{21} - .300033\, a_{31} &= 0 \end{aligned}$$

The coefficient matrix of these equations is $\mathbf{W}^{-1}\mathbf{B} - \lambda_1\mathbf{I}$ and we previously saw that λ_1 was selected to satisfy the condition that $|\mathbf{W}^{-1}\mathbf{B} - \lambda_1\mathbf{I}| = 0$ and hence the coefficient matrix is singular. This means that there is no unique solution to this set of homogeneous equations. The coefficient matrix is of rank two so that one of the values of $\mathbf{a}_1$ can be set at an arbitrary value and the reduced nonhomogeneous equations in the two unknown elements of $\mathbf{a}_1$ can be solved for. Let us set the element $a_{31} = 1$. Substituting this into the set of homogeneous equations, we obtain

$$\begin{aligned} -.205774\, a_{11} + .013152\, a_{21} &= .149060 \\ .131523\, a_{11} - .067674\, a_{21} &= -.035073 \\ -.253183\, a_{11} - .098642\, a_{21} &= .300033 \end{aligned}$$

There are now three equations in two unknowns. Let us drop the last equation because it is a linear combination of the first two linear equations and hence is redundant. The first two equations can be expressed as

$$\begin{bmatrix} -.205774 & .013152 \\ .131523 & -.067674 \end{bmatrix} \begin{bmatrix} a_{11} \\ a_{21} \end{bmatrix} = \begin{bmatrix} .149060 \\ -.035073 \end{bmatrix}$$

Solving for

$$\begin{bmatrix} a_{11} \\ a_{21} \end{bmatrix}$$

we find

$$\begin{bmatrix} a_{11} \\ a_{21} \end{bmatrix} = \begin{bmatrix} -.205774 & .013152 \\ .131523 & -.067674 \end{bmatrix}^{-1} \begin{bmatrix} .149060 \\ -.035073 \end{bmatrix}$$

$$= \begin{bmatrix} -5.548995 & -1.078458 \\ -10.784255 & -16.872469 \end{bmatrix} \begin{bmatrix} .149060 \\ -.035073 \end{bmatrix} = \begin{bmatrix} -.789308 \\ -1.015733 \end{bmatrix}$$

Since we arbitrarily set a_{31} equal to one, the vector

$$\begin{bmatrix} -.78930 \\ -1.01573 \\ 1. \end{bmatrix}$$

is the characteristic vector $\mathbf{a}_1$ associated with $\lambda_1 = .43594$. The reader can verify that this vector satisfies the characteristic equation

$$\mathbf{W}^{-1}\mathbf{B}\mathbf{a}_1 = \lambda_1 \mathbf{a}_1$$

Note that since we can multiply both sides of this characteristic equation by an arbitrary scalar b, the solution for $\mathbf{a}_1$ is unique only up to a scalar multiple of its elements. That is, if $\mathbf{a}_1$ is a characteristic vector, then $b\mathbf{a}_1$ is also a characteristic vector. This is the reason we had to set one of the elements of a_1 equal to 1 in order to obtain a unique solution for $\mathbf{a}_1$. We could have also used the conventional constraint that the length or norm of the vector is equal to one, but our simple constraint made the solution easier to obtain. The elements of $\mathbf{a}_1$ can now be normed so that $\mathbf{a}_1$ is length one by dividing each element of $\mathbf{a}_1$ by

$$\sqrt{\sum_{i=1} a_{i1}^2} = 1.62933$$

This results in

$$\mathbf{a}_1 = \begin{bmatrix} -.48443 \\ -.62340 \\ .61375 \end{bmatrix}$$

It should be noted that any constraint involving an individual element of $\mathbf{a}_1$ or the length of $\mathbf{a}_1$ can be used as a constraint. Constraints are arbitrary, but norming to length one is conventional practice.

Turning now to the second root, λ_2, of $\mathbf{W}^{-1}\mathbf{B}$, we find that by substituting $\lambda_2 = .298399$ into $\mathbf{W}^{-1}\mathbf{B}\mathbf{a}_2 = \lambda_2\mathbf{a}_2$, we can solve for the characteristic vector $\mathbf{a}_2$ associated with the characteristic root $\lambda_2 = .298399$. The procedure is identical to that used to solve for $\mathbf{a}_1$.

The reader can verify that

$$\mathbf{a}_2 = \begin{bmatrix} -.50889 \\ .80537 \\ .30401 \end{bmatrix}$$

The two characteristic vectors together can be expressed by the matrix

$$\mathbf{A} = [\mathbf{a}_1, \mathbf{a}_2] = \begin{bmatrix} -.48443 & -.50889 \\ -.62340 & .80537 \\ .61375 & .30401 \end{bmatrix}$$

This is the transformation matrix for mapping the three test scores into two discriminant function scores. It is a mapping from a Euclidean three space into a Euclidean two space. Thus the discriminant function scores, $\mathbf{z}$, can be expressed as

$$\mathbf{z} = \begin{bmatrix} z_1 \\ z_2 \end{bmatrix} = \mathbf{A}'\mathbf{x} = \begin{bmatrix} -.48443 & -.62340 & .61375 \\ -.50889 & .80537 & .30401 \end{bmatrix} \begin{bmatrix} x_1 \\ x_2 \\ x_3 \end{bmatrix}$$

where z_1 and z_2 are the first and second discriminant function scores, respectively.

5.12 PROPERTIES OF DISCRIMINANT FUNCTIONS

These two discriminant functions are statistically independent of one another. First, we use the fact that the variance-covariance matrix of $\mathbf{z}$ can be expressed as $\mathbf{A}'\mathbf{C}\mathbf{A}$ where $\mathbf{C}$ is the common variance-covariance matrix of the three variables constituting the vector $\mathbf{x}$. Substituting, we find

$$\mathbf{A}'\mathbf{C}\mathbf{A} = \begin{bmatrix} -.48443 & -.62340 & .61375 \\ -.50889 & .80537 & .30401 \end{bmatrix} \begin{bmatrix} 100 & 30 & 40 \\ 30 & 50 & 20 \\ 40 & 20 & 80 \end{bmatrix} \begin{bmatrix} -.48443 & -.50889 \\ -.62340 & .80537 \\ .61375 & .30401 \end{bmatrix}$$

$$= \begin{bmatrix} 52.0633 & 0 \\ 0 & 38.5480 \end{bmatrix}$$

The covariance between the two discriminant functions is zero and therefore they are uncorrelated.

If we desired, the within-group variances of the two discriminant functions could be set to 1 by premultiplying and postmultiplying $\mathbf{A}'\mathbf{C}\mathbf{A}$ by the diagonal matrix

$$\mathbf{D} = \begin{bmatrix} \frac{1}{\sqrt{52.0633}} & 0 \\ 0 & \frac{1}{\sqrt{38.5480}} \end{bmatrix}$$

since

$$\mathbf{DA'CAD} = \begin{bmatrix} \frac{1}{\sqrt{52.0633}} & 0 \\ 0 & \frac{1}{\sqrt{38.5480}} \end{bmatrix} \begin{bmatrix} 52.0633 & 0 \\ 0 & 38.5480 \end{bmatrix} \begin{bmatrix} \frac{1}{\sqrt{52.0633}} & 0 \\ 0 & \frac{1}{\sqrt{38.5480}} \end{bmatrix}$$

$$= \begin{bmatrix} 1 & 0 \\ 0 & 1 \end{bmatrix}$$

But

$$\mathbf{DA}' = \begin{bmatrix} \dfrac{1}{\sqrt{52.0633}} & 0 \\ 0 & \dfrac{1}{\sqrt{38.5480}} \end{bmatrix} \begin{bmatrix} -.48443 & -.62340 & .61375 \\ -.50889 & .80537 & .30401 \end{bmatrix}$$

$$= \begin{bmatrix} -.06714 & -.08640 & .08506 \\ -.08196 & .12972 & .04897 \end{bmatrix}$$

so that each row vector in $\mathbf{A}'$ has been multiplied by a scalar and we have seen that these vectors will still satisfy the characteristic equation and hence are characteristic vectors. We can label the new vectors, which are scalar multiples of the old vectors as $\mathbf{A}_1' = \mathbf{DA}'$. So we have found a new set of characteristic vectors $\mathbf{A}_1$ that satisfy the characteristic equation and are scaled such that $\mathbf{A}_1'\mathbf{CA}_1 = \mathbf{I}$.

These vectors

$$\mathbf{A}_1' = \begin{bmatrix} \mathbf{a}_1' \\ \mathbf{a}_2' \end{bmatrix}$$

make the within-group dispersion for the three patient groups a circular normal standardized distribution. The term "circular normal standardized distribution" comes from the fact that the equal density contours for a bivariate normal distribution with variances equal to one form circles when plotted out. This, of course, assumes that each group has an identical within-group dispersion matrix. In actuality, the within-group dispersion matrices will differ to some extent due to sampling error even if all groups had a common population dispersion matrix. Incidentally, the transformation matrix, $\mathbf{A}_1$, could have been solved for initially by putting the constraint $\mathbf{A}'\mathbf{CA} = \mathbf{I}$ on the elements of the two vectors rather than the two constraints $a_{31} = 1$ and $a_{32} = 1$ that we used to find the initial set of characteristic vectors. On a computer it is just as easy to use these constraints as our simpler constraints, but manual computations are simplified by using the simplest constraints. Note that any matrix of characteristic vectors, $\mathbf{A}$, results in a diagonal covariance matrix since the covariances of $\mathbf{A}'\mathbf{CA}$ must be zero, for the linear discriminant functions are defined to be uncorrelated with one another. The additional requirement that the within-group dispersions on each discriminant function are unity is an appealing property.

Another interesting property is that the ratio of the two characteristic roots is equal to the ratio of the between-groups variance on each of the discriminant functions. That is,

$$\frac{\lambda_1}{\lambda_2} = \frac{.4359}{.2984} = \frac{\mathbf{a}_1'\mathbf{B}\mathbf{a}_1}{\mathbf{a}_2'\mathbf{B}\mathbf{a}_2} = 1.4605$$

since

$$\mathbf{a}_1'\mathbf{B}\mathbf{a}_1 = [-.06714, -.08640, .08506]\begin{bmatrix} 5{,}000 & 2{,}500 & -2{,}500 \\ 2{,}500 & 5{,}000 & 0 \\ -2{,}500 & 0 & 1667 \end{bmatrix}\begin{bmatrix} -.06714 \\ -.08640 \\ .08506 \end{bmatrix}$$
$$= 129.48$$

and

$$\mathbf{a}_2'\mathbf{B}\mathbf{a}_2 = [-.08196, .12972, .04897]\begin{bmatrix} 5{,}000 & 2{,}500 & -2{,}500 \\ 2{,}500 & 5{,}000 & 0 \\ -2{,}500 & 0 & 1667 \end{bmatrix}\begin{bmatrix} -.08196 \\ .12972 \\ .04897 \end{bmatrix}$$
$$= 88.63$$

and therefore

$$\frac{\mathbf{a}_1'\mathbf{B}\mathbf{a}_1}{\mathbf{a}_2'\mathbf{B}\mathbf{a}_2} = \frac{129.48}{88.63} = 1.4605$$

This ratio indicates that the first discriminant function accounts for 46 percent more between-group variation than the second discriminant function.

The means of the three psychiatric patient groups for each of the discriminant functions can be found by applying the transformation matrix $\mathbf{A}'$ to the three vectors of group means. We have

$$\overline{\mathbf{Z}} = \begin{bmatrix} \overline{z}_{11} & \overline{z}_{12} & \overline{z}_{13} \\ \overline{z}_{21} & \overline{z}_{22} & \overline{z}_{23} \end{bmatrix} = \mathbf{A}'\overline{\mathbf{X}} = \mathbf{A}'\begin{bmatrix} \overline{x}_{11} & \overline{x}_{12} & \overline{x}_{13} \\ \overline{x}_{21} & \overline{x}_{22} & \overline{x}_{23} \\ \overline{x}_{31} & \overline{x}_{32} & \overline{x}_{33} \end{bmatrix}$$

where the first subscript of $\overline{z}$ and $\overline{x}$ indicates variable and the second subscript indicates group. Substituting, we find

$$\overline{\mathbf{Z}} = \begin{bmatrix} -.06714 & -.08640 & .08506 \\ -.08196 & .12972 & .04897 \end{bmatrix}\begin{bmatrix} 10 & 20 & 15 \\ 5 & 10 & 15 \\ 15 & 10 & 15 \end{bmatrix}$$

$$= \begin{bmatrix} .1725 & -1.3562 & -1.0272 \\ .5636 & .1477 & 1.4510 \end{bmatrix}$$

These means are plotted in Figure 5.4 in the two-dimensional discriminant function space.

The centroids of the three groups are equally distant from one another in the discriminant function space. Both discriminant functions are needed to separate the groups effectively. Discriminant function 1 (z_1) primarily separates group 1 from groups 2 and 3, while the second discriminant function (z_2) primarily separates group 3 from groups 1 and 2. Since the linear discriminant function space can be considered as a plane passing through the three group centroids, it can easily be seen that the three points in the original variable space of the three test scores do not lie on a straight line and that

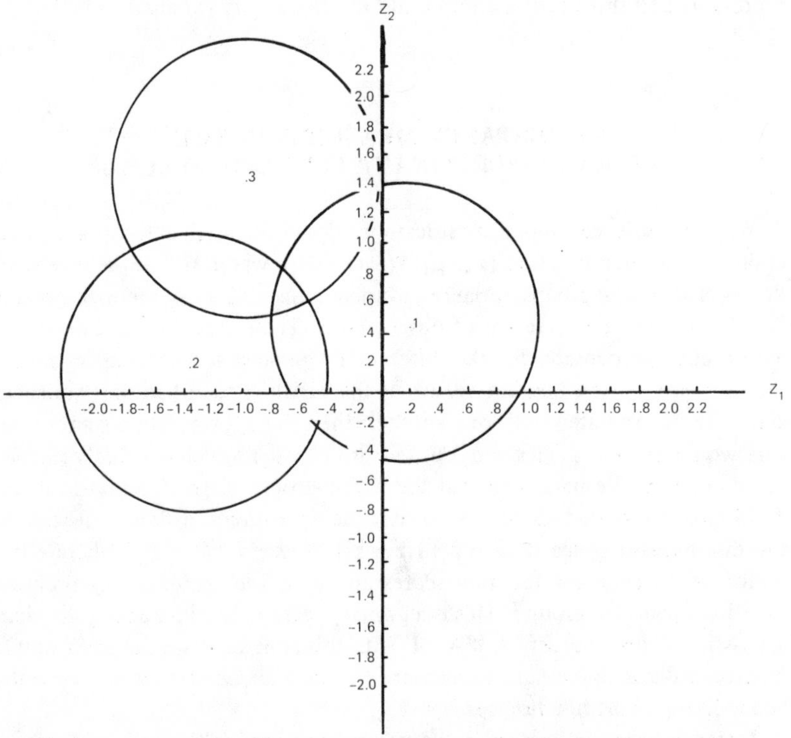

NOTE: Group 1 = neurotic; Group 2 = psychotic; Group 3 = brain damaged.

Figure 5.4 Discriminant Function Centroids and Dispersions for the Three Patient Groups.

two discriminant functions defining a plane are necessary to capture the configuration of the three centroids.

The unit circle surrounding each centroid represents the bivariate dispersion of each group in the discriminant function space. The intersections of the circles indicate that the groups overlap in the discriminant space and hence, as we have previously seen, misclassification errors will arise.

The first discriminant function (z_1) has roughly equal weights for each of the three variables. Since tests 1 and 2 have negative weights, low scores on tests 1 and 2 along with a high score on test 3 result in a high score on z_1. Since group 1 has the lowest means for tests 1 and 2 and ties with group 3 for the highest mean on test 3, it has the highest mean on z_1. The first discriminant function seems to be a contrast of tests 1 and 2 versus test 3.

The second discriminant function has a relatively high positive weight for test 2, a considerably smaller positive weight for test 3, and a moderate sized negative weight for test 1. It can be considered as a contrast primarily between test 1 and test 2. It can be seen from cursory examination of the weight vectors that all three tests are important discriminatory variables.

5.13 DISTANCE MEASURES IN THE LINEAR DISCRIMINANT FUNCTION SPACE

We previously developed classification rules in the original test space based upon the distance function $(\mathbf{x} - \boldsymbol{\mu}_i)'\mathbf{W}^{-1}(\mathbf{x} - \boldsymbol{\mu}_i)$, where $\mathbf{W}^{-1}$ is the inverse of the pooled within-groups variance-covariance matrix, $\boldsymbol{\mu}_i$ is the mean vector for group i, and $\mathbf{x}$ is a vector of observations. The matrix $\mathbf{W}^{-1}$ is a weighting matrix and compensates for the differential variances and covariances among the elements of the random vector. If the variables each had unit variances and were uncorrelated with one another, then the appropriate distance measure would be $(\mathbf{x} - \boldsymbol{\mu}_i)'\mathbf{I}(\mathbf{x} - \boldsymbol{\mu}_i)$ or $(\mathbf{x} - \boldsymbol{\mu}_i)'(\mathbf{x} - \boldsymbol{\mu}_i)$, which is a Euclidean distance measure. We have seen that the within-groups dispersion matrix in the discriminant function space is $\mathbf{I}$, so that the appropriate distance measure in the discriminant space is $(\mathbf{z} - \bar{\mathbf{z}}_i)'\mathbf{I}(\mathbf{z} - \bar{\mathbf{z}}_i)$ or $(\mathbf{z} - \bar{\mathbf{z}}_i)'(\mathbf{z} - \bar{\mathbf{z}}_i)$, where $\mathbf{z}$ is a vector of discriminant function scores and $\bar{\mathbf{z}}_i$ is the vector of discriminant function means for group i. This is a primary reason for constraining the characteristic vectors to satisfy $\mathbf{A}'\mathbf{W}\mathbf{A} = \mathbf{I}$. With this constraint we can use a simple Euclidean distance measure to measure the distance between $\mathbf{z}$ and $\bar{\mathbf{z}}_i$ in the linear discriminant function space.

Distance between vectors in the original test space are equal to distances between the corresponding discriminant function vectors in the discriminant function space. Consequently, identical classification rules in both spaces will lead to identical classification errors. That is, the distance between $\mathbf{x}$ and $\boldsymbol{\mu}_i$,

$(\mathbf{x}-\mu_i)'\mathbf{W}^{-1}(\mathbf{x}-\mu_i)$, in the original test space is equal to the distance between $\mathbf{z}$ and $\bar{\mathbf{z}}_i$, $(\mathbf{z}-\bar{\mathbf{z}}_i)'(\mathbf{z}-\bar{\mathbf{z}}_i)$ in the discriminant function space where $\mathbf{z} = \mathbf{A}'\mathbf{x}$ and $\bar{\mathbf{z}}_i = \mathbf{A}'\mu_i$. Expressing $\mathbf{z}$ and $\bar{\mathbf{z}}_i$ in terms of $\mathbf{x}$ and substituting into the discriminant function space distance measure, we find that

$$\begin{aligned}(\mathbf{z}-\bar{\mathbf{z}}_i)'(\mathbf{z}-\mathbf{z}_i) &= (\mathbf{A}'\mathbf{x}-\mathbf{A}'\mu_i)'(\mathbf{A}'\mathbf{x}-\mathbf{A}'\mu_i)\\ &= (\mathbf{x}'\mathbf{A}-\mu_i'\mathbf{A})(\mathbf{A}'\mathbf{x}-\mathbf{A}'\mu_i)\\ &= (\mathbf{x}'-\mu_i')\,\mathbf{A}\mathbf{A}'(\mathbf{x}-\mu_i)\\ &= (\mathbf{x}-\mu_i)'\mathbf{A}\mathbf{A}'(\mathbf{x}-\mu_i)\end{aligned}$$

Let us illustrate the equivalence of the distances by measuring the distance between the mean vectors for patient groups 1 and 2. The distance between the two vectors of means in the original test space is

$$(\mu_1-\mu_2)'\mathbf{W}^{-1}(\mu_1-\mu_2) = [-10, -5, 5]\begin{bmatrix} .014063 & -.006250 & -.005469\\ -.006250 & .025000 & -.003125\\ -.005469 & -.003125 & .016016\end{bmatrix}\begin{bmatrix}-10\\ -5\\ 5\end{bmatrix}$$

$$= 2.509$$

and the distance in the discriminant function space is

$$(\bar{\mathbf{z}}_1-\bar{\mathbf{z}}_2)'(\bar{\mathbf{z}}_1-\bar{\mathbf{z}}_2) = (\mu_1-\mu_2)'\mathbf{A}\mathbf{A}'(\mu_1-\mu_2)$$

$$= [-10, -5, 5]\begin{bmatrix} -.06714 & -.08196\\ -.08640 & .12972\\ .08506 & .04897\end{bmatrix}\begin{bmatrix} -.06714 & -.98640 & .08506\\ -.08196 & .12972 & .04897\end{bmatrix}\begin{bmatrix}-10\\ -5\\ 5\end{bmatrix}$$

$$[-10, -5, 5]\begin{bmatrix} .01123 & -.00483 & -.00972\\ -.00483 & .02429 & -.00099\\ -.00972 & -.00099 & .00963\end{bmatrix}\begin{bmatrix}-10\\ -5\\ 5\end{bmatrix} = 2.509$$

We can see that although the distances are identical, $\mathbf{W}^{-1} \neq \mathbf{A}\mathbf{A}'$. The matrix $\mathbf{A}\mathbf{A}'$ does, however, properly weight the original data to provide a measure of distance in the original test space.

Some applied problems will have both a large number of variables and a large number of groups. In these situations, a large number of linear discriminant functions will be needed to explain between-group differences completely. In many cases, however, a few discriminant functions will account for most of the between-group variation and the remaining discriminant functions can be ignored. There are multivariate tests available to determine how many discriminant functions should be retained in the analysis. They are similar in nature to the tests of multivariate hypotheses discussed earlier. In fact, multivariate tests in a one-way MANOVA involve the roots of $\mathbf{BW}^{-1}$, the identical roots that are involved in a linear discriminant function analysis. More will be said about statistical tests in the subsequent section on computer software.

5.14 EXAMPLE

Dunteman (1966) used discriminant analysis to isolate the dimensions (discriminant functions) accounting for differences among students in the health-related professions in respect to vocational interests. The number of discriminant functions needed to explain differences among these groups and the nature of the variables defining them can increase our understanding of the role that vocational interests play in selecting a particular curriculum in the health-related professions.

The discriminant function analysis was conducted on four groups of students majoring in occupational therapy (OT), physical therapy (PT), medical technology (MT), and nursing (N). In addition, a fifth group of education majors (E) was included in the analysis as an outside reference group. The sample sizes for the five groups were 46, 27, 41, 61, and 25, respectively. One of the analyses involved eleven vocational interest scales from the Strong Vocational Interest Blank (SVIB). The discriminant function analysis indicated that the first two discriminant functions were statistically significant at the .01 level, while the last two were not significant at the .05 level. The significance of the discriminant functions were determined by a chi-square test due to Bartlett (1947). The largest two discriminant functions accounted for approximately 89 percent of the variation among the five groups. The group centroids, plotted in the discriminant function, are shown in Figure 5.5.

The weights for the two discriminant functions are presented in Table 5.9. The classification matrix for actual and predicted group membership based upon all four discriminant function scores is shown in Table 5.10.

Referring to Figure 5.5, it can be seen that the first discriminant function separates the MTs from the remaining four groups, especially the Ns and OTs. The second discriminant function separates the OTs and Es from the MTs, PTs, and Ns. To interpret the nature of each of the two functions, we need to look at the characteristics of the variables that define them. That is, we must look at the relative size of the variable weights for each linear discriminant function as shown in Table 5.9.

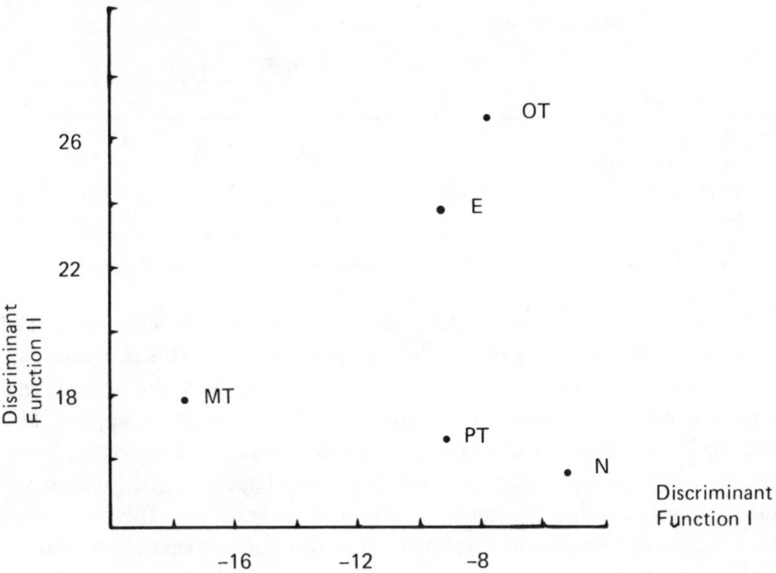

Figure 5.5 Centroids of the Five Curricula Groups in the Discriminant Function Space

TABLE 5.9 Discriminant Function Weights for Interest Scales

	Disciminant Functions	
	I	*II*
Occupational therapist	.57	.48
Laboratory technician	–1.00	–.09
Physician	–.16	.21
Social worker	–.16	.74
Dentist	.03	.07
English teacher	.15	–.25
Math-science teacher	–.33	.18
Music performer	.11	–.13
Music teacher	–.25	.28
Nurse	.51	–1.00
Femininity-masculinity	.01	.27

The weights in this table were calculated by a procedure somewhat different from the procedure described earlier in this chapter. First of all, the scales had different standard deviations and the weights were adjusted by multiplying each weight by the standard deviation of the variable associated with it.

TABLE 5.10 Classification Matrix for Actual and Predicted Goup Membership

	Predicted Group				
Actual Group	*MT*	*OT*	*PT*	*N*	*E*
Medical technology	25	6	4	1	5
Occupational therapy	3	27	2	3	11
Physical therapy	4	3	7	6	7
Nursing	7	13	10	27	4
Education	3	8	3	3	8

This procedure results in weights that are not partly a function of the arbitrary units of measurement for the different variables. This is equivalent to standardizing all of the variables initially and conducting a discriminant analysis on standardized scores. The weights, of course, must be applied to the standardized scores for generating the discriminant function scores. Second, the vectors of weights were normed so that the largest weight for each linear discriminant function was set to an absolute value of one. This is in contrast to norming the weights so that $\mathbf{a}'\mathbf{W}\mathbf{a} = 1$ as was discussed earlier. As discussed earlier, any type of norming results in weight vectors that are proportional to each other.

The largest absolute weight of −1 on the first discriminant function is associated with the laboratory technician scale. The next two largest weights of .57 and .51 are associated with the occupational therapist and nurse scales, respectively. The discriminant function is essentially a contrast of the laboratory technician scale with the occupational therapy and nurse scales. This corresponds nicely with Figure 5.5, which shows OT and N groups on the high end of the first discriminant function and the MT group on the low end. This dimension might be interpreted as representing supportive interests versus nonsupportive interests. The two scales with large positive weights presumably indicate interest in helping other people, while the scale with the large negative weight indicates interests of a more introverted, task-oriented nature.

The second discriminant function is essentially defined by the highest absolute weight of −1 on the nurse scale and positive weights of .74 and .48 on the social worker and occupational therapy scales, respectively. The Ns had the lowest score on the second discriminant function and the OTs had the highest score, as can be seen in Figure 5.5. A correspondence between the group means on the second discriminant function and the weights on the second discriminant function can again be seen. The second dimension was more difficult to interpret. In the full study with 29 SVIB scales it was interpreted as a dimension that defined interest in abstract-unstructured job situations versus interest in concrete-structured job situations.

Classification was performed using the total discriminant function space. This is equivalent to classifying individuals in the original variable space. As can be seen from Table 5.10, group membership can be fairly well predicted on the basis of these 11 SVIB scales. There were 94 correct classfications out of a possible 200. Only 40 correct classifications would be expected by chance alone. This is encouraging, since the groups are so extrinsically similar. The results also support the validity of SVIB and its use as a counseling instrument.

5.15 COMPUTER SOFTWARE

There are a number of software packages that can be used to conduct a linear discriminant function analysis. The most popular packages are probably SAS and SPSS. Both packages produce the following key outputs: the standardized coefficients for each discriminant function; the latent roots associated with each discriminant function; the centroids of the groups in the discriminant function space; and the multivariate tests to determine the statistical significance of successive discriminant functions.

Let us discuss the key SAS output in somewhat more detail. We will begin with a discussion of how SAS tests the statistical significance of the discriminant functions. The hypothesis that is tested is that the latent root associated with a particular discriminant function and all that follow are zero. The first test is a test of the hypothesis that the first discriminant function and all succeeding discriminant functions have a latent root equal to zero or, equivalently, a zero between-group sum of squares on each linear discriminant function. This is also equivalent to testing the hypothesis in a one-way analysis of variance that the mean vectors across the groups are equal. The first test uses the largest root criteria, discussed previously, as well as three other test criteria.

If the first test is significant, then the hypothesis that the second and succeeding discriminant functions do not account for any between-group variation is tested. If the second test is significant, then the procedure is continued until either the test turns out to be nonsignificant or all discriminant functions have been tested. These tests are based upon a likelihood ratio that is transformed to an approximate F statistic.

The canonical correlation associated with each discriminant function, a technique discussed in Chapter 8, is also presented. The first canonical correlation is the maximum correlation that can be generated between a linear combination of the discriminatory variables and a linear combination of the groups that are represented by $g - 1$ dummy variables where g is the number of groups. The coefficients that are associated with the discriminatory variables and that produce the maximum correlation are equal to the linear discriminant function weights. The canonical correlation approach is equivalent to the linear discriminant function approach. The second canonical correlation is the maximum correlation that can be generated between a linear combination of the discriminatory variables and a linear combination of the group dummy variables given that the second pair of canonical variables (one for variables and one for groups) is uncorrelated with the first pair. The weights associated with the discriminatory variables and that maximize the second canonical correlation are the coefficients of the second linear discriminant function. The procedure is continued as far as necessary.

Large canonical correlations indicate a high correlation between the variables and the groups or, equivalently, a large ratio of between to within sums of squares on the associated linear discriminant function. In fact, the latent root associated with a particular discriminant function and the corresponding canonical correlation (r) are related by the formula

$$\frac{r^2}{1 - r^2} = \lambda.$$

The SAS output includes the discriminant coefficients for both standardized and unstandardized variables. As mentioned earlier, the standardized coefficients are independent of the metrics of the variables and hence give a better indication of the importance of the variables than the unstandardized score coefficients. The output also includes the correlation of each variable with each discriminant function for both the total sample and within groups. These matrices are referred to as "canonical structure matrices." They are nothing more than the correlations between the variables and the linear composites, which in this case are the linear discriminant functions. The group means on each discriminant function are presented and the centroids are plotted in the discriminant function space.

5.16 PROBLEMS

(1) Using the sample data in the Appendix, conduct a multiple discriminant analysis of the four college-level groups defined by variable 9 using the six ability measures as the discriminatory variables. How many discriminant functions are needed to account for most of the between-group variation? What ability measures are most important in discriminating between the four groups? Plot the group centroids in the space of the two largest discriminant functions.

(2) Develop a quadratic classification equation for each of the four groups using a common covariance matrix. Classify each individual on the basis of these equations and estimate the classification efficiency. Develop a quadratic classification for each of the four groups using each group's unique covariance matrix. Compare the classification efficiency of the two classification procedures.
(3) Assuming a common covariance matrix, transform the quadratic classification equations into linear classification equations.
(4) Estimate the prior probability of being a member of each of the four college-level groups. Assuming a common covariance matrix, develop new classification procedures. Compare the classification efficiency of this procedure with the classification efficiency of the first procedure in problem 2.
(5) Let us return to the classic data from problem 4 in Chapter 4. It was pointed out that these data were used to illustrate the technique of linear discriminant function analysis developed by R. A. Fisher.
    (a) Compute the three quadratic classification equations. (Hint: Don't forget to convert **E** into a pooled within-group dispersion matrix by dividing all of the elements in **E** by 147 degrees of freedom.) Assume equal costs of misclassification and equal prior probabilities.
    (b) On the basis of these equations, assign each of the following vectors of measurements to one of the three groups:
        (i) [3.5, 2, 4, 2.3]
        (ii) [1.5, 1, 2.2, .8]
        (iii) [7.2, 5.3, 2.1, 3]
    (c) Find two independent linear classification equations and assign the above three vectors to one of the three groups. Check to see that both procedures yield the same assignments.
    (d) Discuss the relative importance of the variables in discriminating among the three flower populations.
    (e) Based upon normal distribution theory, estimate the classification efficiency of the linear classification equations.
(6) Conduct a linear discriminant function analysis on the flower data.
    (a) How many linear discriminant functions would you retain?
    (b) Plot the centroids for the three flower species.
    (c) What is the relative importance of the four variables in discriminating among the three groups? Compare your answer to that for question 5d, above.
    (d) Which two species are closest to each other?
(7) Another classic data set that has been used to illustrate the utility of discriminant analysis was presented by Rao and Slater (1949). It involved five neurotic groups plus a normal group who were measured on three tests. The pertinent data are presented below.

Group	Sample Size	Mean Test Score 1	2	3
Anxiety state	114	2.9298	1.1667	.7281
Hysteria	33	3.0303	1.2424	.5455
Psychopathy	32	3.8125	1.8438	.8125
Obsession	17	4.7059	1.5882	1.1176
Personality change	5	1.4000	.2000	.0000
Normal	55	.6000	.1455	.2182

Pooled Within-Group Variance-Covariance Matrix

		1	2	3
Test	1	2.3009	.2516	.4742
	2		.6075	.0358
	3			.5951

(a) Derive the five linear classification equations assuming equal prior probabilities and costs of misclassification.

(b) Estimate the probability of misclassifying a person as a member of the normal group when that person is actually a member of the anxiety state group.

(c) Which group would you assign each of the following test score vectors?

(i) [2.1, 3.2, .8]
(ii) [1.2, .9, .6]
(iii) [4.1, 2.3, 1.8]

(8) Conduct a linear discriminant function analysis of the neurotic group data set.

(a) How many linear discriminant functions would you retain? What are the relative importances of the discriminant functions?

(b) Plot the group centroids in the space of the first two linear discriminant functions.

(c) On the basis of the configuration of the centroids in the linear discriminant function space, how would you cluster these groups?

(d) Which neurotic group is closest to the normal group?

(e) What is the relative importance of the three variables in discriminating among the six groups?

(f) What implications do the relatively small sample sizes for some of the groups have on the discriminant analyses?

NOTES

1. If a child's score turned out to be exactly 25, then we would flip a coin to assign him or her to a group.

2. The three principal minor determinants of $\mathbf{W}^{-1}\mathbf{B}$ are formed by deleting the row and column 1, row and column 2, and row and column 3, respectively.

6 Principal Components Analysis

6.1 INTRODUCTION

There are any number of rationales that could be used to weight a vector of variables (to obtain a linear composite). For example, we could weight a set of test scores in any of the following ways:

(1) Make the weights proportional to the reliabilities of the individual tests making up the composite.
(2) Weight the tests in regard to their hypothesized relation to an underlying construct.
(3) Weight the tests in regard to their contribution in explaining the variation in another variable (for example, weights determined through regression analysis).

The reader may be able to think of other ways to assign the weights to variables for constructing a linear composite. Another reason for forming composites is to summarize and simplify the data. Instead of working with a large set of variables, we could transform those variables into a much smaller set of variables by a linear transformation. For summarization and simplification purposes, we would want a relatively small number of linear composites that would provide most of the information residing in the larger set of original variables. Putting it another way, we would want linear composites that have high correlations with the original variables or, equivalently, that explain a lot of the variation in the original variables. For example, we could weight a set of tests, as shown later with real data, such that the composite has, overall, the highest possible correlations with the original variables. This is equivalent to maximizing the variance of the linear composite.

Principal components analysis involves the selection of a set of weights such that the variance of the linear composite is a maximum. Statistically, the problem can be formulated as maximizing the variance of $\mathbf{b}'\mathbf{x} = b_1 x_1 + b_2 x_2 + b_p x_p$ subject to the condition

$$\mathbf{b}'\mathbf{b} = \sum_{i=1}^{p} b_i^2 = 1$$

The restriction $\mathbf{b}'\mathbf{b} = 1$ is necessary for a unique solution to exist. If we did not impose this restriction, then, intuitively, the weights would become so large that the variance of the composite would itself become infinite. After the first principal component, the composite with maximum variance, is calculated, a second principal component that is uncorrelated with the first component and has maximum variance (but less variance than the first component) can be calculated. The process can be continued until all of the variation in the original variables is accounted for. Sometimes a large percentage (as much as 80 percent) of the variation in the original variables can be accounted for by the first few largest principal components. This is the goal for which principal components analysis strives.

Section 6.2 contains an intuitive and informal discussion of principal components analysis. The principal components analysis of two variables is discussed in section 6.3 so that geometry can further help us understand the nature of principal components. With the background of the first three sections, section 6.4 gives a theoretical derivation of principal components so that the general case of p variables can be addressed. The derivation uses calculus, but the reader with no calculus should be able to follow the main themes in the derivation. This section is important because it derives the general matrix equation that must be solved in order to determine the weighting vectors for the principal components. An algebraic solution is demonstrated for the case of two variables. For larger variable sets, however, iterative computer procedures are required. One of these procedures is discussed in section 6.5 and is illustrated in detail on a small variable set. Deciding how many principal components to retain is discussed in section 6.6. Section 6.7 discusses some applications of principal components, including an example using some actual data collected on the Wechsler Adult Intelligence Scale. Section 6.8 concludes this chapter with a few statements concerning computer software.

6.2 PRINCIPAL COMPONENTS

In most situations the number of principal components needed to completely exhaust the information in a set of variables is equal to the number of variables under consideration. This is true if the covariance (correlation) matrix corresponding to the variables is nonsingular (that is, its inverse exists). If the rank of the covariance (correlation) matrix is less than the dimension of the covariance matrix (that is, number of variables), then the number of principal components is equal to the rank of the covariance matrix. But, hopefully, as mentioned above, the first few components will account for most of the variation in the original variables. If so, we have effectively reduced the dimensionality of the data set. This simplification can, in turn, as we shall see in the examples ahead, lead to a better understanding of the nature of the original variables. Quite frequently, principal components can be substantively interpreted as dimensions underlying a data set.

Let us further explain what we mean by the number of principal components. After we have found the largest principal component, then we can find a second principal component that has maximum variance given the constraint that its vector of weights also satisfies the restriction $\mathbf{b}_2'\mathbf{b}_2 = 1$ and in addition satisfies a restriction that the correlation between the two principal components is zero. Similarly, if the rank of the covariance matrix is large enough, we may then solve for a third principal component that has maximum variance given that its vector of weights satisfies the restriction that $\mathbf{b}_3'\mathbf{b}_3 = 1$ and in addition is statistically uncorrelated with the first two principal components. We could continue extracting principal components until all of the information in the covariance (correlation) matrix was exhausted; that is, until the number of principal components extracted is equal to the rank of the covariance matrix.

The above verbal description can be expressed statistically as follows: Find $\mathbf{b}_1$ such that the variance of $(\mathbf{b}_1'\mathbf{x} = b_{11}x_1 + b_{12}x_2 + \ldots + b_{1p}x_p) = \mathbf{b}_1'\mathbf{C}\mathbf{b}_1$ is a maximum given that $\mathbf{b}_1'\mathbf{b}_1 = 1$. Then find $\mathbf{b}_2$ such that the variance of $(\mathbf{b}_2'\mathbf{x} = b_{21}x_1 + b_{22}x_2 + \ldots + b_{2p}x_p) = \mathbf{b}_2'\mathbf{C}\mathbf{b}_2$ is a maximum given that $\mathbf{b}_2'\mathbf{b}_2 = 1$ and $\mathbf{b}_2\mathbf{C}\mathbf{b}_1 = 0$. Next, find $\mathbf{b}_3$ such that the variance of $(\mathbf{b}_3'\mathbf{x} = b_{31}x_1 + b_{32}x_2 + ..+ b_{3p}) = \mathbf{b}_3'\mathbf{C}\mathbf{b}_3$ is a maximum given that $\mathbf{b}_3'\mathbf{b}_3 = 1$, $\mathbf{b}_3'\mathbf{C}\mathbf{b}_1 = 0$, and $\mathbf{b}_3'\mathbf{C}\mathbf{b}_2 = 0$. $\mathbf{C}$ is the covariance or correlation matrix and the constraints that $\mathbf{b}_3'\mathbf{C}\mathbf{b}_1 = 0$, and $\mathbf{b}_3'\mathbf{C}\mathbf{b}_2 = 0$ mean that the third principal component is uncorrelated with both the first and second principal components. In general, each successively computed principal component has less variance associated with it than the previous principal component. That is, the first principal component has the largest variance, the second principal component has the second largest variance, the third principal component has the third largest variance, and so on.

Principal components can be extracted from either a covariance or correlation matrix. But if the units of the variables are arbitrary (such as scales for tests), then it is best to work with the correlation matrix. For example, if we had a number of tests, one of which had an extremely large variance relative to the remaining tests, then the assigning of weights through principal components would give that variable with the large variance a large weight because to do so would help accomplish the goal of maximizing the variance of the composite. But since the variance of a test score is a function of the arbitrary unit of measurement, the principal component weights become more a function of the units of measurement than of the underlying structure of the observations. Consequently, in many instances the covariance matrix is transformed into a correlation matrix before a principal components analysis is conducted. A major problem with extracting principal components from a sample correlation matrix is that since we are now working with elements such as

$$\frac{\hat{\sigma}_{ij}}{\hat{\sigma}_i \hat{\sigma}_j}$$

instead of $\hat{\sigma}_{ij}$, the sampling distribution theory becomes quite complex. Notice that $\hat{\sigma}_{ij}$, $\hat{\sigma}_i$, and $\hat{\sigma}_j$ are all sample estimates. This problem of making population inferences from the correlation matrix is somewhat alleviated if we are working with large samples.

Although multivariate normality assumptions are not necessary to apply principal components analysis, we shall make this assumption so that certain statistical tests can be applied to the sample. We shall examine a few bivariate situations in order to further our understanding of principal components. We shall then look at some trivariate situations before generalizing to any arbitrary-sized vector of dimension p.

6.3 PRINCIPAL COMPONENTS OF TWO VARIABLES

If two bivariate normally distributed variables are highely correlated, then the scatter plot of the sample standardized variables (that is,

$$z_1 = \frac{y_1 - \hat{\mu}_1}{\hat{\sigma}_1}, \quad z_2 = \frac{y_2 - \hat{\mu}_2}{\hat{\sigma}_2}$$

would look like that in Figure 6.1. The first (larger) principal component is represented as the line p_1, while the second principal component (smaller) is represented as the line p_2. The line representing the first principal component (p_1) for this sample is roughly the principal axis of the ellipse formed by the sample points.

The cosine of the angles α and β that the principal component line makes with the z_1 and z_2 axes, respectively, are equal to the principal component weights. In the case of two standardized variables, the principal component line has to bisect the angle $z_1 o z_2$ and hence the angles α and β are each 45°. The cosine of 45° is .71 and, hence, the appropriate principal component weights are each .71, so that the linear composite $.71z_1 + 71z_2$ has maximum variance. No other set of weights with the restriction that $b_1^2 + b_2^2 = 1$ will produce a composite score with as much variation. Let us suppose that the

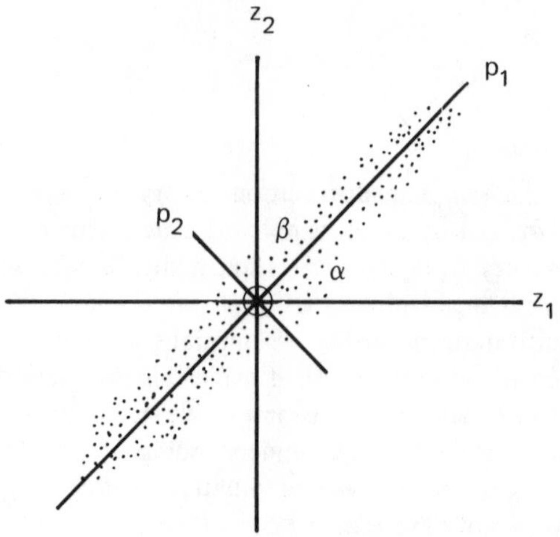

Figure 6.1 Principal Components of Two Highly Correlated Bivariate Normally Distributed Standardized Variables

correlation between z_1 and z_2 was .80. Then the sample variance of the first principal component $.71z_1 + .71z_2$ is

$$\hat{\sigma}^2_{p_1} = [.71,\ .71] \begin{bmatrix} 1.00 & .80 \\ .80 & 1.00 \end{bmatrix} \begin{bmatrix} .71 \\ .71 \end{bmatrix} = 1.80$$

while another similar set of weights such as [.80, .60] would yield a variance of

$$[.80,\ .60] \begin{bmatrix} 1.00 & .80 \\ .80 & 1.00 \end{bmatrix} \begin{bmatrix} .80 \\ .60 \end{bmatrix} = 1.77$$

which is less than 1.80. The calculation of these variances made use of the formulas for the variances of a linear composite discussed in Chapter 3.

Since the second principal component, p_2, is uncorrelated with the first principal component, p_1, the line p_2 must be perpendicular to p_1. Consequently, p_2 makes an angle of $90° + 45° = 135°$ with z_1 and $45°$ with z_2. The cosine of 135° is −.71 and the cosine of 45° is .71. The second principal component would thus be $-.71z_1 + .71z_2$. The second principal component line is equivalent to the minor axis of the ellipse. The variance of the second principal component would be

$$\hat{\sigma}^2_{p_2} = [-.71,\ .71]\begin{bmatrix} 1.00 & .80 \\ .80 & 1.00 \end{bmatrix}\begin{bmatrix} -.71 \\ .71 \end{bmatrix} = .20$$

The second principal component has considerably less variance than the first principal component. Because of the relatively high correlation between z_1 and z_2, the largest principal component itself does a fairly good job in summarizing the information in z_1 and z_2. We may be able to see this better by just looking at the bivariate distribution on our new derived variables, p_1 and p_2, as illustrated in Figure 6.2. Notice that the sum of the variances of the original variables is 1 + 1 = 2, which is identical to the sum of the new derived principal components variables, 1.80 + .20 = 2. A characteristic of principal components analysis is that the sum of the variances of the original variables is equal to the sum of the variances of the principal components. If one of the principal components has a large variance relative to the sum of the variances of all of the principal components, then that principal component captures most of the information lying in the original set of variables. For our example, the first principal component accounts for 1.80/2.00 = 90% of the variation in the two variables z_1 and z_2.

Let us now verify that p_1 and p_2 are uncorrelated by observing that

$$\hat{\sigma}_{p_1,p_2} = [.71,\ .71]\begin{bmatrix} 1.00 & .80 \\ .80 & 1.00 \end{bmatrix}\begin{bmatrix} -.71 \\ .71 \end{bmatrix} = 0$$

There is another useful way of looking at principal components. Since we have transformed the original variables z_1 and z_2 to principal components p_1 and p_2 by the transformation $\mathbf{Az} = \mathbf{p}$, which in our example is

$$\begin{bmatrix} .71 & .71 \\ -.71 & .71 \end{bmatrix}\begin{bmatrix} z_1 \\ z_2 \end{bmatrix} = \begin{bmatrix} p_1 \\ p_2 \end{bmatrix}$$

we can express the original variables z_1 and z_2 in terms of the principal components by observing that $\mathbf{z} = \mathbf{A}^{-1}\mathbf{p}$, which is

$$\begin{bmatrix} z_1 \\ z_2 \end{bmatrix} = \begin{bmatrix} .71 & .71 \\ -.71 & .71 \end{bmatrix}^{-1}\begin{bmatrix} p_1 \\ p_2 \end{bmatrix} = \begin{bmatrix} .71 & -.71 \\ .71 & .71 \end{bmatrix}\begin{bmatrix} p_1 \\ p_2 \end{bmatrix}$$

Thus $z_1 = .71p_1 - .71p_2$ and $z_2 = .71p_1 + .71p_2$ and we have expressed each of the variables in terms of a linear combination of the principal components.

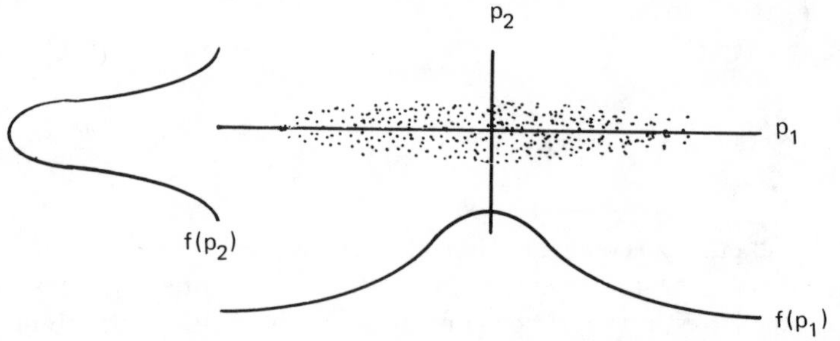

Figure 6.2 Bivariate Distribution of the Two Principal Components

Next, we can verify that these two principal components completely explain the variation in each of the original variables z_1 and z_2 by noting that

$$1 = \hat{\sigma}^2_{z_1} = (.71)^2 \hat{\sigma}^2_{p_1} + (-.71)^2 \hat{\sigma}^2_{p_2} = .50(1.80) + .50(.20) = 1$$

and

$$1 = \hat{\sigma}^2_{z_2} = (.71)^2 \hat{\sigma}^2_{p_1} + (.71)^2 \hat{\sigma}^2_{p_2} = 1$$

Since $\hat{\sigma}_{p_1,p_2} = 0$, there is no covariance term in these composite score expressions.

From our above equations we can also see that the largest principal component alone accounts for 90 percent of the variation for both z_1 and z_2, since if we attempt to reproduce z_1 and z_2 from p_1 alone we would find that

$$\hat{z}_1 = .71p_1 \text{ so that } \sigma^2_{\hat{z}_1} = (.71)^2 \sigma^2_{p_1} = .50(1.80) = .90 \text{ or } 90\% \text{ of } \hat{\sigma}^2_{z_1}$$

and

$$\hat{z}_2 = .71p_1 \text{ so that } \sigma^2_{\hat{z}_2} = .90 \text{ or } 90\% \text{ of } \hat{\sigma}^2_{z_2}$$

The circumflexes over z_1 and z_2 signify that p_1 alone will not reproduce z_1 and z_2 exactly. They are the predicted values based upon only the first principal component. Since p_1 explains 90 percent of the variation in both z_1 and z_2, both of the latter correlate $\sqrt{.90} = .95$ with p_1.

Similarly, p_2 explains only 10 percent of the variance in z_1 and z_2 and hence has an absolute correlation of only $\sqrt{.10} = .31$ ($-.31$ with z_1, and .31 with z_2) with each of these variables. We again see that nothing much is lost in trying to represent both z_1 and z_2 in terms of the largest principal component alone. We can verify that $r_{z_1,p_2} = -.31$ by observing that

$$r_{z_1,p_2} = r_{.71p_1-.71p_2,p_2} = \frac{\sigma_{.71p_1-.71p_2,p_2}}{\sigma_{.71p_1-.71p_2}\sigma_{p_2}}$$

$$= \frac{[.71,-.71]\begin{bmatrix}0\\.20\end{bmatrix}(1)}{\sqrt{[.71,-.71]\begin{bmatrix}1.80 & 0\\0 & .20\end{bmatrix}\begin{bmatrix}.71\\-.71\end{bmatrix}}\sqrt{.20}} = \frac{-.142}{(1)\sqrt{.20}} = -.31$$

The reader can easily verify the remaining correlations r_{z_1,p_1}, r_{z_2,p_1}, and r_{z_2,p_2}.

We mentioned earlier that the principal component weights are highly dependent upon the units of measurement associated with each of the variables. For example, if we rescaled (linear transformed) z_2 by arbitrarily multiplying each score by 2 (that is, $z_2' = 2z_2$, then our new variable z_2' would have a variance of 4. Since the correlation between z_1 and z_2' would still be .80, the bivariance scatter plot of z_1 and z_2' and the associated principal components would resemble Figure 6.3.

Cursory examination of Figure 6.3 reveals that the largest principal component p_1 is oriented more in the direction of z_2' than z_1, that is, $\beta < \alpha$ and hence z_2' would get a larger weight than z_1 in the principal component, p_1. Our solution to the new problem would be different than for our original problem. The results of a principal components analysis are not invariant with regard to changes in scale (that is, unit of measurement). It should be emphasized that the weights of the largest principal component for an analysis of two variables are identical for all values of the correlation coefficient if both variables are standardized. The weights would be the same even if the correlation between the two variables was close to zero, but the largest principal component would not do an adequate job in reproducing the two original variables.

For example, let us suppose that the correlation between the two sample standardized variables z_1 and z_2 was only .10. Then, we know that

$$p_1 = .71z_1 + .71z_2$$

and

$$p_2 = -.71z_1 + .71z_2$$

and the variance of p_1 is $(.71)^2 + (.71)^2 + 2(.71)(.71)(.10) = 1.10$ and the variance of p_2 is $(-.71)^2 + (.71)^2 + 2(-.71)(.71)(.10) = .90$. The reader should verify that this indicates that only 55 percent of the variation in both z_1 and

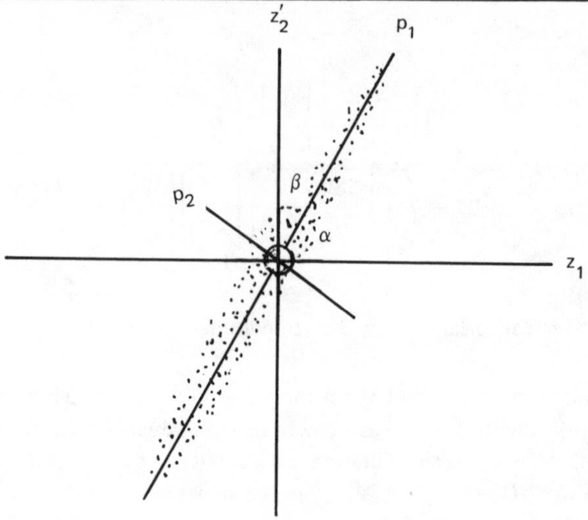

Figure 6.3 Principal Components of z_1 and z_2'

z_2 is explained by using only the largest principal component. The remaining 45 percent of the variation in both variables is explained by the remaining principal component. In this case we would not want to summarize the information in z_1 and z_2 by only the largest principal component. We need to use both of them to do an adequate job.

An important goal of principal components analysis is to reduce the dimensionality of the problem under consideration. If we need both principal components to explain the variation in two variables, then we have not reduced the dimensionality of the problem. For all practical purposes, we might just as well use our original two variables. If one or a few principal components explain most of the variation in a large set of variables, then we have effectively reduced the dimensionality of our data set.

6.4 THEORETICAL DERIVATION OF PRINCIPAL COMPONENTS

We have used a rather intuitive approach up to this point in our two-dimensional discussion of principal components. To enable us to generalize easily to three- and higher-dimensional (that is, number of variables) situations, we need to be a bit more rigorous. The reader who has not had any calculus should not be discouraged by the following discussion. Rather, the reader can take some things on faith and take comfort in the fact that the analytical solution of the principal components problem makes use of many of the matrix operations that we have continuously applied throughout this book. The problem of finding the weights for the largest principal component involves multivariate calculus and the theory of latent roots and latent vectors. The problem is to find $\mathbf{b}_1' = [b_{11}, b_{12} \ldots, b_{1p}]$ such that the variance of $\mathbf{b}_1'\mathbf{x} = b_{11}x_1 + b_{12}x_2 + \ldots + b_{1p}x_p$ is maximized subject to the constraint that

$$\mathbf{b}_1'\mathbf{b}_1 = \sum_{i=1}^{p} b_{1i}^2 = 1$$

From calculus, we first form the Lagrangian

$$y = \mathbf{b}'\mathbf{V}\mathbf{b} - \lambda(\mathbf{b}'\mathbf{b} - 1)$$

where y is the function to be maximized and $\mathbf{V}$ is the $p \times p$ covariance (correlation) matrix of the original variables. The matrix expression $\mathbf{b}'\mathbf{V}\mathbf{b}$ is simply the variance of the composite to be maximized, λ is an unknown constant called a "Lagrange multiplier," and $\mathbf{b}'\mathbf{b} - 1$ reflects the constraint that $\mathbf{b}'\mathbf{b} - 1 = 0$. The next step is to find $\mathbf{b}'$ and λ such that y is maximized. From the theory of partial differentiation we first differentiate with respect to the vector $\mathbf{b}$ and set the expression equation to 0. This yields

$$\frac{\partial y}{\partial \mathbf{b}} = 2\mathbf{V}\mathbf{b} - 2\lambda\mathbf{b} = \mathbf{0}$$

or

$$(\mathbf{V} - \lambda\mathbf{I})\mathbf{b} = \mathbf{0}$$

Since $(\mathbf{V} - \lambda\mathbf{I})\mathbf{b} = \mathbf{0}$ and $\mathbf{b} \neq \mathbf{0}$, the matrix $\mathbf{V} - \lambda\mathbf{I}$ must be singular because the columns of $\mathbf{V} - \lambda\mathbf{I}$ must be linearly dependent if $\mathbf{b} \neq 0$. This means that $|\mathbf{V} - \lambda\mathbf{I}| = 0$ (that is, the determinant of $\mathbf{V} - \lambda\mathbf{I}$ vanishes since the matrix is singular). The equation $|\mathbf{V} - \lambda\mathbf{I}| = 0$ is often called a characteristic equation. In the case of two variables,

$$|\mathbf{V} - \lambda\mathbf{I}| = \left| \begin{bmatrix} \sigma_1^2 & \sigma_{12} \\ \sigma_{21} & \sigma_2^2 \end{bmatrix} - \lambda \begin{bmatrix} 1 & 0 \\ 0 & 1 \end{bmatrix} \right| = \begin{vmatrix} \sigma_1^2 - \lambda & \sigma_{12} \\ \sigma_{21} & \sigma_2^2 - \lambda \end{vmatrix}$$

$$= (\sigma_1^2 - \lambda)(\sigma_2^2 - \lambda) - \sigma_{21}\sigma_{12}$$

$$= \lambda^2 - \lambda(\sigma_1^2 + \sigma_2^2) + \sigma_1^2\sigma_2^2 - \sigma_{21}\sigma_{12} = 0$$

You will note that this is a quadratic form in λ or a second-degree polynomial. It has two solutions for λ or roots. If we premultiply $(\mathbf{V} - \lambda\mathbf{I})\mathbf{b} = 0$ by $\mathbf{b}'$ we get $\mathbf{b}'(\mathbf{V} - \lambda\mathbf{I})\mathbf{b} = 0$ or $\mathbf{b}'\mathbf{V}\mathbf{b} = \lambda\mathbf{b}'\mathbf{b}$. Since $\mathbf{b}'\mathbf{b} = 1$ and we want to maximize $\mathbf{b}'\mathbf{V}\mathbf{b} = \lambda$ (that is, the variance of the composite), the root or solution of $\lambda^2 - \lambda(\sigma_1^2 + \sigma_2^2) + \sigma_1^2\sigma_2^2 - \sigma_{11}\sigma_{12} = 0$ that we want is the largest of the two roots. We can then find the vector, $\mathbf{b}$, associated with the largest root.

Let us return to our example, where

$$\mathbf{V} = \begin{bmatrix} 1.00 & .80 \\ .80 & 1.00 \end{bmatrix}$$

In this case, we have standardized variables and hence the covariance matrix turns out to be a correlation matrix. Continuing, we have

$$|\mathbf{V} - \lambda\mathbf{I}| = \begin{bmatrix} 1.00 - \lambda & .80 \\ .80 & 1.00 - \lambda \end{bmatrix} = \lambda^2 - 2\lambda + .36 = 0$$

This second-degree polynomial has two solutions: $\lambda_1 = 1.80$ and $\lambda_2 = .20$. The largest root is 1.80 and is equal to the variance of the principal component with the largest variance. We can also verify that the latent vector $\mathbf{b}'$ corresponding to the largest root is [.71, .71], the vector whose solution we found earlier on the basis of geometrical considerations. That is,

$$\mathbf{V}\mathbf{b} = \begin{bmatrix} 1.00 & .80 \\ .80 & 1.00 \end{bmatrix} \begin{bmatrix} .71 \\ .71 \end{bmatrix} = 1.80 \begin{bmatrix} .71 \\ .71 \end{bmatrix} = \lambda\mathbf{b}$$

or

$$\begin{bmatrix} 1.278 \\ 1.278 \end{bmatrix} = \begin{bmatrix} 1.278 \\ 1.278 \end{bmatrix}$$

The second largest root in this example is .20 and its associated latent vector is [−.71, .71] because

$$\begin{bmatrix} 1.00 & .80 & -.71 \\ .80 & 1.00 & .71 \end{bmatrix} = .20 \begin{bmatrix} -.71 \\ .71 \end{bmatrix}$$

or

$$\begin{bmatrix} -.142 \\ .142 \end{bmatrix} = \begin{bmatrix} -.142 \\ .142 \end{bmatrix}$$

These values correspond to those we previously derived from geometrical considerations; we are merely verifying that they are the solutions to $(\mathbf{V} - \lambda\mathbf{I})\mathbf{b} = \mathbf{0}$ corresponding to our two-dimensional example.

TABLE 6.1 Correlations Among Tests

	1	2	3	4
(1) Intelligence	1.00	.80	.70	.60
(2) Reading	.80	1.00	.70	.50
(3) Arithmetic reasoning	.70	.70	1.00	.60
(4) Mechanical aptitude	.60	.50	.60	1.00

6.5 AN ALGORITHM FOR CONDUCTING PRINCIPAL COMPONENTS ANALYSIS

When we are working with three or more variables, we cannot rely on simple geometrical solutions. In addition, we cannot rely upon algebraic solutions in the case of large variable sets. Rather, we need some computing algorithm. We will demonstrate an iterative computing algorithm on the hypothetical 4×4 correlation matrix presented in Table 6.1.

The problem is to see if we can account for the variation of these four test scores by a smaller subset of independent basic dimensions (that is, principal components). The number of nonzero principal components is equal to the rank of the correlation matrix. The correlation matrix in Table 6.1 is of rank 4, so that there are 4 nonzero principal components. However, we would like to be able to explain most of the variation in these 4 tests by one or two principal components.

The first step in the iterative procedure is to compute successive powers of the correlation matrix. We start with $\mathbf{R}$, then we compute $\mathbf{RR} = \mathbf{R}^2$, $\mathbf{R}^2\mathbf{R}^2 = \mathbf{R}^4$, $\mathbf{R}^4\mathbf{R}^4 = \mathbf{R}^8$, $\mathbf{R}^8\mathbf{R}^8 = \mathbf{R}^{16}$ and so on, until we find that the elements of the vectors $\mathbf{a}'\mathbf{R}^i$ and $\mathbf{a}'\mathbf{R}^{2i}$ are proportional to each other. The vector $\mathbf{a}'$ can be any arbitrary vector and when $\mathbf{a}'\mathbf{R}^i$ is proportional to $\mathbf{a}'\mathbf{R}^{2i}$ for some i (power to which R is raised) we say that the solution has converged and that $\mathbf{a}'\mathbf{R}^i$ is proportional to the largest latent vector, $\mathbf{b}$. That is, we continue the iterative procedure until $\mathbf{a}'\mathbf{R}^i = k\mathbf{a}'\mathbf{R}^{2i}$ for some i. The arbitrary vector $\mathbf{a}'$ and the number of variables influence the rate of convergence. For more rapid convergence, it is best to have the elements of $\mathbf{a}'$ proportional to the row totals of the correlation matrix. With a small number of variables and a reasonable selection of $\mathbf{a}'$ the solution converges rapidly, as we shall see.

In our problem the sums of the rows of the correlation matrix are fairly close to each other, so that we can set $\mathbf{a}' = [1, 1, 1, 1]$. The next step is to compute $\mathbf{R}^2$, $\mathbf{R}^4$ and see if $\mathbf{a}'\mathbf{R}^2$ and $\mathbf{a}'\mathbf{R}^4$ satisfy the proportionality requirements, thus signifying a solution for the latent vector.

$$\mathbf{R}^2 = \begin{bmatrix} 1.00 & .80 & .70 & .60 \\ .80 & 1.00 & .70 & .50 \\ .70 & .70 & 1.00 & .60 \\ .60 & .50 & .60 & 1.00 \end{bmatrix} \begin{bmatrix} 1.00 & .80 & .70 & .60 \\ .80 & 1.00 & .70 & .50 \\ .70 & .70 & 1.00 & .60 \\ .60 & .50 & .60 & 1.00 \end{bmatrix}$$

$$= \begin{bmatrix} 2.49 & 2.39 & 2.32 & 2.02 \\ 2.39 & 2.38 & 2.26 & 1.90 \\ 2.32 & 2.26 & 2.34 & 1.97 \\ 2.02 & 1.90 & 1.97 & 1.97 \end{bmatrix}$$

and

$$\mathbf{a}'\mathbf{R}^2 = [1,\ 1,\ 1,\ 1] \begin{bmatrix} 2.49 & 2.39 & 2.32 & 2.02 \\ 2.39 & 2.38 & 2.26 & 1.90 \\ 2.32 & 2.26 & 2.34 & 1.97 \\ 2.02 & 1.90 & 1.97 & 1.97 \end{bmatrix}$$

$$= [9.22,\ 8.93,\ 8.89,\ 7.86]$$

We can standardize this vector by dividing each element by the largest element, 9.22. This gives

$$[1.0000,\ .9685,\ .9642,\ .8525]$$

Next,

$$\mathbf{R}^4 = \begin{bmatrix} 2.49 & 2.39 & 2.32 & 2.02 \\ 2.39 & 2.38 & 2.26 & 1.90 \\ 2.32 & 2.26 & 2.34 & 1.97 \\ 2.02 & 1.90 & 1.97 & 1.97 \end{bmatrix} \begin{bmatrix} 2.49 & 2.39 & 2.32 & 2.02 \\ 2.39 & 2.38 & 2.26 & 1.90 \\ 2.32 & 2.26 & 2.34 & 1.97 \\ 2.02 & 1.90 & 1.97 & 1.97 \end{bmatrix}$$

$$= \begin{bmatrix} 21.3750 & 20.7205 & 20.5864 & 18.1206 \\ 20.7205 & 20.0941 & 19.9550 & 17.5450 \\ 20.5864 & 19.9550 & 19.8265 & 17.4711 \\ 18.1206 & 17.5450 & 17.4711 & 15.4522 \end{bmatrix}$$

and

$$[1,\ 1,\ 1,\ 1]\mathbf{R}^4 = [80.8025,\ 78.3146,\ 77.8390,\ 68.5889]$$

Standardizing this vector by dividing each element by 80.8025, we obtain

$$[1.000,\ .9692,\ .9633,\ .8489]$$

If we compare this vector with the previous vector, then we can see that the two vectors agree with each other to the second decimal place. Let us now see if we can obtain closer agreement by computing $[1, \; 1, \; 1, \; 1]\mathbf{R}^8$ and comparing it with $[1, \; 1, \; 1, \; 1]\mathbf{R}^4$ after both vectors have been standardized. Continuing, we find

$$\mathbf{R}^8 = \mathbf{R}^4\mathbf{R}^4$$

$$= \begin{bmatrix} 21.3750 & 20.7205 & 20.5864 & 18.1206 \\ 20.7205 & 20.0941 & 19.9550 & 17.5450 \\ 20.5864 & 19.9550 & 19.8265 & 17.4711 \\ 18.1206 & 17.5450 & 17.4711 & 15.4522 \end{bmatrix} \begin{bmatrix} 21.3750 & 20.7205 & 20.5864 & 18.1206 \\ 20.7205 & 20.0941 & 19.9550 & 17.5450 \\ 20.5864 & 19.9550 & 19.8265 & 17.4711 \\ 18.1206 & 17.5450 & 17.4711 & 15.4522 \end{bmatrix}$$

$$= \begin{bmatrix} 1638.3858 & 1587.9880 & 1578.2550 & 1390.5392 \\ 1587.9880 & 1539.1410 & 1529.7065 & 1347.7635 \\ 1578.2550 & 1529.7065 & 1520.3313 & 1339.5061 \\ 1390.5392 & 1347.7635 & 1339.5061 & 1180.1930 \end{bmatrix}$$

and

$$[1, \; 1, \; 1, \; 1]\mathbf{R}^8 = [6195.1680, \; 6004.5990, \; 5967.7989, \; 5258.0018]$$

and upon standardizing, we have

$$[1.0000, \; .9692, \; .9633, \; .8487]$$

We can see that all elements of this last vector agree to the third decimal place with $[1, \; 1, \; 1, \; 1]\mathbf{R}^4$ after standardization. Another iteration or two would probably lead to agreement to the fourth decimal place. The first three elements of these last two vectors already agree to the fourth decimal place. If p was extremely large, then we would have to deal with matrices such as $\mathbf{R}^{32}$, $\mathbf{R}^{64}$, $\mathbf{R}^{128}$, and so on in order to obtain convergence and hence would need a computer to solve our problem.

For our purposes, we will accept this agreement to the third decimal place and convert this last vector into a latent vector by dividing each element by the square root of the sum of squares of the four elements. (Remember, the latent vector is restricted to be of unit length, that is, $\mathbf{b}'\mathbf{b} = 1$.) Dividing each element of [1.000, .969, .963, .849] by

$$\sqrt{(1.000)^2 + (.969)^2 + (.963)^2 + (.849)^2} = 1.893972$$

we have the unit length latent vector

$$[.528, \; .512, \; .508, \; .448]$$

Since $\mathbf{Rb} = \lambda \mathbf{b}$,

$$[1.00,\ .80,\ .70,\ .60]\begin{bmatrix} .528 \\ .512 \\ .508 \\ .448 \end{bmatrix} = \lambda(.528)$$

and consequently $\lambda = 2.958$. Since this equality holds for all rows of $\mathbf{R}$, we chose to solve for λ in terms of the first row.

This λ of 2.958 is the largest latent root of $|\mathbf{R} - \lambda \mathbf{I}| = 0$, so the associated latent vector is [.528, .512, .508, .448]. This latent vector is also the weighting vector for the largest principal component and its associated λ is equal to the variance of the largest principal component.

Let us now examine the correlation of each of these four tests with the largest principal component. From our previous discussion concerning variances, covariances, and correlations of composites, we know that the correlation of the first test with the largest (first) principal component is

$$\frac{\mathbf{b}'\mathbf{r}_1}{\sqrt{\lambda}} = \frac{[.528,\ .512,\ .508,\ .448]\begin{bmatrix} 1.00 \\ .80 \\ .70 \\ .60 \end{bmatrix}}{\sqrt{2.958}} = \frac{1.562}{1.720} = .908$$

where $\mathbf{b}'$ is the latent vector, $\mathbf{r}_1$ is the first column from the correlation matrix $\mathbf{R}$, and $\sqrt{\lambda}$ is the standard deviation of the first principal component. This calculation can be simplified by noting that $\mathbf{b}'\mathbf{r}_1 = \lambda b_1$ where b_1 is the first element of the latent vector. This fact enables us to express the correlation of test 1 with the first principal component as

$$\frac{\lambda b_1}{\sqrt{\lambda}} \text{ or } \sqrt{\lambda} b_1$$

In our example, $\sqrt{\lambda} b_1 = 1.720(.528) = .908$.

The correlation of test 2 with the first principal component can be expressed as

$$\frac{\mathbf{b}'\mathbf{r}_2}{\sqrt{\lambda}} = \sqrt{\lambda} b_2$$

where $\mathbf{r}_2$ is the second column of the correlation matrix and b_2 is the second element of the latent vector. Similarly, it can be shown that the correlations of test 3 and test 4 with the first principal components are $\sqrt{\lambda}b_3$ and $\sqrt{\lambda}b_4$, respectively, where b_3 and b_4 are the third and fourth elements of the latent vector, respectively. We can see that the correlations of the four tests with the first principal component can be jointly expressed in one matrix expression as

$$\sqrt{\lambda}\mathbf{b} = \sqrt{2.958}\begin{bmatrix} .528 \\ .512 \\ .508 \\ .448 \end{bmatrix} = \begin{bmatrix} .908 \\ .881 \\ .874 \\ .771 \end{bmatrix}$$

Since all four of these tests correlate highly with the first principal component, a researcher might interpret this component to represent general aptitude or general intelligence. There are some similarities between the principal component model being considered here and the factor analysis model to be considered later. Both models attempt to represent a set of manifest variables such as test scores by a smaller set of more basic latent or underlying factors. However, principal component analysis attempts to reproduce the test scores while factor analysis attempts to reproduce the original correlations that reflect what the variables have in common. Also, the factors derived from principal components analysis are based upon maximizing the variance of the components while the factors derived from factor analysis are based upon satisfying certain structural properties that are desirable from a theoretical or conceptual viewpoint. For example, some viewpoints concerning factor analysis are that each original variable should be explained by as few factors as possible and that each factor should account for the variation of a subset of variables but not all variables. Many factor analysts would not accept our first principal component as a psychologically meaningful underlying trait since the factor correlates substantially with all four tests rather than a subset of them. For example, should the variation in both reading and mechanical aptitude be explained by the same underlying factor? We shall see later that rotating the factors so that they have desirable conceptual properties is a basic component of factor analysis.

Returning to our example, we can see that if we square each element in the above vector of test correlations with the first principal component, then we have the proportion of test variance that the principal component explains for each of the four tests. These are presented in Table 6.2.

Adding up the proportion of variance accounted for by the first principal component for each of the four tests, we find that this sum equals 2.958. This value is equal to the largest latent root or, equivalently, to the variance of the first principal component. The first principal component does a pretty good job of accounting for the variation in all four tests. It explains 2.958/4.000, or 74 percent, of the variation in the test scores. However, 26 percent of the variance in the test scores has yet to be explained. Our next step will be to derive a second principal component that is orthogonal to the first and the variance of which is maximized. The first step in doing this is to calculate a residual correlation matrix. The residual correlation matrix reflects what is left of the variance and covariance terms of the original correlation matrix after the influence of the first principal component is subtracted out. For example, if we subtract out the effects of the first principal component, then the residual variance remaining for the four tests are .176, 224, .236, and .406, respectively. Also, the original correlation between tests 1 and 2 was .80. But if test 1 correlates .908 with the first principal component and test 2 correlates .881 with the first principal component, then the correlation between the two test scores as estimated by the first principal component would be (.908)(.881), or .800; the residual correlation between these two tests after the effects of the first principal component have been subtracted out would then be .800 − .800 = 0. Using a similar argument for the remaining correlations, it can be seen that the residual correlation matrix ($\mathbf{R}_s$) can be computed as $\mathbf{R}_s = \mathbf{R} - \lambda\mathbf{b}\mathbf{b}'$, where $\mathbf{R}$ is the original correlation matrix, λ is the latent root corresponding to the largest (first) principal component, and $\mathbf{b}$ is the column latent vector. For our example,

$$\mathbf{R}_s = \begin{bmatrix} 1.00 & .80 & .70 & .60 \\ .80 & 1.00 & .70 & .50 \\ .70 & .70 & 1.00 & .60 \\ .60 & .50 & .60 & 1.00 \end{bmatrix} - 2.958 \begin{bmatrix} .528 \\ .512 \\ .508 \\ .448 \end{bmatrix} [.528,\ .512,\ .508,\ .448]$$

$$= \begin{bmatrix} 1.000 & .800 & .700 & .600 \\ .800 & 1.000 & .700 & .500 \\ .700 & .700 & 1.000 & .600 \\ .600 & .500 & .600 & 1.000 \end{bmatrix} - \begin{bmatrix} .825 & .800 & .793 & .707 \\ .800 & .775 & .769 & .678 \\ .793 & .769 & .763 & .673 \\ .707 & .678 & .673 & .594 \end{bmatrix}$$

$$= \begin{bmatrix} .175 & .000 & -.093 & -.107 \\ .000 & .235 & -.069 & -.178 \\ -.093 & -.069 & .237 & -.073 \\ -.107 & -.178 & -.073 & .406 \end{bmatrix}$$

The matrix $\lambda\mathbf{b}\mathbf{b}'$ that is subtracted from $\mathbf{R}$ is simply the covariance matrix based upon the test scores as estimated from the first principal component. Note that $\mathbf{R}_s$ is actually a covariance matrix rather than a correlation matrix. Note that the principal diagonal contains elements considerably less than 1. It

TABLE 6.2 Proportion of Variance Accounted for by First Principal Component

	Proportion of Variance
Test 1: Intelligence	.824
Test 2: Reading	.776
Test 3: Arithmetic reasoning	.764
Test 4: Mechanical aptitude	.594

is the residual covariation among the tests after the effects of the first principal component have been partialled out.

To obtain the second principal component, we can use the exact same iterative procedure that was used to find the first principal component. As successive principal components are extracted, the residual matrix comes closer and closer to a null matrix. Upon applying this procedure to $\mathbf{R}_s$, we find that

$$\lambda_2 = .532 \text{ and } b_2 = \begin{bmatrix} -.240 \\ -.404 \\ -.015 \\ .835 \end{bmatrix}$$

The correlation of each of the four test variables with the second principal component is given by

$$\sqrt{\lambda_2}\mathbf{b}_2 = \sqrt{.532}\begin{bmatrix} -.240 \\ -.494 \\ -.015 \\ .835 \end{bmatrix} = \begin{bmatrix} -.175 \\ -.360 \\ -.011 \\ .609 \end{bmatrix}$$

The second principal component has a variance of .532 and accounts for .532/4.00, or 13.3 percent, of the variance in the test scores. This is considerably less than the 74 percent of the test variance accounted for by the first principal component. We can see that the second principal component is most effective in explaining some additional variation in test 4. The latent roots and the component-test correlations (loadings) were computed for the third and fourth principal components and the loadings are presented in Table 6.3 along with the corresponding results for the first two principal components. The latent roots and associated vectors for the third and fourth principal components are computed in the same manner used to calculate the latent root and vector for the second principal component. That is, we work with successive residual correlation matrices.

We can see from Table 6.3 that principal component 1 does a pretty good job of explaining variance for each of the four tests. The second principal component mainly contributes by explaining some additional variation in test 4. Likewise, the third principal component mainly contributes by explaining some additional variance in test 3. The fourth and last principal component adds a small contribution in explaining the variation in the first two tests. On the basis of this principal components analysis, a researcher might conclude that he or she should use only the first principal component since the other principal components individually and totally accounted for considerably less variation. It should be pointed out that if we label the matrix presented in Table 6.3 as **P**, then $\mathbf{R} = \mathbf{PP}'$. In other words, the original correlation matrix has been decomposed into the product of two matrices, one being the transpose of the other. The matrix **P** that we solved for is not the only matrix that satisfies this condition. There are an infinite number of matrices that would satisfy this condition. However, there is only one matrix **P** that has the maximization of variance property of principal components that satisfies these conditions. We shall see in the chapter on factor analysis that **R** can be factored like this in an infinite number of ways. We can easily verify that $\mathbf{R} = \mathbf{PP}'$ as follows: First, $\mathbf{B}'\mathbf{RB} = \mathbf{D}_\lambda$ where **B** is the matrix containing the four latent vectors and $\mathbf{D}_\lambda$ is a diagonal matrix of latent roots. Next, pre- and postmultiplying both sides of the equation by **B** and $\mathbf{B}'$, respectively, we have $\mathbf{BB}'\mathbf{RBB}' = \mathbf{BD}_\lambda\mathbf{B}'$ or $\mathbf{R} = \mathbf{BD}^{1/2}\mathbf{D}^{1/2}\mathbf{B}'$ since $\mathbf{BB}' = \mathbf{I}$ and $\mathbf{D}_\lambda = \mathbf{D}_\lambda^{1/2}\mathbf{D}_\lambda^{1/2}$. Since $\mathbf{BD}_\lambda^{1/2} = \mathbf{P}$ and $\mathbf{D}_\lambda^{1/2}\mathbf{B}' = \mathbf{P}'$, we can see that $\mathbf{R} = \mathbf{PP}'$. The matrix $\mathbf{D}_\lambda^{1/2}$ is a diagonal matrix containing the square roots of the latent roots.

6.6 DECIDING HOW MANY PRINCIPAL COMPONENTS TO RETAIN

The problem of statistical inference for principal components extracted from a sample correlation matrix is extremely complex. The statistical hypotheses that a particular population latent root is zero or that the population latent roots for a subset are all zero are both meaningless. If a sample

TABLE 6.3 Correlations (Loadings) of Four Tests with the Four Principal Components

	Principal Components			
Tests	1	2	3	4
(1) Intelligence	.908	−.175	−.233	.309
(2) Reading	.881	−.360	−.130	−.295
(3) Arithmetic reasoning	.874	−.011	.481	.049
(4) Mechanical aptitude	.771	.609	.122	−.083
λ_i = variance	2.958	.532	.318	.192

latent root is nonzero, then the corresponding latent root must also be nonzero. This follows from the fact that the dimensionality of the sample space cannot be greater than the dimensionality of the space from which the sample was generated. There is a statistical test that tests the hypothesis that the last k latent roots of a correlation matrix are equal. If the null hypothesis of equal latent roots is accepted, then each of the corresponding principal components contains the same amount of information. Consequently, they should be either thrown out or retained as a group. The reader desiring more information on statistical inference concerning principal components is referred to Mardia, Kent, and Bibby (1979).

In most cases, deciding on how many principal components to obtain is based upon rules of thumb. The following are three popular rules:

(1) Graph the latent roots (that is, plot λ_i versus i) and determine where large latent roots cease and small latent roots begin. (This rule is due to Cattell (1966) and is called a "scree graph.")
(2) Include enough components to explain, say, 90 percent of the total variation.
(3) Exclude principal components the latent roots of which are less than the average of the latent roots. For a correlation matrix, latent roots less than one would be discarded. This means that a principal component would be discarded if it had less variance than one of the original variables since the variance of standardized variables is one (for more information, see Kaiser, 1958).

For our previous hypothetical example, the latent roots were 2.958, .532, .318, and .192, respectively. Both Cattell's scree graph procedure and Kaiser's criterion would lead to discarding the last three principal components. However, if one wanted to account for, say, 90 percent of the total variation in the four tests, then the first three principal components would need to be retained.

6.7 APPLICATIONS

Morrison (1976) conducted a principal components analysis of a correlation matrix given by Birren and Morrison (1961) for 11 subscales of the Wechsler Adult Intelligence Scale (WAIS) along with age and years of formal education. The sample was composed of 933 white, native male and female participants in a community testing program. The basic idea was to isolate the dimensions underlying the WAIS subscales and see how age and education were related to them. The correlation matrix will not be presented here, but most of the correlations were high. It is possible to extract thirteen principal components from the correlation matrix, making the reasonable assumption that the correlation matrix is nonsingular. The principal components analysis indicated only two latent roots greater than one, so, using Kaiser's criterion, only these two components are displayed in Table 6.4.

All of the WAIS subtests had high and nearly equal correlations with the first principal component. The pattern of correlations suggests that the first principal component is a measure of general intellectual ability. Years of education also had an equally high positive correlation with this dimension. This indicates that more educated people perform better on intelligence subtests. This does not necessarily mean that more education causes better performance on intelligence subtests. In could be that the same underlying factors (such as family socioeconomic status) that "explain" intelligence scores also promote educational attainment. Age has a substantially smaller and negative correlation with this dimension. This indicates that general intellectual functioning declines to a small extent with advancing age.

This principal component explains over 51 percent of the variance of the original thirteen variables. This is clearly an important and interpretable dimension. Scores on this single principal component summarize over half of the information contained in the original thirteen variables. For some purposes, this component alone might be adequate. For example, combined with other variables, it might be a good predictor of occupational attainment.

The second principal component explains considerably less of the total variance (11 percent) than the first principal component. Cattell's scree test might suggest that the second and subsequent principal components should be discarded since there is such a big break between the first and second latent roots. Since λ_2 is greater than 1, the variance of any one of the standardized variables, Kaiser would recommend retaining and interpreting the second component. The interpretability of a principal component as well as the size of its associated latent root should be considered in retaining or discarding components.

The second principal component is clearly interpretable. Verbal subtest scores have positive correlations with this component; performance subtest scores have negative correlations. It seems to be a contrast between verbal and performance subtests. High scores on this dimension come about from high verbal subtest scores and low performance subtest scores. (Remember we are dealing with standardized scores, so that low scores have negative signs.) Conversely, low scores on this dimension come about from low verbal subtest scores and high performance subtest scores. Education is virtually unrelated to this dimension. On the other hand, age has a high correlation with this component. This indicates that older people are more likely to have high verbal scores combined with low performance scores. In other words, the difference (contrast) between verbal and performance subtests increases with age.

TABLE 6.4 Correlation of WAIS Subtests, Age, and Education with the Two Largest Principal Components

Variables	*Principal Component*	
WAIS Subtest	1	2
Verbal		
Information	.83	.33
Comprehension	.75	.31
Arithmetic	.72	.25
Similarities	.78	.14
Digit Span	.62	.00
Vocabulary	.83	.38
Performance		
Digit Symbol	.72	–.36
Picture Completion	.78	–.10
Block Design	.72	–.26
Picture Arrangement	.72	–.23
Object Assembly	.65	–.30
Age	–.34	.80
Education	.75	.01
Latent root (variance)	6.69	1.42
Percentage of total variance	51.47	10.90

Together these two principal components account for over 62 percent of the variance in the original 13 variables. These two dimensions summarize the data nicely. Two easily interpretable dimensions of intellectual functioning have been uncovered that are related to education and age, respectively. If we wanted to explain, say, 90 percent of the total variation in the variables, then considerably more principal components would need to be retained since the third and succeeding components each have small variances.

If these thirteen variables were predictors of, for instance, educational performance, then a multicolinearity problem could occur because of the high intercorrelations among the variables. Some researchers circumvent the multicolinearity problem by transforming the original variables to principal components since they are uncorrelated. This transformation does not help much, however, if we are interested in the effects of the original variables. Others use principal components for discarding redundant variables from a data set. The rationale is that variables highly correlated with the smallest principal components represent practically insignificant variation.

Sometimes only the largest principal components are retained as predictors of a dependent variable. There is no compelling reason to suspect that larger components are better predictors of some dependent variable than smaller components. Fortunately, it seems to be the case empirically that the larger components explain more variation in a dependent variable than smaller components.

If the data can be summarized by a few principal components, then the data can be plotted and visually inspected. The visual inspection might reveal that the data have certain peculiarities such as nonnormality, nonlinearity, and extreme data points (outliers). The plotting may also reveal that the data are multimodal and consist of clusters of points.

Principal components analysis is particularly useful in the life sciences for summarizing the measurements made on the parts of various organisms, both plant and animal. Typically, a large principal component reflecting the size of the organism is found with all body part measures having high positive correlations. Subsequent principal components typically have some variables correlating negatively with them. These are contrasts that are usually interpreted as shape factors. For example, a particular principal component might contrast length measures of body parts with breadth measures. The situation is similar to the pattern of correlations of the WAIS subtests with the second principal component.

6.8 COMPUTER SOFTWARE

There are a number of software packages that can satisfactorily perform principal components analyses. The outputs for the different programs are quite similar. For example, SAS output includes the following: means and standard deviations of the variables; the variable correlation matrix; the complete set of latent roots and their associated latent vectors; a listing of the principal components scores; and graphical plots of scores for pairs of principal components.

6.9 PROBLEMS

(1) Using the sample data in the Appendix, conduct a principal components analysis of variables 1 through 6. How many principal components would you retain? How much of the total ability score variation do the retained components explain?

(2) Verify that the six principal components are uncorrelated.

(3) Calculate the determinant of the correlation matrix for the six ability measures. Show that the value of that determinant equals the value of the determinant of the variance-covariance matrix of the principal components. What does this relationship between the two determinants indicate?

(4) Let us reexamine the correlation matrix of Kenny (1979) presented in problem 5 at the end of Chapter 3.

(a) Find the latent roots and associated latent vectors of the correlation matrix
(b) What are the principal component scores associated with the following vector of original concern variables $(-.5, 1, .3, -.8)$?
(c) How many principal components would you retain for interpretation? How much of the variation in the four variables do they account for?
(d) Calculate the correlation of each of the four variables with the principal components that you retained.
(e) What does each retained component seem to measure?
(f) How well does the equally weighted composite derived in problem 5 at the end of Chapter 3 correlate with the largest principal component? Would you say that the equally weighted composite is a good approximation to the largest principal component?

(5) Crano, Kenny, and Campbell (1972) presented the intercorrelations among six subtests of the Iowa Test of Basic Skills:

		X_1	X_2	X_3	X_4	X_5	X_6
Language usage (capitalization)	$-X_1$	1.000					
Language usage (punctuation)	$-X_2$	.611	1.000				
Work skills (map reading)	$-X_3$	.459	.437	1.000			
Work skills (use of graphs)	$-X_4$	.468	.416	.438	1.000		
Arithmetic (concepts)	$-X_5$	.482	.460	.470	.469	1.000	
Arithmetic (problems)	$-X_6$	.478	.403	.423	.432	.574	1.000

(a) Find the latent roots and associate latent vectors of the correlation matrix.
(b) Calculate the correlations of the six test scores with the principal components that you would retain and interpret them.

(6) Conduct a principal components analysis of Milburn's (1978) smoking data presented as problem 6 in Chapter 3. Discuss and interpret your results.

(7) Harman (1967) presents raw data on five socioeconomic variables from twelve census tracts taken from the Los Angeles standard metropolitan statistical area.

	Variables				
Tract	*Total Population (in thousands)*	*Median School Years*	*Total Employment (in thousands)*	*Miscellaneous Professional Services (in hundreds)*	*Median Value of House (in thousands)*
	1	2	3	4	5
1	5.7	12.8	2.5	2.7	25
2	1.0	10.9	.6	.1	10
3	3.4	8.8	1.0	.1	9
4	3.8	13.6	1.7	1.4	25
5	4.0	12.8	1.6	1.4	25
6	8.2	8.3	2.6	.6	12
7	1.2	11.4	.4	.1	16
8	9.1	11.5	3.3	.6	14
9	9.9	12.5	3.4	1.8	18
10	9.6	13.7	3.6	3.9	25
11	9.6	9.6	3.3	.8	12
12	9.4	11.4	4.0	1.0	13

Summarize this data matrix by carrying out the following steps:

(a) Do a principal components analysis of the sample variance-covariance matrix for the five socioeconomic variables. (Note: Divide the sum of squares and cross-products by n rather than n − 1.)
(b) Plot the five latent roots on a graph. On the basis of this plot, how many principal components would you retain? What percentage of the original variances of the five variables do your retained principal components explain.
(c) Compute the 12 × 5 matrix of principal component scores.
(d) Plot the bivariate distribution of the two largest principal components.
(e) Describe the characteristics of this bivariate distribution of principal component scores.
(f) How has this analysis simplified the original data matrix?

7 Factor Analysis

7.1 INTRODUCTION

Factor analysis was originally developed by Charles Spearman (1904), a psychologist, who noticed that the intercorrelations among exam scores in subjects such as classics, French, and English fell into a pattern that could be accounted for by a single underlying factor. That is, the observed score on the ith exam, x_i, can be expressed as $x_i = l_i f + \epsilon_i$, where f is an underlying factor, l_i is the weight (commonly called "loading") of the ith test on the underlying factor, and ϵ_i reflects the variation that is unique to x_i. Spearman called this factor, f, general intelligence. The unique variance, ϵ_i, is composed of two components: a component specific to the ith test and a component due to measurement error in the ith test. For the purposes of factor analysis, we do not have to distinguish between these two components.

Later, it was found that a single underlying factor could not account for the intercorrelations among other sets of ability and achievement measures. Consequently, the model was generalized to include two or more underlying factors. For example, a factor analysis model with two underlying factors can be expressed as $x_i = l_{i1} f_1 + l_{i2} f_2 + \epsilon_i$ and a model with m factors can be expressed as

$$x_i = \sum_{k=1}^{m} l_{ik} f_k + \epsilon_i$$

This is the model that we shall develop further in this chapter.

Factor analysis has been heavily employed over many years to isolate the dimensions (factors) underlying human abilities. It has also been used in many other contexts. For example, it has been used to isolate the factors underlying organizational behavior in industrial firms and to isolate the factors explaining the intercorrelations of tests measuring various aspects of psychopathology.

While principal components and factor analysis are related techniques, there are some important differences between the two. Principal components analysis is oriented toward explaining the total variation in the original measures, while factor analysis is concerned only with explaining the covariation among the original measures. Principal components analysis is merely a transformation of the original variables into principal components. It does not have an underlying model, as in factor analysis, where, for example, common and unique variances are distinguished. In line with this, note that the principal components model is formulated as maximizing the variance of a linear composite of the original variables (that is, $p = \Sigma l_i x_i$), while factor analysis expresses the original variables as a linear combination of underlying factors plus a residual term—that is,

$$x_i = \sum_{k=1}^{m} l_{ik} f_k + \epsilon_i$$

Note the difference. Principal components analysis determines weights for the variables, while factor analysis estimates loadings for the factors. These and other differences will become more apparent as the reader progresses through this chapter.

Notice that in our discussion of factor analysis we did not say that these underlying components had to be orthogonal or that the factors should be defined upon the basis of maximizing explained variance. However, in this book we are concerned mostly with orthogonal factor-analytic models. We will also concentrate on principal factor analysis, which uses principal component techniques so that each successively extracted factor explains less of the covariation among the observed variables. We shall see, however, that these factors based upon principal components techniques might not be as conceptually meaningful as another set of underlying factors. This problem of yielding a more conceptually satisfying set of underlying factors is handled by what are termed "factor rotation" techniques. That is, once a set of principal component factors are extracted, we may want to transform (rotate) these orthogonal components to yet another set of orthogonal components that may have more desirable properties from a substantive viewpoint.

Section 7.2 formalizes the general common factor analysis model. The discussion includes the assumptions of the model and the definition of key concepts. The common factors can be extracted from the correlation matrix by numerous techniques. Two factor extraction procedures are developed, illustrated, and compared in section 7.3. The problem of deciding upon the number of factors to retain from the analysis is discussed in section 7.4. There are an infinite number of factor analysis solutions that can account for the intercorrelations among a given set of variables. This leads naturally to the problem of finding one or more of the infinite number of solutions that have appealing conceptual and statistical properties. The solution to this problem involves the application of a transformation matrix to transform one solution to a more appealing final solution. This is equivalent to rotating the original factor axes and is accordingly called factor rotation. It is discussed in section 7.5. Section 7.6 discusses the estimation of factor scores. A practical application of factor analysis is demonstrated in section 7.7. The chapter concludes with a discussion of computer software.

7.2 THE FACTOR ANALYSIS MODEL

The common factor-analytic model may be expressed algebraically as

$$y_i = l_{i1} f_1 + l_{i2} f_2 + \ldots + l_{im} f_m + U_i p_i$$

or

$$y_i = \sum_{j=1}^{m} l_{ij} f_j + U_i p_i$$

where y_i is the ith variable, l_{ij} is the weight for variable i on the jth factor, f_j is the score on the jth common factor, U_i is the weight for the factor unique to variable i, and p_i is the score on the factor unique to variable i.

It can be seen from the above model that common factor analysis assumes that each variable is a function of the same set of underlying common factors plus a factor unique to that variable. However, each variable has a different set of weights associated with the factors. The weights associated with the common factors are called "loadings," and we shall refer to them as such throughout this chapter. For the sake of parsimony, it is hoped that the number of common factors, m, is substantially less than the number of original variables, p. Even then, there will be more factors than variables needed to account for the variance of the variables because each variable is explained by a set of m common factors and a unique factor. Consequently, p + m factors are needed to account completely for the variation in all of the original variables. In principal components analysis only p factors are needed to account completely for the variance in the original p variables. As mentioned earlier, principal components analysis does not distinguish between common and unique variations; these variances are lumped together in the principal components analysis.

Let us use our example of the four psychological tests to construct a hypothetical common factor analysis model. Let us assume that only two common factors are needed to explain the variation in the four test scores. Our model could then be written as

$$y_1 = l_{11} f_1 + l_{12} f_2 + U_1 p_1 + 0p_2 + 0p_3 + 0p_4 \quad \text{(intelligence)}$$

$$y_2 = l_{21} f_1 + l_{22} f_2 + 0p_1 + U_2 p_2 + 0p_3 + 0p_4 \quad \text{(reading)}$$

$$y_3 = l_{31}f_1 + l_{32}f_2 + 0p_1 + 0p_2 + U_3p_3 + 0p_4 \quad \text{(arithmetic reasoning)}$$

$$y_4 = l_{41}f_1 + l_{42}f_2 + 0p_1 + 0p_2 + 0p_3 + U_4p_4 \quad \text{(mechanical aptitude)}$$

We can see that six underlying factors are needed to account for the variation in the four tests. However, only one unique factor is needed in addition to the two common factors for explaining the variation of a variable. The remaining unique factors have zero weights. Each of the four tests is a function of the same two common factors, but different tests have different loadings associated with the common factors. For example, intelligence has a loading of l_{11} on factor 1 while reading has a loading of l_{21} on factor 1.

The object of factor analysis is to estimate the matrix of factor loadings;

$$\begin{bmatrix} l_{11} & l_{12} \\ l_{21} & l_{22} \\ l_{31} & l_{32} \\ l_{41} & l_{42} \end{bmatrix}$$

In order to do this, certain assumptions are made: (1) The original variables are linearly related; (2) the common and unique factors have means of 0 and standard deviations of 1; (3) the common factors are orthogonal; (4) the unique factors are orthogonal; (5) the common and unique factors are orthogonal; and (6) the original variables have means of 0 and standard deviations of 1. These assumptions can be expressed algebraically as

(1) $y_i = by_{i'} + \epsilon$ for all pairs of variables

(2) $E(f_j) = 0,\ E(f_j^2) = 1;\ E(p_i) = 0,\ E(p_i^2) = 1$ for all i and j

(3) $E(f_jf_k) = 0$ for $j \neq k$

(4) $E(p_jp_k) = 0$ for $j \neq k$

(5) $E(f_jp_i) = 0$ for all i and j

(6) $E(y_i) = 0,\ E(y_i^2) = 1$ for all i

Let **f** be the vector of common factor scores, and **p** be the vector of unique factor scores, then assumptions 2 through 5 can be more economically expressed in matrix form as

$$E(\mathbf{f}) = \mathbf{0},\ E(\mathbf{p}) = \mathbf{0},\ E[\mathbf{ff}'] = \mathbf{I},\ E(\mathbf{pp}') = \mathbf{I}$$

and

$$E[\mathbf{fp}'] = \mathbf{0}$$

Given these assumptions, let us examine some derived properties of the factor-analytic model. First, let us express the variance of a particular original variable in terms of the common and unique factors. The variance of y_1 is

$$\begin{aligned}\sigma^2_{y_1} = 1 &= E[l_{11}f_1 + l_{12}f_2 + U_1p_1 - E(l_{11}f_1 + l_{12}f_2 + U_1p_1)]^2 \\ &= E(l_{11}f_1 + l_{12}f_2 + U_1p_1)^2\end{aligned}$$

since

$$\begin{aligned}E(l_{11}f_1 + l_{12}f_2 + U_1p_1) &= l_{11}E(f_1) + l_{12}E(f_2) + U_1E(p_1) \\ &= l_{11}0 + l_{12}0 + U_10 = 0\end{aligned}$$

Next,

$$\begin{aligned}E(l_{11}f_1 + l_{12}f_2 + U_1p_1)^2 &= E(l^2_{11}f^2_1 + l^2_{12}f^2_2 + U^2_1p^2_1 + 2l_{11}l_{12}f_1f_2 \\ &\quad + 2l_{11}U_1f_1p_1 + 2l_{12}U_1f_2p_1) \\ &= l^2_{11}E(f^2_1) + l^2_{12}E(f^2_2) + U^2_1E(p^2_1) \\ &\quad + 2l_{11}l_{12}E(f_1f_2) + 2l_{11}U_1E(f_1p_1) \\ &\quad + 2l_{12}U_1E(f_2p_1) \\ &= l^2_{11} + l^2_{12} + U^2_1\end{aligned}$$

since the E( )s in the remaining terms are zero because of our original assumptions. Consequently, $\sigma^2_{y_1} = l^2_{11} + l^2_{12} + U^2_1$. We have shown that the variance of y_1 can be divided into two components: one attributable to the common factors $(l^2_{11} + l^2_{12})$ and one attributable to the unique factor (U^2_1). Furthermore, the reader should verify that l_{11} is the correlation of variable y_1 with common factor 1; l_{12} is the correlation of variable y_1 with common factor 2; and U_1 is the correlation of y_1 with the unique factor p_1.

Generalizing, we have

$$\sigma^2_i = l^2_{i1} + l^2_{i2} + \ldots + l^2_{im} + U^2_i = 1$$

where σ^2_i is the variance of the kth variable, l_{ij} is the correlation of the ith variable with the jth common factor, and U_i is the correlation of the ith variable with the factor unique to the ith variable. The loadings, then, are the correlations of the variables with the factors. Since the factors are uncorrelated, the loadings associated with each variable are actually the multiple regression weights for predicting the variable from the underlying factors. The component, $l_{i1}^2 + l_{i2}^2 + \ldots + l_{im}^2$, is called the "communality" of variable i, and the term U_i^2 is called the "uniqueness" of variable i. In our example above, $l_{11}^2 + l_{12}^2$ is the communality of test 1 and U_1^2 is the uniqueness of test 1. The communality is the proportion of variance of a particular variable that is predictable from the common factors, and the uniqueness of the respective variable is that part of the variance of the variable that is not predictable from the common factors. A major problem in factor analysis is estimating the communalities for each of the variables.

We have shown how to break up the variance of a variable in terms of components due to common and unique factors. Let us now express the correlation between any two variables in terms of the underlying factors. The correlation between test 1 and test 2 can be expressed as

$$\begin{aligned} r_{12} &= E[(l_{11}f_1 + l_{12}f_2 + U_1p_1)(l_{21}f_1 + l_{22}f_2 + U_2p_2)] \\ &= E[l_{11}l_{21}f_1^2 + l_{11}l_{22}f_1f_2 + l_{11}U_2f_1p_2 + l_{12}l_{21}f_2f_1 + l_{12}l_{22}f_2^2 \\ &\quad + l_{12}U_2f_2p_2 + U_1l_{21}p_1f_1 + U_1l_{22}p_1f_2 + U_1U_2p_1p_2] \end{aligned}$$

Since $E(f_1f_2) = E(f_1p_2) = E(f_2f_1) = E(f_2p_2) = E(p_1f_1) = E(p_1f_2) = E(p_1p_2) = 0$ and $E(f_1^2) = E(f_2^2) = 1$, we find that bringing E into the parentheses and taking the expectation of each term results in

$$r_{12} = l_{11}l_{21} + l_{12}l_{22}$$

The term $l_{11}l_{21}$ is the contribution of factor 1 in "explaining" the correlation between tests 1 and 2, and the term $l_{12}l_{22}$ is the contribution of factor 2 in "explaining" the correlation between tests 1 and 2. Notice that the unique factors U_1 and U_2 play no role in explaining the correlation between tests 1 and 2. In general, if r_{jk} is the correlation between variables j and k, then this correlation can be expressed in terms of the factor-analytic model as

$$\begin{aligned} r_{jk} &= l_{j1}l_{k1} + l_{j2}l_{k2} + l_{j3}l_{k3} + \ldots + l_{jm}l_{km} \\ &= \sum_{i=1}^{m} l_{ji}l_{ki} \end{aligned}$$

where m is the number of common factors, i is the subscript for factors, and j and k are the variable subscripts.

Let us attempt to express the correlations of our four subtests in terms of our hypothesized two-factor model. The correlations would be

$$r_{12} = r_{21} = l_{11}l_{21} + l_{12}l_{22} = \sum_{i=1}^{2} l_{1i}l_{2i}$$

$$r_{13} = r_{31} = l_{11}l_{31} + l_{12}l_{32} = \sum_{i=1}^{2} l_{1i}l_{3i}$$

$$r_{14} = r_{41} = l_{11}l_{41} + l_{12}l_{42} = \sum_{i=1}^{2} l_{1i}l_{4i}$$

$$r_{23} = r_{32} = l_{21}l_{31} + l_{22}l_{32} = \sum_{i=1}^{2} l_{2i}l_{3i}$$

$$r_{24} = r_{42} = l_{21}l_{41} + l_{22}l_{42} = \sum_{i=1}^{2} l_{2i}l_{4i}$$

$$r_{34} = r_{43} = l_{31}l_{41} + l_{32}l_{42} = \sum_{i=1}^{2} l_{3i}l_{4i}$$

We can easily express the above equations in matrix form. Let us define

$$\mathbf{F} = \begin{bmatrix} l_{11} & l_{12} \\ l_{21} & l_{22} \\ l_{31} & l_{32} \\ l_{41} & l_{42} \end{bmatrix}$$

The reader can easily verify that $\mathbf{FF}' = \mathbf{R} - \mathbf{U}^2$ where $\mathbf{U}^2$ is a diagonal matrix of the unique variances in the original variables. That is, the diagonal elements of $\mathbf{U}^2$ are the U_i^2's corresponding to the respective variables. The matrix product $\mathbf{FF}'$ exactly reproduces the intercorrelations and results in communalities

$$\sum_{i=1}^{m} l_{ki}^2$$

in the principal diagonal rather than 1's. The important point is that if we can estimate the factor loading matrix, **F**, then we can reproduce the correlations among the original variables. Here again it should be emphasized that factor analysis is focused on explaining correlations, not variances. In actual practice, as we shall see, a small number of factors might not explain the correlations perfectly, but yet yield a close enough fit from a statistical and practical perspective. Some major problems in factor analysis involve estimating the uniqueness or, equivalently, the communalities of the original variables and estimating the number of common factors needed to explain the correlation coefficients adequately.

7.3 EXTRACTING COMMON FACTORS

There are a number of techniques that can be used to extract factors from a correlation matrix. One of the most popular approaches is to estimate the communalities of each of the variables and apply the principal component technique to the reduced correlation matrix. The reduced correlation matrix is defined as $\mathbf{R} - \mathbf{U}^2$, which has the original correlations as off-diagonal elements and communalities $(1 - U_i^2)$ in the principal diagonal. The substitution of communalities for 1's in the principal diagonal reflects the fact that in the common factor analysis model we are trying to explain the correlations among variables or, equivalently, what the variables have in common. The communalities in the principal diagonal reflect the amount of variance that each variable has in common with the remaining variables in the set. There are a number of highly technical issues associated with the definition and estimation of the communality for a test or other variable in a given domain. One practical approach has been to define the communality of a test or variable as the amount of its variance that can be predicted by the remaining tests or variables in the set. Consequently, the communality is estimated as R_i^2 where R_i^2 is the squared multiple correlation coefficient for variable i as predicted from the remaining variables in the set.

Besides principal components factor analysis, there are a number of factor-analytic models used to solve for $\mathbf{F}$ and $\mathbf{U}$. One method involves finding an $\mathbf{F}$ such that $\mathbf{FF}'$ minimizes the sum of squares on the off-diagonal elements of $\mathbf{R} - \mathbf{FF}'$. Then, $\mathbf{U}^2$ is estimated on the basis of the $\mathbf{F}$ that satisfies this property. Maximum likelihood factor analysis simultaneously solves for $\mathbf{F}$ and $\mathbf{U}^2$ such that for a given number of common factors, the $\mathbf{F}$ and $\mathbf{U}^2$ solved for maximize the likelihood of the sample of multivariate observations.

For illustrative purposes we will assume that the communalities are known or have been estimated by, say, multiple regression and have been inserted into the diagonal of our test score correlation matrix as shown below.

$$
\begin{array}{l}
\text{mechanical aptitude} \\
\text{intelligence} \\
\text{arithmetic reasoning} \\
\text{reading}
\end{array}
\quad
\begin{bmatrix}
.36 & .42 & .48 & .54 \\
.42 & .65 & .68 & .71 \\
.48 & .68 & .73 & .78 \\
.54 & .71 & .78 & .85
\end{bmatrix} = \mathbf{R} - \mathbf{U}^2
$$

We will begin with a rather simple factor extraction process called the diagonal method. The diagonal method of factoring begins with taking factor 1 to be colinear with variable 1 of the reduced correlation matrix. Variable 1 of the reduced correlation matrix, however, is a residual variable with its unique variance, U_1^2, already partialled out. Consequently, we are making factor 1 colinear (that is, correlated perfectly) with the residual variable 1 of the reduced correlation matrix. This correlation matrix is called reduced because the unique variances have been partialled out of the original variables. Since only the unique variance has been partialled from each variable, this should have no effect on the off-diagonal correlations, which reflect what pairs of variables have in common.

If we make factor 1 colinear with the residual variable 1 of the reduced correlation matrix, then the original variable 1 would have a correlation of $\sqrt{.36} = .60$ with factor 1 since this is the correlation between variable 1 and the predictable or common part of variable 1 (that is, variable 1 with its unique variance partialled out). Since factor 1 is colinear with the common part of variable 1, factor 1 must account for the total correlation between variable 1 and the remaining three variables. From the assumption of the factor analysis model, $r_{12} = l_{11} l_{21}$, where r_{12} is the correlation between variables 1 and 2, l_{11} is the correlation of variable 1 with factor 1, and l_{21} is the correlation of variable 2 with factor 1. Substituting our example data into this equation, we find that $.42 = .60 l_{21}$ and l_{21}, the correlation between variable 2 and factor 1, is .70. Likewise, $r_{13} = l_{11} l_{31}$, which gives, for our example, $.48 = .60 l_{31}$ or $l_{31} = .80$. Similarly, since $r_{14} = l_{11} l_{41}$ or $.54 = .60 l_{41}$, then $l_{41} = .90$. We have thus solved for the test correlations with factor 1 where factor 1 was defined to be variable 1 with its unique variance partialled out or the total common variance of variable 1. These four correlations or loadings with factor 1 are summarized in Table 7.1.

From Table 7.1, we can see that all four tests correlate substantially with factor 1. We would, of course, expect this because variable 1 correlates substantially with the remaining three variables and factor 1 was defined as the common part (that is, predictable part) of variable 1. Let us now determine how well we can reproduce the reduced correlation matrix with just one factor. The assumptions of factor analysis lead to the result that $\mathbf{R} - \mathbf{U}^2 = \mathbf{FF}'$ where $\mathbf{F}$ is the factor-loading matrix. For the sake of parsimony, we would

TABLE 7.1 **Correlations of Four Tests with Factor 1 from Diagonal Factoring**

	Factor 1
(1) Mechanical aptitude	.60
(2) Intelligence	.70
(3) Arithmetic reasoning	.80
(4) Reading	.90

hope that the rank of **F** would be considerably less than the number of original variables. For our example, **F** is provisionally set at rank 1 and we find that

$$\mathbf{FF}' = \begin{bmatrix} .60 \\ .70 \\ .80 \\ .90 \end{bmatrix} [.60,\ .70,\ .80,\ .90] = \begin{bmatrix} .36 & .42 & .48 & .54 \\ .42 & .49 & .56 & .63 \\ .48 & .56 & .64 & .72 \\ .54 & .63 & .72 & .81 \end{bmatrix}$$

The agreement between $\mathbf{FF}'$ and $\mathbf{R} - \mathbf{U}^2$ can be measured by computing the residual matrix, $\mathbf{R}_1$, where

$$(\mathbf{R} - \mathbf{U}^2) - \mathbf{FF}' = \mathbf{R}_1$$

which, for our example, yields

$$\underset{\mathbf{R} - \mathbf{U}^2}{\begin{bmatrix} .36 & .42 & .48 & .54 \\ .42 & .65 & .68 & .71 \\ .48 & .68 & .73 & .78 \\ .54 & .71 & .78 & .85 \end{bmatrix}} - \underset{\mathbf{FF}'}{\begin{bmatrix} .36 & .42 & .48 & .54 \\ .42 & .49 & .56 & .63 \\ .48 & .56 & .64 & .72 \\ .54 & .63 & .72 & .81 \end{bmatrix}} = \underset{\mathbf{R}_1}{\begin{bmatrix} 0 & 0 & 0 & 0 \\ 0 & .16 & .12 & .08 \\ 0 & .12 & .09 & .06 \\ 0 & .08 & .06 & .04 \end{bmatrix}}$$

There are a number of things that can be noted about the first residual matrix, $\mathbf{R}_1$, when factors are extracted by the diagonal method. First, the residual matrix, $\mathbf{R}_1$, is a covariance matrix whose elements are the variances and covariances among the four test variables after partialling out the effects of factor 1. In other words, it is a covariance matrix of residual variables. Actually, it is a second residual matrix because the unique variance was previously partialled out of the original variables to yield the reduced matrix, $\mathbf{R} - \mathbf{U}^2$. However, $\mathbf{R}_1$ is the first matrix in which common factor variance was partialed out. Second, the $\mathbf{R}_1$ matrix produced from the diagonal method of factor extraction leaves the first row and first column of $\mathbf{R}_1$ full of zeros. In other words, the first factor extracted by the diagonal method accounts completely for the correlation between the first variable and the remaining variables. Third, from $\mathbf{R}_1$ it can be noted that, in addition to accounting completely for these correlations, it also reduces the intercorrelations among the remaining variables. That is, the residual variables have considerably smaller correlations than the original variables. Fourth, one common factor does a pretty good job of accounting for the original correlations, but we might still suspect that we could do a better job (that is, having a residual matrix containing zeros or near zeros) if we extracted another common factor.

Proceeding with the diagonal method of factoring, we would define our second factor as perfectly colinear (that is, having a correlation of 1) with the residual variable 2 (variable 2 with the unique variance and predictable variance from factor 1 partialled out). Since the residual variable 2 or, equivalently, our new second common factor has only .16 of its variance in common with variable 2, it must correlate $\sqrt{.16} = .40$ with variable 2. Since residual variable 1 correlates 0 with residual variable 2, it must correlate 0 with factor 2. In order to satisfy the factor-analytic model, $r'_{23} = .12 = l_{22}l_{32} = .40\,l_{32}$ or $l_{32} = .30$. Similarly, $r'_{24} = .08 = l_{22}l_{42} = .40l_{42}$ or $l_{42} = .20$. The primes on the correlations indicate that they are residual correlations. Thus the correlations of the original four variables with factor 2 are given by the vector $\mathbf{f}'_2 = [0, .40, .30, .20]$.

Let us now see how well factor 2 accounts for the residual correlations in $\mathbf{R}_1$ by computing

$$\mathbf{R}_2 = \mathbf{R}_1 - \mathbf{f}_2\mathbf{f}'_2 = \begin{bmatrix} 0 & 0 & 0 & 0 \\ 0 & .16 & .12 & .08 \\ 0 & .12 & .09 & .06 \\ 0 & .08 & .06 & .04 \end{bmatrix} - \begin{bmatrix} 0 \\ .40 \\ .30 \\ .20 \end{bmatrix} [0, .40, .30, .20]$$

$$= \begin{bmatrix} 0 & 0 & 0 & 0 \\ 0 & 0 & 0 & 0 \\ 0 & 0 & 0 & 0 \\ 0 & 0 & 0 & 0 \end{bmatrix}$$

Factor 2 has completely accounted for the residual correlations in $\mathbf{R}_1$; consequently, the first two common factors extracted by the diagonal method have completely accounted for the correlations among the four tests. The rank of the 4×4 reduced correlation matrix, $\mathbf{R} - \mathbf{U}^2$, is 2, while the reader

TABLE 7.2 Diagonal Factor Matrix F for Four Tests

	Factor 1	*Factor 2*	h_i^2
(1) Mechanical aptitude	.60	0	.36
(2) Intelligence	.70	.40	.65
(3) Arithmetic reasoning	.80	.30	.73
(4) Reading	.90	.20	.85
$\sum_{i=1}^{4} l_{ij}^2$	2.30	.29	

can verify that the rank of the original correlation matrix (1's in principal diagonal) is 4 (that is, it has 4 nonzero latent roots). In most cases, especially when working with sample correlation matrices, we will not have a null residual matrix as we had in this hypothetical example. We would expect, however, that after m common factors have been extracted from the reduced correlation matrix, a residual matrix would be obtained such that the elements were close to zero. We simplified the hypothetical example to a certain extent by assuming that we knew the communalities. In applied problems we must estimate the communalities jointly with the **F** matrix or at least initially estimate the communalities by some common accepted procedure such as multiple regression. The common factor matrix that reproduces the off-diagonal correlations exactly is presented below in Table 7.2.

The entries in the h_i^2 column of Table 7.2 are the communalities and, under the assumption of the common factor analysis model, are equal to the sums of squares of the elements in the respective rows of the factor matrix. The row at the bottom of Table 7.2 indicates the amount of common variance in the original variables for which each of the two factors accounts. It can be easily seen that factor 1 accounts for 2.30/2.59, or 89 percent, of the common variance. The denominator of 2.59 in these two fractions is the total common variance for all four tests or the trace

$$\left(\sum_{i}^{4} h_i^2\right)$$

of $\mathbf{R} - \mathbf{U}^2$. Note that while these two factors together account for 100 percent of the common variance in the four tests, they only account for 2.59/4.00, or 65 percent of the total variation in the tests. This illustrates nicely that the goal of factor analysis, as contrasted to principal components analysis, is to explain common variation and not total variation in the variables.

A major problem in factor analysis is that an infinite number of orthogonal two-factor solutions can be found that will exactly reproduce the correlation coefficients. This is called the problem of indeterminacy. For example, a

TABLE 7.3 Principal Factor Analysis for Four Tests

	Factor 1	*Factor 2*	h_i^2
(1) Mechanical aptitude	.57	−.18	.36
(2) Intelligence	.78	.17	.65
(3) Arithmetic reasoning	.85	.05	.73
(4) Reading	.92	−.08	.85
$\sum_{i=1}^{4} l_{ij}^2$	2.52	.07	

principal components analysis of the reduced correlation matrix yields the solution for the **F** matrix presented in Table 7.3. A principal components analysis of $\mathbf{R} - \mathbf{U}^2$ proceeds in identically the same manner as a principal components analysis of **R** itself, as discussed in the previous chapter. (A principal components analysis of a reduced correlation matrix is sometimes referred to as a "principal factor analysis.")

If we compare the diagonal solution with the principal factor solution, we can note a number of similarities. First, both solutions yield two factors since the rank of the reduced correlation matrix is 2. Second, both solutions completely explain the correlations. (The reader should verify that $\mathbf{R} - \mathbf{U}^2 = \mathbf{F}_D\mathbf{F}_D' = \mathbf{F}_P\mathbf{F}_P'$ where $\mathbf{F}_D$ and $\mathbf{F}_P$ are the diagonal and principal factor matrices, respectively.) Third, although the factors are different for the two solutions, the communalities are invariant (that is, identical). The first factor of the principal factor analysis solution accounts for more of the common variance than the first factor of the diagonal solution. A characteristic of the principal factor solution is that each successively extracted factor accounts for a maximum amount of the common variance. This is similar to the property of the principal components of a correlation matrix where each successively extracted principal component accounts for a maximum amount of the total variance in the original variables.

7.4 DETERMINING THE NUMBER OF FACTORS

The rules of thumb used in deciding how many factors to retain are the same as those discussed previously in deciding how many principal components to retain. That is, we examine the latent roots of the correlation matrix. For example, we may decide to retain only those factors that have an associated latent root equal to or greater than 1.

There is a formal statistically based method of determining the number of factors. It is based on maximum likelihood factor analysis, as discussed briefly earlier in this chapter. Maximum likelihood factor analysis assumes that the variables have a multivariate normal distribution. For a specified number of factors it estimates the factor loading matrix and communalities. These parameter estimates are those that maximize the likelihood of realizing the sample observations.

The procedure begins by fitting one common factor to the correlation matrix and then testing the goodness of fit using a χ^2 approximation. (The closer that $\hat{\mathbf{F}}\hat{\mathbf{F}}' + \hat{\mathbf{U}}^2 = \hat{\mathbf{R}}$ comes to $\mathbf{R}$, the better the fit. Here, $\hat{\mathbf{R}}$ is the estimated correlation matrix based upon the maximum likelihood estimates of the factor loading matrix, $\hat{\mathbf{F}}$, and the diagonal matrix of unique variances, $\hat{\mathbf{U}}$. $\mathbf{R}$ is the sample correlation matrix.) If the χ^2 is not significant, then the hypothesis of one factor is accepted. If the χ^2 is significant, indicating a lack of fit, then two factors are fitted to the correlation matrix and the goodness of fit of the two-factor model is tested by the χ^2 approximation. If the χ^2 is insignificant, then a two-factor solution is accepted. If it is significant, then a three-factor solution is fitted and tested for significance. The procedure continues until the χ^2 is insignificant. At this point we have determined both the number of factors needed to fit the correlation matrix and the associated factor matrix.

7.5 TRANSFORMATIONS OF FACTOR ANALYSIS SOLUTIONS (FACTOR ROTATION)

These two-factor solutions for the reduced correlation matrix are only two of an infinite number of solutions. Any orthogonal transformation of a particular factor matrix yields a new factor matrix, $\mathbf{F}_N$, which also satisfies the relationship $\mathbf{R} - \mathbf{U}^2 = \mathbf{F}_N\mathbf{F}_N'$. This can be shown as follows. Let $\mathbf{F}_N = \mathbf{F}_O\mathbf{T}$ where $\mathbf{F}_N$ is the new $p \times m$ factor matrix, $\mathbf{F}_O$ is the old factor matrix, and $\mathbf{T}$ is an $m \times m$ orthogonal transformation matrix. (An orthogonal matrix $\mathbf{T}$ has the property that $\mathbf{T}'\mathbf{T} = \mathbf{T}\mathbf{T}' = \mathbf{I}$. That is, the column vectors of $\mathbf{T}$ are orthogonal and have a length or norm of 1.) Then, $\mathbf{R} - \mathbf{U}^2 = \mathbf{F}_N\mathbf{F}_N' = (\mathbf{F}_O\mathbf{T})(\mathbf{F}_O\mathbf{T})' = \mathbf{F}_O\mathbf{T}\mathbf{T}'\mathbf{F}_O'$ $= \mathbf{F}_O\mathbf{F}_O'$ since $\mathbf{T}\mathbf{T}' = \mathbf{I}$ by definition.

Since both the diagonal solution and principal factor solution in our example are admissible solutions to the problem, then there must be an orthogonal transformation matrix that relates these two solutions. That is,

$$\mathbf{F}_D\mathbf{T} = \mathbf{F}_P$$

where

$$\mathbf{F}_D = \begin{bmatrix} .60 & .00 \\ .70 & .40 \\ .80 & .30 \\ .90 & .20 \end{bmatrix}$$

$$\mathbf{F}_P = \begin{bmatrix} .57 & -.18 \\ .79 & .17 \\ .85 & .05 \\ .92 & -.08 \end{bmatrix}$$

and

$$\mathbf{T} = \begin{bmatrix} a_{11} & a_{12} \\ a_{21} & a_{22} \end{bmatrix}$$

and $\mathbf{T}$ satisfies the relationship $\mathbf{TT}' = \mathbf{I}$. Let us proceed to find the orthogonal transformation matrix, $\mathbf{T}$, for our example. Since $\mathbf{F}_D\mathbf{T} = \mathbf{F}_P$, $\mathbf{F}_D'\mathbf{F}_D\mathbf{T} = \mathbf{F}_D'\mathbf{F}_P$, then consequently, $\mathbf{T} = (\mathbf{F}_D'\mathbf{F}_D)^{-1}\mathbf{F}_D'\mathbf{F}_P$. In our example,

$$\mathbf{F}_D'\mathbf{F}_D = \begin{bmatrix} .60 & .70 & .80 & .90 \\ .00 & .40 & .30 & .20 \end{bmatrix} \begin{bmatrix} .60 & .00 \\ .70 & .40 \\ .80 & .30 \\ .90 & .20 \end{bmatrix} = \begin{bmatrix} 2.30 & .70 \\ .70 & .29 \end{bmatrix}$$

and

$$\mathbf{F}_D'\mathbf{F}_P = \begin{bmatrix} .60 & .70 & .80 & .90 \\ .00 & .40 & .30 & .20 \end{bmatrix} \begin{bmatrix} .57 & -.18 \\ .79 & .17 \\ .85 & .05 \\ .92 & -.08 \end{bmatrix} = \begin{bmatrix} 2.4039 & -.0210 \\ .7547 & .0670 \end{bmatrix}$$

The reader can verify that

$$(\mathbf{F}_D'\mathbf{F}_D)^{-1} = \begin{bmatrix} 1.6384 & -3.9548 \\ -3.9548 & 12.9944 \end{bmatrix}$$

so that

$$\mathbf{T} = \begin{bmatrix} 1.6384 & -3.9548 \\ -3.9548 & 12.9944 \end{bmatrix} \begin{bmatrix} 2.4039 & -.0210 \\ .7547 & .0670 \end{bmatrix} = \begin{bmatrix} .954 & -.300 \\ .300 & .954 \end{bmatrix}$$

where

$$\mathbf{TT}' = \mathbf{I}$$

Let us plot these two solutions graphically so that we may better understand the meaning of this orthogonal transformation matrix. Figure 7.1 presents the two-dimensional diagonal and principal factor solutions.

From Figure 7.1 it can be noted that we can obtain the principal factor solution by rotating the diagonal factor axes approximately 17 degrees. If we examine our transformation matrix, it can be seen that the diagonal entries are each .954, which happens to be the cosine of 17 degrees. Furthermore, the sine of 17 degrees is approximately .300, which are the absolute values of the off-diagonal elements of the transformation matrix. Consequently, we may write the general 2 x 2 transformation matrix as

$$\mathbf{T} = \begin{bmatrix} \cos\theta & -\sin\theta \\ \sin\theta & \cos\theta \end{bmatrix}$$

where in our example

$$\mathbf{T} = \begin{bmatrix} \cos 17^\circ & -\sin 17^\circ \\ \sin 17^\circ & \cos 17^\circ \end{bmatrix} = \begin{bmatrix} .954 & -.300 \\ .300 & .954 \end{bmatrix}$$

Note that

$$\mathbf{TT}' = \begin{bmatrix} \cos\theta & -\sin\theta \\ \sin\theta & \cos\theta \end{bmatrix} \begin{bmatrix} \cos\theta & \sin\theta \\ -\sin\theta & \cos\theta \end{bmatrix} = \begin{bmatrix} 1 & 0 \\ 0 & 1 \end{bmatrix}$$

for all possible θ's since $\cos\theta^2 + \sin\theta^2 = 1$ and $\cos\theta \sin\theta - \cos\theta \sin\theta = 0$. Suppose that we wanted to rotate our axes 45° from the diagonal factor axis, then our transformation matrix would be

$$\mathbf{T} = \begin{bmatrix} \cos 45^\circ & -\sin 45^\circ \\ \sin 45^\circ & \cos 45^\circ \end{bmatrix} = \begin{bmatrix} .707 & -.707 \\ .707 & .707 \end{bmatrix}$$

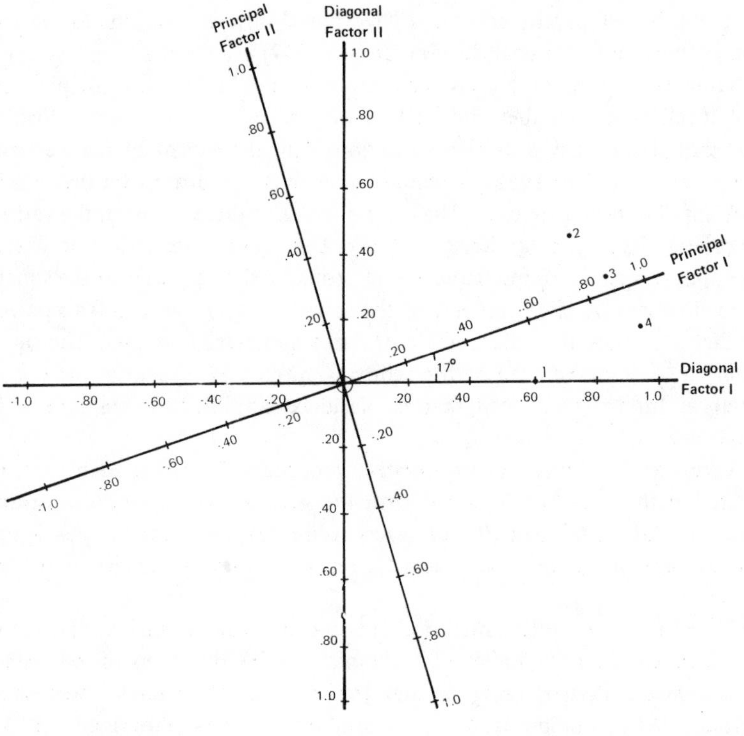

Figure 7.1 Graphical Presentation of Diagonal and Principal Factor Solutions

and our new factor loading matrix would be

$$\underset{\mathbf{F_D}}{\begin{bmatrix} .60 & .00 \\ .70 & .40 \\ .80 & .30 \\ .90 & .20 \end{bmatrix}} \underset{\mathbf{T}}{\begin{bmatrix} .707 & -.707 \\ .707 & .707 \end{bmatrix}} = \underset{\mathbf{F_N}}{\begin{bmatrix} .42 & -.42 \\ .78 & -.21 \\ .78 & -.35 \\ .78 & -.50 \end{bmatrix}}$$

The reader can easily verify that this factor matrix also exactly reproduces $\mathbf{R} - \mathbf{U}^2$, that is, $\mathbf{F_N F_N'} = \mathbf{R} - \mathbf{U}^2$. So we have shown three different solutions for $\mathbf{F}$ that satisfy the basic equation of factor analysis, $\mathbf{F\,F'} = \mathbf{R} - \mathbf{U}^2$. How do we solve this indeterminacy problem? We begin with an arbitrary factor extraction procedure such as principal factor analysis. Then we determine a final rotated factor matrix that has certain desirable properties as described below.

A number of psychometricians have posed various solutions to the rotation problem in factor analysis. Thurstone (1947) proposed a simple structure criterion for determining a proper rotation of the factor axes. Simple structure specifies the number and pattern of zero or near-zero factor loadings that should appear in a desirable rotation. With the advent of the electronic computer in the late 1950s, a number of analytical solutions for the rotation problem have been proposed. The most popular of these has been the varimax procedure developed by Kaiser (1958). The varimax procedure in a sense attempts to specify simple structure in terms of the variances of the squared factor loadings. A large variance of the squared factor loadings for a particular factor implies that there are both large and small loadings. The overall criterion to be maximized by the varimax approach is the sum of the squared variances for the m rotated factors. Varimax simplifies the columns of the factor matrix.

Varimax does this by an iterative procedure in which each factor is rotated with every other factor with the goal of maximizing the varimax criterion. After each pair of factors has been rotated once, the angles of rotation are computed and the process is repeated until the angles of rotation converge.

There are many other analytical rotation procedures. Like varimax, they are all based upon maximizing or minimizing some functions of the loadings in the factor matrix using an iterative process. Quartimax (Newhaus & Wrigley, 1954) minimizes the cross-products of the factor loadings. This method simplifies the rows of the factor loading matrix since small cross-products of factor loadings imply that each variable is related to as few factors as possible.

So far, we have been concerned only with orthogonal solutions to factor analysis problems. That is, factors that are uncorrelated or independent. The factors were extracted by orthogonal methods and rotated orthogonally. An orthogonal rotation means that the factor axes are kept at right angles to one another when they are rotated. There is no reason, however, that the final rotated factors have to be uncorrelated. Some factor analysts prefer correlated factors if they allow a more parsimonious or plausible explanation of the observed correlation matrix. For example, Thurstone's (1947) pioneering factor-analytic research concerning the primary mental abilities involved the use of oblique (that is, correlated) factor analysis models. In fact, some of his primary mental ability factors had correlations in the .60s and .70s.

In oblique rotations, the factor axes are not restricted to be rigidly set at right angles to one another. They can be set at arbitrary angles (that is, correlated) in trying to maximize or minimize various functions of the factor loading matrix. This flexibility sometimes results in more parsimonious factor solutions. However, it must be remembered that the parsimony in factor structure is traded off for correlations among the factors.

The situation becomes more complex for an oblique solution. The correlations of the variables with the factors are not the same as the standardized regression weights for predicting variables from factors, as is the case for an orthogonal solution. Hence, we need three matrices to summarize an oblique solution: a factor loading matrix (sometimes referred to as a factor pattern matrix) summarizing the variable-factor correlations; a factor structure matrix summarizing the standardized regression weights for predicting variables from the oblique factors; and a matrix of intercorrelations among the oblique factors. While all of these matrices are important in interpreting an oblique factor analysis, most attention is focused on the factor structure matrix.

Like orthogonal rotations, there are oblique procedures that simplify rows (for example, quartimin) of the factor loading matrix. They also use an iterative procedure to maximize or minimize a function of the factor loadings.

An orthogonal extraction method such as principal components factor analysis or maximum likelihood factor analysis can be combined with any type of orthogonal or oblique rotation. The most common combination seems to be a principal components factor analysis with squared multiple correlations in the principal diagonal followed by a varimax rotation.

One reason for this indeterminacy of the factor matrix is that our factor model involves the estimation of more parameters than observed correlations in order to explain the correlation matrix. In our example, we need to estimate eight parameters (factor loadings) in order to explain the six correlations between all possible pairs of the four tests. If we also had to estimate the communalities (remember they were given for our example), then we have to estimate twelve parameters in order to explain the six correlations. The situation would become even worse if three factors were needed to explain these six correlations. The indeterminacy could be reduced if we could specify beforehand the value of a sufficient number of parameters so that fewer parameters would have to be estimated from the data. For example, if we could have specified beforehand that test 3 has a loading of .80 on factor 1 and a loading of .30 on factor 2, then a unique solution for the other six parameters of the factor matrix would have been possible. Techniques have recently been developed that allow the investigator to hypothesize the values of certain parameters of the factor model and then estimate the remaining parameters under the constraints given by the hypothesized parameters. The fit of the model under the hypothesis can then be tested statistically.

7.6 FACTOR SCORES

Sometimes a researcher might want to use the factors as independent variables in another model. For example, factors derived from a factor analysis of test scores could be used to predict future school achievement. In order to do this the scores on the factors must be estimated for each individual. In principal components analysis, the principal components scores can be calculated exactly since they are defined as a linear combination of the variables. In factor analysis, however, there is no such a transformation matrix relating the factors to the variables so that exact factor scores can be calculated. They have to be estimated. We can estimate the factor scores from the original variables since we know both the intercorrelations among the variables (**R**) and their correlations with the factors (**F**). Consequently, we can use multivariate regression analysis to estimate the ith person's vector of factor scores, $\mathbf{f}_i$ from his or her vector of variable scores, $\mathbf{x}_i$ by $\mathbf{f}_i = \mathbf{F}'\mathbf{R}^{-1}\mathbf{x}_i$. There are other more complicated procedures for estimating factor scores, but this method is easy to understand and yields desirable results.

7.7 A PRACTICAL APPLICATION OF FACTOR ANALYSIS

The Stanford Achievement Test (SAT), Primary Battery I, consists of seven subtests. These are combined to form three subtotal scores (total auditory, total reading, and total mathematics) as well as one total battery score. Previous research by Klein (1977) led to the suspicion that the SAT was not measuring independent abilities. In order to test this hypothesis, Klein (1979) factor analyzed the intercorrelation matrix of the seven subtests for a sample of 927 beginning second-grade students in a large suburban school district. The intercorrelation matrix is presented in Table 7.4.

It can be seen from Table 7.4 that the subtests were highly intercorrelated with one another. If three subtotal scores could be legitimately formed from the seven subtests, then three common factors should be isolated in the factor analysis. If the subtests were highly redundant, as Klein suspected, then only one common factor would be needed to account for the common variation. There was only one latent root of the correlation matrix greater than one. The two largest roots were 4.861 and .771. When communalities were estimated and placed in the principal diagonal, the latent roots of the reduced correlation matrix were 4.609 and .511. Since the second latent root of .511 was appreciably smaller than the highest communality estimate of .904 (see Table 7.5), Klein decided to accept a one-factor solution. That is, the second

TABLE 7.4 Intercorrelations Among SAT Subtests

	1	2	3	4	5	6	7
(1) Vocabulary		.634	.622	.625	.636	.617	.612
(2) Reading, Part A			.872	.860	.614	.615	.493
(3) Reading, Part B				.830	.597	.625	.511
(4) Word Study Skills					.635	.625	.517
(5) Mathematics Concepts						.733	.614
(6) Mathematics Computation and Application							.573
(7) Listening Comprehension							

principal factor explained less common variance than was present in just one variable. The criterion of rejecting factors with a latent root of less than one would also lead to the rejection of the second factor. The loadings on the first two principal factors are presented in Table 7.5.

The first principal factor had high loadings by all seven subtests. The second factor, as previously mentioned, was rejected so there was no reason for rotating the two factors. The results indicate that one factor essentially explains the intercorrelations among the subtests. The results put into question the use of the three subtotals since all of the tests seem to be measuring one common factor. Questions about the cost and time effectiveness of the SAT are also raised because of the redundancy among the subtests. There does not seem to be much differential information in the subtests.

7.8 COMPUTER SOFTWARE PACKAGES

There are a number of computer software packages that can successfully perform factor analyses. Two widely used packages are SPSS and SAS. Both of these programs will provide a principal factor analysis with squared multiple correlations in the principal diagonal followed by a varimax rotation. This is, by far, the most popular combination of factor extraction and rotation. However, both of these programs provide a full range of alternative factor analysis and rotation options. SAS will be briefly described below.

The SAS input can be raw data, the covariance matrix, or the correlation matrix. Factors can be extracted by principal components factor analysis, maximum likelihood factor analysis, as well as a number of techniques that we have not discussed. These two methods seem to be the most popular. However, maximum likelihood factor analysis can be more expensive than principal factor analysis because the communalities are estimated iteratively and the factor analysis must be repeated for different numbers of factors.

TABLE 7.5 First Two Principal Factors for the SAT

	I	II	h^2
(1) Vocabulary	.765	.166	.613
(2) Reading, Part A	.890	−.334	.904
(3) Reading, Part B	.873	−.284	.843
(4) Word Study Skills	.875	−.238	.821
(5) Mathematics Concepts	.798	.304	.728
(6) Mathematics Computations and Application	.782	.236	.668
(7) Listening Comprehension	.675	.295	.543
Latent root	4.609	.511	

Before a factor analysis is undertaken, prior communality estimates must be specified. The user can select squared multiple correlations or the highest correlation that each variable has with another variable as communality estimates.

The user can specify the number of factors to be extracted and can also use the latent root equal to or greater than one criteria or specify that the extracted factors have to account for a given proportion of common variance. In maximum likelihood factor analysis, the user can fit different numbers of common factors and test the goodness of fit for each solution.

There are numerous rotation options, both orthogonal and oblique. The most popular orthogonal rotation is varimax. Promax is an oblique rotation to simple structure and involves a two-stage procedure. First, the unrotated matrix is orthogonally rotated to a varimax solution. Then, the orthogonal varimax matrix is rotated to an oblique promax solution. Because of the two-stage procedure, the user can ask for a promax rotation and obtain both a varimax and promax solution. Consequently, this tends to be a popular rotation option.

The user can specify a wide variety of outputs depending upon the extraction and rotation technique selected. The means, standard deviations, and correlations can be printed out. The latent roots can be printed out in a scree plot and the associated latent vectors can be printed out.

The unrotated factor loading matrix and rotated factor loading matrix (matrices) can be printed out for orthogonal solutions. For oblique solutions, both a factor loadings matrix (correlations of variables with factors, referred to as a factor structure matrix) and a matrix of the standardized multiple regression weights for predicting the variables from the oblique factors (referred to as a factor pattern matrix) are printed out. It should be kept in mind that an oblique solution is obtained from an initial orthogonal solution. In the case of an orthogonal solution, these two matrices are identical because the standardized regression weights for uncorrelated independent variables (that is, the factors) are simply the correlations. Consequently, only the factor loading matrix (referred to by SAS as the factor pattern matrix) is printed out. The intercorrelations among the oblique factors are also printed out. The oblique or orthogonal transformation matrix, whichever the case, used to rotate the factors will also be printed out.

The factor score coefficient matrix can also be requested. Pairs of factors can be plotted against each other before and after rotation. Residual correlations among the variables after the factors have been extracted can also be printed.

7.9 PROBLEMS

(1) Using the sample data in the Appendix, conduct a principal factor analysis of the six ability measures using multiple $\mathbf{R}^2$s as communality estimates. How many common factors would you retain? Graphically rotate the retained factors to a conceptually appealing solution.

(2) Derive the transformation matrix, **T**, for transforming the principal factor analysis solution into your rotated solution.

(3) Find an oblique rotation that would be conceptually appealing. Estimate the factor loadings and the correlation among the factors by graphical means.

(4) Let us return to the correlation matrix of Kenny (1979) presented in problem 5 at the end of Chapter 3.

(a) Conduct a principal components factor analysis using squared multiple correlations as the communality estimates. Find the latent roots, associated latent vectors, and the factor loading matrix.

(b) How many factors would you retain for interpretation?

(c) How do the results of the principal components factor analysis compare to the results of the principal components analysis of the same matrix (see problem 4 at the end of Chapter 6)?

(d) Factor the intercorrelation matrix by the diagonal method and compare your results to 4a above.

(5) Let us return to the Crano et al. (1972) data concerning the intercorrelations of the six subtests of the Iowa Test of Basic Skills presented in problem 5 of Chapter 6.

(a) Conduct a principal components factor analysis using squared multiple correlations as the communality estimates. Find the latent roots, associated latent vectors, and the factor loading matrix.

(b) How many factors would you retain for interpretation?
(c) Plot the factor loadings for each pair of retained factors.
(d) Examine these plots and orthogonally rotate (graphically) the axes such that the transformed solution is more conceptually appealing than the original principal components factor analysis solution. Construct the rotated factor solution from your plots.
(e) From these same plots, do an oblique rotation. Estimate the factor loading matrix and the intercorrelations among the oblique factors from these plots.
(f) Which rotated factor solution is more conceptually appealing? Why?

8 Canonical Correlation Analysis

8.1 INTRODUCTION

In a previous chapter, we developed the concepts and procedures necessary in the calculation of the correlation between any two linear composites of arbitrary dimensions. In this chapter we will be concerned with finding a vector of weights for each of two sets of variables such that the correlation between the two linear composites using these weights is a maximum. This is the problem of canonical correlation, which was described by its originator, Harold Hotelling (1935), as a way of determining the most predictable criterion.

In the case of multiple regression, there is only one dependent variable; hence there is no weighting problem on the dependent variable side. On the other hand, the canonical correlation situation involves at least two variables on the dependent variable side as well as at least two variables on the independent variable side. The variables on the dependent variable side are weighted in such a way that the linear composite of the dependent variables has a maximum correlation with a linear composite derived from the independent variables. If these dependent variables are considered as criteria (for example, grades, performance measures, and the like), then these unique weights yield the most predictable criterion for a linear combination of the dependent variables. Statistically, the problem is to find a vector **a** and a vector **b** such that the correlation between the composites $\mathbf{a}'\mathbf{x}$ and $\mathbf{b}'\mathbf{y}$ is a maximum where **x** is a vector of random variables and **y** is another vector of random variables. The correlation between $\mathbf{a}'\mathbf{x}$ and $\mathbf{b}'\mathbf{y}$ for an arbitrary **a** and **b** as discussed in a previous chapter can be written as

$$r_{a'x,b'y} = \frac{a'C_{x,y}b}{\sqrt{a'C_x a}\,\sqrt{b'C_y b}}$$

where $\mathbf{C}_{\mathbf{x},\mathbf{y}}$ is the cross-covariance matrix between the variables in **x** and the variables in **y**, $\mathbf{C}_{\mathbf{x}}$ is the covariance matrix of the variables in **x**, and $\mathbf{C}_{\mathbf{y}}$ is the covariance matrix of the variables in **y**.

Although some researchers may consider one set of variables as independent variables and another set of variables as dependent variables, the method itself makes no such distinctions among the two variable sets. Canonical correlation analysis is merely a tool for examining the interrelationships between two sets of variables. The method is usually used with continuous variables, with some exceptions to be noted later. Multivariate normality needs to be assumed if currently available tests of statistical significance are to be used.

Some examples of research situations where canonical correlation analysis has been applied are in examining the interrelationships between a set of personality and a set of interest measures (Dunteman & Bailey, 1967); in examining the interrelationships between a set of drug abuse measures and a set of personality and personal background variables (Forsyth & Sadava, 1977); and in examining the interrelationships between a large set of job values and a large set of perceived job characteristics for a sample of skilled factory workers (Wood & Erskine, 1976).

Canonical correlation analysis is closely related to discriminant analysis as discussed in Chapter 5. In discriminant analysis, interest is focused on the relationship between a set of groups and a set of continuous variables. In fact, if the groups are coded into dummy variables (excluding one dummy variable to prevent a singular covariance matrix of the dummy variables), then the application of canonical correlation analysis to the set of dummy variables and the set of continuous discriminatory variables produces canonical weights for the discriminatory variables that are identical to the linear discriminant function weights.

The technique is also closely related to multivariate regression analysis, where, as we have seen, each continuous dependent variable is regressed upon a set of independent variables. If we consider one set of variables as dependent variables, then the canonical weights for the independent variables are the regression weights that would predict the linear combination of the dependent variables (that is, the canonical variate representing the dependent variables obtained from the canonical correlation analysis). We have only talked about one canonical correlation in representing the relationship between two sets of variables, but, as we shall subsequently see, it is possible, as in principal components, to generate additional canonical correlations between two variable sets.

The canonical correlation problem is formalized in section 8.2. Section 8.3 illustrates step by step the computational procedures needed to determine the numerical values of the canonical correlations and their associated weighting vectors. Section 8.4 discusses tests of significance. A practical application is discussed in Section 8.5. The last section discusses the output from canonical correlation programs.

8.2 FORMULATION OF CANONICAL CORRELATION PROBLEM

Similar to principal components analysis, the problem can be formulated as a maximization problem. Algebraically, the problem is to maximize $\mathbf{a}'\mathbf{C}_{\mathbf{x},\mathbf{y}}\mathbf{b}$ subject to the constraints that $\mathbf{a}'\mathbf{C}_{\mathbf{x}}\mathbf{a} = 1$ and $\mathbf{b}'\mathbf{C}_{\mathbf{y}}\mathbf{b} = 1$. These constraints are needed to solve for unique weighting vectors **a** and **b** and simply indicate that each linear composite is constrained to have a variance of one. Thus the problem is to find the vectors **a** and **b** that maximize

$$z = \mathbf{a}'\mathbf{C}_{\mathbf{x},\mathbf{y}}\mathbf{b} - \lambda_1(\mathbf{a}'\mathbf{C}_{\mathbf{x}}\mathbf{a} - 1) - \lambda_2(\mathbf{b}'\mathbf{C}_{\mathbf{y}}\mathbf{b} - 1)$$

where λ_1 and λ_2 are Lagrange multipliers.

Since in many instances in the social and behavioral sciences the units of measurement are arbitrary, we can standardize the variables and maximize

$$z = \mathbf{a}'\mathbf{R}_{12}\mathbf{b} - \lambda_1(\mathbf{a}'\mathbf{R}_1\mathbf{a} - 1) - \lambda_2(\mathbf{b}'\mathbf{R}_2\mathbf{b} - 1)$$

where $\mathbf{R}_{12}$ represents the cross-correlations between the first set of variables (that is, **x**) and the second set of variables (that is, **y**); $\mathbf{R}_1$ represents the intercorrelations among the first set of variables (**x**), and $\mathbf{R}_2$ represents the intercorrelations among the second set of variables (**y**).

Applying multivariate differential calculus to the function z results in two characteristic equations that can be solved for λ, **a**, and **b**. They are

$$(\mathbf{R}_1^{-1}\mathbf{R}_{12}\mathbf{R}_2^{-1}\mathbf{R}_{12}' - \lambda\mathbf{I})\mathbf{a} = \mathbf{0}$$

and

$$(\mathbf{R}_2^{-1}\mathbf{R}_{12}'\mathbf{R}_1^{-1}\mathbf{R}_{12} - \lambda\mathbf{I})\mathbf{b} = \mathbf{0}$$

There are two latent roots and associated vectors **a** and **b** that satisfy these characteristic equations. The largest latent root turns out to be the largest canonical correlation squared and the associated weighting vectors are **a** and **b**. The next largest latent root, λ_2, is the next largest canonical correlation squared and has another pair of canonical weight vectors, $\mathbf{a}_2$ and $\mathbf{b}_2$, such that the correlation beween $\mathbf{a}_2'\mathbf{x}$ and $\mathbf{b}_2'\mathbf{y}$ is maximal given certain conditions discussed below. The number of possible nonzero latent roots or, equivalently, canonical correlations is equal to the dimension of the smallest variable set. For our example, the dimension of the smallest variable set is two, so that the two nonzero canonical correlations are possible. The size of the canonical correlations is, of course, a function of the intercorrelations within and between the variable sets. As in principal components and linear discriminant function analysis, some of the canonical correlations might be too small to be of any practical significance. A test for the statistical significance of canonical correlations is presented in a later section.

Other properties of the solution to the two characteristic equations associated with canonical correlational analysis are discussed below. First of all, note that the dimensions of **a** and **b** will be different unless the number of variables in the two variable sets is equal. Let $\mathbf{a}_i$ be the set i^{th} set of canonical weight vectors associated with one set (**x**) and $\mathbf{b}_j$ be the jth set of canonical weight vectors associated with the other set (**y**). Then the $\mathbf{a}_j\mathbf{x}$ of the first set are uncorrelated with each other, that is, $\mathbf{A}'\mathbf{R}_x\mathbf{A} = \mathbf{I}$ where **A** has as column vectors the set of canonical weight vectors associated with the set **x** and $\mathbf{R}_x$ is the correlation matrix for **x**. Similarly, the $\mathbf{b}_j\mathbf{y}$ of the second set satisfies the property that $\mathbf{B}'\mathbf{R}_y\mathbf{B} = \mathbf{I}$ and, hence, the canonical variates associated with **y** are uncorrelated with one another. Most important is the fact that the correlation between $\mathbf{a}_j\mathbf{x}$ and $\mathbf{b}'_j\,\mathbf{y}$ is zero for $i \neq j$ and equal to the canonical correlations for $i = j$. This can be summarized as $\mathbf{A}'\mathbf{R}_{x,y}\mathbf{B} = \mathbf{D}_p$ where $\mathbf{R}_{x,y}$ is the cross-correlation matrix between **x** and **y** and $\mathbf{D}_p$ is a diagonal matrix of canonical correlation coefficients.

Note that the maximization of multivariate functions associated with both linear discriminant function analysis and principal components analysis also resulted in characteristic equations for which characteristic (latent) roots and their associated latent vectors needed to be solved. As in the other characteristic equations, there may be more than one nonzero latent root. For principal components, the latent roots turned out to be the variances of the associated principal components. For linear discriminant function analysis, the latent roots turned out to be the ratio of the between- to the within-group sum of squares for the associated linear discriminant functions. It is not surprising, then, that the latent roots in the two characteristic equations associated with canonical correlation analysis turn out to be the squares of the canonical correlations. The latent roots for both of the characteristic equations associated with canonical correlation analysis are identical. Once these are solved for, their associated vectors, the $\mathbf{a}_i$'s, associated with the first set of variables (that is, **x**) can be solved for by substituting, in turn, the latent roots into the first characteristic equation. Similarly, substituting the latent roots, in turn, into the second characteristic equation yields the associated latent vectors, the $\mathbf{b}_j$'s, for the second set of variables (**y**).

8.3 SOLVING FOR THE CANONICAL CORRELATIONS AND THEIR ASSOCIATED WEIGHTING VECTORS

Suppose that we had two subsets of variables, **x** and **y**, where **x** was three personality measures $[x_1, x_2, x_3]$ that had the following correlation matrix

$$\begin{array}{lc} & \begin{array}{ccc} x_1 & x_2 & x_3 \end{array} \\ \begin{array}{ll} \text{dominance} & x_1 \\ \text{autonomy} & x_2 \\ \text{freedom from anxiety} & x_3 \end{array} & \begin{bmatrix} 1.00 & .40 & .30 \\ .40 & 1.00 & .40 \\ .30 & .40 & 1.00 \end{bmatrix} = \mathbf{R}_1 \end{array}$$

and **y** was a measure of two interest measures $[y_1, y_2]$ that had the following correlation matrix

$$\begin{array}{lc} & \begin{array}{cc} y_1 & y_2 \end{array} \\ \begin{array}{ll} \text{people} & y_1 \\ \text{things} & y_2 \end{array} & \begin{bmatrix} 1.00 & .30 \\ .30 & 1.00 \end{bmatrix} = \mathbf{R}_2 \end{array}$$

Furthermore, suppose that the cross-correlation matrix for these sets of variables was

$$\begin{array}{lc} & \begin{array}{cc} y_1 & y_2 \end{array} \\ \begin{array}{l} x_1 \\ x_2 \\ x_3 \end{array} & \begin{bmatrix} .30 & .40 \\ .20 & .50 \\ .40 & .10 \end{bmatrix} = \mathbf{R}_{12} \end{array}$$

If **a** is a nonnull vector, then the determinant of $\mathbf{R}_1^{-1}\mathbf{R}_{12}\mathbf{R}_2^{-1}\mathbf{R}_{12}' - \lambda\mathbf{I}$ must vanish since the columns of this matrix must be linearly dependent to meet the conditions of the characteristic equation. Substituting the appropriate matrices from our example into $|\mathbf{R}_1^{-1}\mathbf{R}_{12}\mathbf{R}_2^{-1}\mathbf{R}_{12}' - \lambda\mathbf{I}|$, we find

$$\left| \begin{bmatrix} 1.00 & .40 & .30 \\ .40 & 1.00 & .40 \\ .30 & .40 & 1.00 \end{bmatrix}^{-1} \begin{bmatrix} .30 & .40 \\ .20 & .50 \\ .40 & .10 \end{bmatrix} \begin{bmatrix} 1.00 & .30 \\ .30 & 1.00 \end{bmatrix}^{-1} \begin{bmatrix} .30 & .20 & .40 \\ .40 & .50 & .10 \end{bmatrix} - \lambda \begin{bmatrix} 1 & 0 & 0 \\ 0 & 1 & 0 \\ 0 & 0 & 1 \end{bmatrix} \right|$$

$$= \begin{vmatrix} .130747 - \lambda & .139493 & .077147 \\ .152389 & .220902 - \lambda & -.018390 \\ .013008 & -.059879 & .144651 - \lambda \end{vmatrix} = 0$$

Upon expanding the above determinant, we have the following polynomial:

$$\lambda^3 - .4963\,\lambda^2 + .0564\,\lambda = \lambda(\lambda^2 - .4963\lambda + .0564) = 0$$

Applying the quadratic formula, we find the two roots $\lambda_1 = .3202$ and $\lambda_2 = .1761$. The square roots of these two roots yields the two canonical correlations of .5659 and .4196.

The next step is to find the vectors $\mathbf{a}_1$ and $\mathbf{b}_1$ associated with the largest canonical correlation. The vector $\mathbf{a}_1$ is found by solving the homogeneous equations

$$\mathbf{R}_1^{-1}\mathbf{R}_{12}\mathbf{R}_2^{-1}\mathbf{R}'_{12}\mathbf{a}_1 - \lambda_1\mathbf{a}_1 = \mathbf{0}$$

Substituting, we find

$$\begin{bmatrix} 1.00 & .40 & .30 \\ .40 & 1.00 & .40 \\ .30 & .40 & 1.00 \end{bmatrix}^{-1} \begin{bmatrix} .30 & .40 \\ .20 & .50 \\ .40 & .10 \end{bmatrix} \left[\begin{bmatrix} 1.00 & .30 \\ .30 & 1.00 \end{bmatrix}^{-1} \begin{bmatrix} .30 & .20 & .40 \\ .40 & .50 & .10 \end{bmatrix} \right] \mathbf{a}_1 - .3202\mathbf{a}_1 = \mathbf{0}$$

$$\begin{bmatrix} .130747 & .139493 & .077147 \\ .152389 & .220902 & -.183900 \\ .013008 & -.059879 & .144651 \end{bmatrix} \begin{bmatrix} a_{11} \\ a_{21} \\ a_{31} \end{bmatrix} - .3202 \begin{bmatrix} a_{11} \\ a_{21} \\ a_{31} \end{bmatrix} = \begin{bmatrix} 0 \\ 0 \\ 0 \end{bmatrix}$$

This expression reduces to the following set of homogeneous equations

$$-.189453\,a_{11} + .139493\,a_{21} + .077147\,a_{31} = 0$$

$$.152389\,a_{11} - .099298\,a_{21} - .018390\,a_{31} = 0$$

$$.013008\,a_{11} - .059879\,a_{21} - .175549\,a_{31} = 0$$

The reader can verify that the rank of this matrix is two, so that one of the elements of $\mathbf{a}_1$ may be arbitrarily set to any nonzero value. Setting $a_{31} = 1$, the first two equations reduce to the full rank and nonhomogeneous equations

$$-.189453\,a_{11} + .139493\,a_{21} = -.077147$$

$$.152389\,a_{11} - .099298\,a_{21} = .018390$$

and

$$\begin{bmatrix} a_{11} \\ a_{21} \end{bmatrix} = \begin{bmatrix} -.189453 & .139493 \\ .152389 & -.099298 \end{bmatrix}^{-1} \begin{bmatrix} -.077147 \\ .018390 \end{bmatrix}$$

$$= \begin{bmatrix} 40.6144 & 57.0548 \\ 62.3295 & 77.4892 \end{bmatrix} \begin{bmatrix} -.0771 \\ .0184 \end{bmatrix} = \begin{bmatrix} -2.0840 \\ -3.3835 \end{bmatrix}$$

The solution for $\mathbf{a}_1$ is

$$\begin{bmatrix} -2.0840 \\ -3.3835 \\ 1 \end{bmatrix}$$

For interpretive convenience, we can rescale the vector by multiplying all the elements by the unique scalar that will set the element with the largest absolute value to one. The other elements or weights in the vector may then be easily compared relative to the most important variable in the canonical variate $\mathbf{a}_1'\mathbf{x}$. The rescaled vector is

$$\begin{bmatrix} .6159 \\ 1. \\ -.2956 \end{bmatrix}$$

so the first canonical variate for the first set of variables, $\mathbf{x}$, is $.6159x_1 + x_2 - .2956x_3$.

To solve for $\mathbf{b}_1$, we must substitute in and solve the equation

$$\mathbf{R}_2^{-1}\mathbf{R}_{12}'\mathbf{R}_1^{-1}\mathbf{R}_{12}\mathbf{b}_1 - \lambda_1\mathbf{b}_1 = \mathbf{0}$$

Substituting, we find

$$\begin{bmatrix} 1.00 & .30 \\ .30 & 1.00 \end{bmatrix}^{-1} \begin{bmatrix} .30 & .20 & .40 \\ .40 & .50 & .10 \end{bmatrix} \begin{bmatrix} 1.00 & .40 & .30 \\ .40 & 1.00 & .40 \\ .30 & .40 & 1.00 \end{bmatrix}^{-1} \begin{bmatrix} .30 & .40 \\ .20 & .50 \\ .40 & .10 \end{bmatrix} \mathbf{b}_1 - .3202\mathbf{b}_1 = \mathbf{0}$$

or

$$\begin{bmatrix} .180309 & .011326 \\ .052029 & .315990 \end{bmatrix} \begin{bmatrix} b_{11} \\ b_{12} \end{bmatrix} - .3202 \begin{bmatrix} b_{11} \\ b_{12} \end{bmatrix} = \begin{bmatrix} 0 \\ 0 \end{bmatrix}$$

which reduces to

$$-.1399\,b_{11} + .0113\,b_{12} = 0$$

$$.0520\,b_{11} - .0046\,b_{12} = 0$$

Each equation is a multiple of the other, so we may set one of the elements of $\mathbf{b}_1$ equal to an arbitrary value and solve the single equation for the other element of $\mathbf{b}_1$. Setting $b_{12} = 1$, and solving for b_{11} in the first equation, we find

$$-.1399b_{11} = -.0113$$

or

$$b_{11} = .0810$$

Therefore,

$$\mathbf{b}_1 = \begin{bmatrix} b_{11} \\ b_{21} \end{bmatrix} = \begin{bmatrix} .0810 \\ 1. \end{bmatrix}$$

and the first canonical variate associated with the second set of variables, $\mathbf{y}$, is $.0810y_1 + y_2$.

We have found a set of weights for both sets of variables resulting in two composites that have the maximum correlation among all possible pairs of composites. As an exercise the reader can verify that the correlation between the composite $.6159x_1 + x_2 - .2956x_3$ and $.0810y_1 + y_2$ is .5659 by using the formula for the correlation between two linear composites. The first canonical variable, which is a composite of the personality variables, is primarily defined by x_1 and x_2 (dominance and autonomy) with a relatively small negative weight for x_3 (freedom from anxiety). The second canonical variable is primarily defined by the second interest measure, y_2 (interest in things). Cursory examination of the cross-correlation matrix of the personality and interest measures clearly indicates that the correlations of the personality variables x_1 and x_2 with the interest measure y_2 are the highest in this matrix. The highest cross-correlation is .50, which is between variables x_1 and y_2 and is quite close in magnitude to the largest canonical correlation between the two sets of measures.

Let us now turn to the second and final set of canonical variables. The root associated with the second set of canonical weights was found to be .1761 and the associated second canonical correlation was $\sqrt{.1761}$ or .4196. We can solve for the set of weights associated with the vector **x** by setting λ_2 equal to .1761 in

$$\mathbf{R}_1^{-1}\mathbf{R}_{12}\mathbf{R}_2^{-1}\mathbf{R}'_{12}\mathbf{a}_2 - \lambda_2\mathbf{a}_2 = \mathbf{0}$$

and solving for the vector $\mathbf{a}_2$.

Using the procedure previously illustrated, we find that

$$\mathbf{a}_2 = \begin{bmatrix} a_{21} \\ a_{22} \\ a_{23} \end{bmatrix} = \begin{bmatrix} .2586 \\ -.4690 \\ 1. \end{bmatrix}$$

The $\mathbf{b}_2$ vector can be solved for by setting λ_2 equal to .1761 in the characteristic equation

$$\mathbf{R}_2^{-1}\mathbf{R}'_{12}\mathbf{R}_1^{-1}\mathbf{R}_{12}\mathbf{b}_2 - \lambda_2\mathbf{b}_2 = \mathbf{0}$$

and solving for $\mathbf{b}_2$. We find that

$$\mathbf{b}_2 = \begin{bmatrix} 1. \\ -.3716 \end{bmatrix}$$

so that the second pair of canonical variates is $.2586x_1 - .4690x_2 + x_3$ and $y_1 - .3716y_2$.

These two composites have a correlation of .420. They are quite different in character from the first pair of canonical variables. In fact, as we have seen, the canonical correlation paradigm constrains the solution vectors so that each respective pair of canonical variables is uncorrelated. The reader can verify this by substituting into the formula for calculating the covariance between each of the pairs of canonical variates. Consequently, we would expect the second set of canonical variables to be quite different from the first set. The first pair of canonical variables primarily reflects correlation of a linear composite of x_1 and x_2 of the first set of variables with y_2 from the second set of variables. The second pair of canonical variables primarily reflects the correlation of a linear composite of x_2 and x_3 of the first set of variables with y_1 from the second set of variables. The two variables y_1 and y_2 from the second set of variables have a low correlation and hence the two pairs of canonical variables reflect essentially the prediction of y_1 and y_2, respectively, from the first set of variables, **x**.

8.4 TESTS OF SIGNIFICANCE

The sampling distributions associated with canonical correlation analysis are extremely complicated. There are, however, some approximate tests of significance based on the χ^2 distribution. The first hypothesis that would normally be tested is that $p_1 = p_2 = \ldots = p_k = 0$. This is the hypothesis that all possible canonical correlations are zero. This is equivalent to the hypothesis that $\mathbf{R}_{12} = 0$ or that there is no relationship between the two sets of variables. This hypothesis is tested by computing

$$-[n - \tfrac{1}{2}(p + q + 3)] \log_e \prod_{i=1}^{k} (1 - r_i^2)$$

which when n, the sample size, is large is distributed as χ^2 with pq degrees of freedom where p is the number of variables in one set and q is the number in the other set. The r_i's are the sample canonical correlations and the number of canonical correlations, k, is equal to the dimension of the smallest variable set. The test is due to Bartlett (1947).

Since there are only two canonical correlations in our example, we would be testing the hypothesis that $p_1 = p_2 = 0$. Let us assume that the sample size for our hypothetical example was 100. Substituting in the above formula, we have

$$-[100 - \tfrac{1}{2}(3 + 2 + 3)] \log_e [1 - (.5659)^2)(1 - (.4196)^2)] = 55.64$$

Referring to a χ^2 table with pq = (3)(2) = 6 degrees of freedom, we see that the value of χ^2 is highly significant (.001). If this test were insignificant, we would accept the hypothesis that $p_1 = p_2 = \ldots = p_k = 0$ in the general case or $p_1 = p_2 = 0$ for our example. If we reject this hypothesis, as we have done here, then we may want to continue further testing.

From our first test we know that at least one canonical correlation is greater than zero (that is, $p_1 > 0$), but we do not know if any of the remaining canonical correlations are greater than zero. (In our example we do not know if p_2 is also greater than zero.) In the general case, we test the hypothesis that $p_2 = p_3 = \ldots = p_k = 0$ and $p_1 > 0$. (In our example we test the hypothesis $p_2 = 0$ and $p_1 > 0$.) If this hypothesis is accepted, then we know that p_1 is the only significant canonical correlation. If it is rejected, then we know that p_2 is greater than zero, but we do not know if p_3 and subsequent correlations are greater than zero. We then test the hypothesis that $p_3 = p_4 = \ldots = p_k = 0$, $p_1 > 0$, and $p_2 > 0$. We continue this sequence of testing until a test turns out to be insignificant. We can do this sequence of testing by using the following formula, which is a generalization of the first formula:

$$-[n - \tfrac{1}{2}(p + q + 3)] \log_e \prod_{i=s+1}^{k} (1 - r_i^2) \sim \chi^2_{(p-s)(p-q)}$$

The term s is associated with the hypothesis that only s of the canonical correlation are greater than zero. When $s = 0$, we have the previous formula that tests the hypothesis that none of the canonical correlations are greater than zero. When $s = 1$, we are testing the hypothesis that $p_1 > 0$, $p_2 = p_3 = \ldots = p_k = 0$; when $s = 2$, we are testing the hypothesis that $p_1 > 0$, $p_2 > 0$, and $p_3 = p_4 = \ldots = p_k = 0$; and so on.

In our example, by stating $s = 0$ we have rejected the hypothesis that $p_1 = p_2 = 0$. If we let $s = 1$, then we are testing the hypothesis that $p_1 > 0$, $p_2 = 0$. Substituting into the above formula, we have

$$-[100 - \tfrac{1}{2}(3 + 2 + 3)] \log_e(1 - .4196)^2 \sim \chi^2_{(2)(1)}$$

since

$$\log_e \prod_{i=s+1}^{k} (1 - r_i^2) = \log_e \prod_{i=2}^{2} (1 - r_2^2) = \log_e(1 - r_2^2)$$

We find a χ^2 of 18.59, which, according to a χ^2 table with 2 degrees of freedom, is highly significant (.001). We would reject the hypothesis that $p_1 > 0$, $p_2 = 0$ and conclude that both p_1 and p_2 are significantly greater than zero.

8.5 AN APPLICATION

Canonical correlational analysis was originally developed for use with continuous variables. Furthermore, testing the statistical significance of the canonical correlations assumes that the variables have a multivariate normal distribution. Canonical correlational analysis can also be used when the variables are a mixture of continuous and categorical variables or are all categorical variables. Applying canonical correlational analysis in these situations can also be informative; the major drawback is that the currently available significance tests are no longer appropriate since they are based upon multivariate normal distribution theory.

We shall give an example of how canonical correlational analysis can be used to summarize the relationship between two categorical variables with r and c levels, respectively. In this case, the data are represented by a two-way contingency table with r rows and c columns in which the sample is distributed over the rc cells. A chi-square statistic can be used to test the hypothesis that the row and column variables are independent. Numerous indices of relationship have been proposed to summarize the relationship between two categorical variables. Some are based on transformations of χ^2; most range from 0 to 1 where 0 represents no relationship and 1 represents a perfect relationship.

Mardia, Kent, and Bibby (1979) illustrate the use of canonical correlational analysis in summarizing the relationship between the socioeconomic status of fathers and sons. The data are taken from Glass (1954) and are presented in Table 8.1.

For both father and son, 1 represents the highest socioeconomic status and 5 the lowest. The total sample size is 3497. While the table indicates some correspondence between father's and son's socioeconomic status, there is also appreciable upward and downward social mobility. The application of canonical correlational analysis to this table will yield three pieces of information: an index of relationship between father's and son's status (that is, canonical correlation), scale values or scores (that is, canonical weights for the son's status levels) for the five status levels of the son, and scale values or canonical weights for the father. We will now illustrate the procedure.

The five socioeconomic status levels of both father and son can be represented by five dummy variables. For each father, a set of five dummy variables is created for which $x_1 = 1$ if father belongs to socioeconomic status 1, 0 otherwise; $x_2 = 1$ if father belongs to socioeconomic status 2, 0 otherwise; and so on. Likewise, for the corresponding son of each father, a set of five dummy variables is created for which $y_1 = 1$ if the corresponding son belongs to socioeconomic status 1, 0 otherwise; $y_2 = 1$ if the corresponding son belongs to socioeconomic status 2, 0 otherwise; and so on.

For each observation (that is, father-son pair), there are five x variables and five y variables. The x variables represent the father's socioeconomic status and the y variables represent the corresponding son's socioeconomic status. We can consider $\mathbf{x}' = [x_1, x_2, x_3, x_4, x_5]$ to be one set of variables and $\mathbf{y}' = [y_1, y_2, y_3, y_4, y_5]$ to be another set of variables and canonical correlational analysis can express the relationship between the two sets of variables, father's socioeconomic status and son's socioeconomic status. We have seen dummy variables used to represent a categorical independent variable in regression analysis. In this situation, we saw that the dummy variables were linearly dependent so that one dummy variable had to be dropped in order to solve the inverse of $\mathbf{X}'\mathbf{X}$. The same principle applies here since the formula for computing the sample canonical correlations involves the inverse of both the covariance matrix of $\mathbf{x}$ and the covariance matrix of $\mathbf{y}$. Covariance rather than correlation matrices are used in this canonical correlational analysis because we want the canonical weights to correspond to the status levels represented by the dummy variables rather than standardized versions of them.

Let us drop the first dummy variable (x_1 and y_1), which represents the highest socioeconomic status level, for both fathers and sons. Our new vectors are then $\mathbf{x}^{*\prime} = [x_2, x_3, x_4, x_5]$ and $\mathbf{y}^{*\prime} = [y_2, y_3, y_4, y_5]$ and the problem is to find the canonical weight vectors $\mathbf{a}_{(4\times1)}$ and $\mathbf{b}_{(4\times1)}$ such that the correlation between $\mathbf{a}'\mathbf{x}^*$ and $\mathbf{b}'\mathbf{y}^*$ is maximized. The vectors $\mathbf{a}$ and $\mathbf{b}$ are the scores attached to socioeconomic status levels 2 through 5 for fathers and sons, respectively, so that the correlation between the father's and son's socioeconomic status is maximized. The first or largest canonical correlation was .504 so that, just as we expected, there is a moderate relationship between the socioeconomic status of father and son. The canonical weight vectors for father's status and son's status are presented in Table 8.2.

TABLE 8.1 Social Mobility Contingency Table (n = 3497)

	Son's Status				
Father's Status	1	2	3	4	5
1	50	45	8	18	8
2	28	174	84	154	55
3	11	78	110	223	96
4	14	150	185	714	447
5	0	42	72	320	411

Socioeconomic status 1 for both fathers and sons has a weight or score of zero since it was dropped from the analysis. The remaining four weights, for both fathers and sons, give the score associated with each status level that maximizes the correlation between the status of father or son. Note that the scores, for both fathers and sons, are in the same rank order as the status levels. Also, the difference between the scores representing status levels 1 and 2, for both fathers and sons, is noticeably larger than the distance between any other two adjacent status levels. For example, the score difference between status levels 1 and 2, for fathers, is $3.15 - 0 = 3.15$, while the difference between status levels 4 and 5 is $4.96 - 4.55 = .41$. Similar differences exist for sons. It seems that the two highest status levels are considerably more distinct than, say, the two lowest status levels. We could, of course, compute the remaining three canonical correlations and their associated canonical weight vectors, but, for the sake of parsimony, we have considered only one set of score vectors and their associated canonical correlation.

8.6 COMPUTER PACKAGES

SPSS and SAS, as well as other computer packages, can perform canonical correlational analysis. Both SPSS and SAS will generate the means, variances, and intercorrelations of all the variables. Both programs compute all possible canonical correlations and test for their significance. The weight vectors for each pair of canonical variates is also computed. Two sets of weights are computed: one for raw scores and one for standardized scores.

The correlations of the original variables in each set with each pair of canonical variates can also be generated. The interpretation of these correlations is similar to interpreting factor loadings in factor analysis. The squared correlations indicate how much of the variation in the variables can be accounted for by a particular canonical variate. Summing the squared correlations for a particular canonical variate and dividing by the number of variables indicates the proportion of the variation in the variable set that is accounted

TABLE 8.2 Canonical Weight Vectors

Canonical Weights or Scores	*Status*				
	1	2	3	4	5
Father's	0	3.15	4.12	4.55	4.96
Son's	0	3.34	4.49	4.87	5.26

for by a particular canonical variate. The correlations of one set of variables with the opposite set of canonical variates indicate how well one set of canonical variates can predict the other set of original variables. These types of analyses involving the patterns of correlations of the original variables with the canonical variates is called "canonical redundancy analysis." For more information, the reader is referred to Stewart and Love (1968).

8.7 PROBLEMS

(1) Using the sample data in the Appendix, conduct a canonical correlation analysis between the six ability measures (variables 1 through 6) and the four personal orientation scales (variables 13 through 16). What is the largest canonical correlation and what are the weighting vectors for each set of variables producing the maximal correlation? How many pairs of canonical variates would you retain for interpreting the interrelationships between the two sets of variables?

(2) Verify the orthogonality properties of the canonical variates.

(3) Why do you think canonical correlational analysis is sometimes called exernal factor analysis?

(4) Let us return to problem 3 at the end of Chapter 4. The data were take from Hauser (1973). The variables can logically be partitioned into two sets: the three x variables involving family background measures and the two y variables involving mental ability and high school grades.

   (a) Compute the two canonical correlations between the x and the y variables.
   (b) Compute the pair of weight vectors associated with each canonical correlation.
   (c) Do you think that you need both pairs of canonical variates to account adequately for the interrelationships among the x and y variables?
   (d) Interpret the nature of the canonical variates associated with the significant canonical correlations.

Appendix

Variable Description of Sample Data Base

Variable	*Description*
(1) SCVOCSC	Scaled Vocabulary Score (01-99)
(2) SCPICT	Scaled Score-Picture Numbers Total (01-99)
(3) SCRDSC	Scaled Reading Score (01-99)
(4) SCLGSC	Scaled Letter Groups Score (01-99)
(5) SCMATSC	Scaled Mathematics Score (01-99)
(6) SCMSCMT	Scaled Mosaic Comparisons Total (01-99)
(7) SEX	0 = male, 1 = female
(8) RACE	0 = white, 1 = nonwhite
(9) COLLEGE STATUS	1 = vocational, trade, or business school 2 = junior, community college 3 = four-year college/university 4 = not in school
(10) SES	Socioeconomic Status 1 = low 2 = medium 3 = high
(11) HSPGM	High School Program 0 = general, vocational-technical 1 = academic
(12) HSGRDS	High School Grades 1 = mostly A 2 = half A-B 3 = mostly C 4 = half B-C 5 = mostly C 6 = half C-D 7 = mostly D 8 = below D
(13) CREATIVE	Personal Orientation Towards Creativity scale (3-9)
(14) PRESSURE	Personal Orientation Towards Avoiding Pressure Scale (2-6)
(15) PEOPLE	Personal Orientation Towards People (2-6)
(16) PRESTIGE	Personal Orientation Towards Prestige (3-9)

APPENDIX
Sample of 300 NLS Respondents

ID	SCVOCSC	SCPICT	SCRDSC	SCLGSC	SCMATSC	SCMSCMT	SEX	RACE	COLLEGE	SES	HSPGM	HSGRDS	CREATIVE	PRESSURE	PEOPLE	PRESTIGE
1	52	48	48	63	56	57	0	0	4	2	1	5	5	4	4	4
2	66	48	68	55	56	57	1	0	2	3	1	2	4	3	5	4
3	45	45	39	45	46	52	1	0	2	3	0	6	6	4	4	7
4	58	53	54	62	58	49	0	0	2	3	1	4	5	3	4	5
5	45	65	46	59	53	54	1	0	2	2	0	4	7	5	5	6
6	51	58	46	55	50	58	1	0	4	3	1	3	5	4	5	5
7	40	50	42	55	49	41	0	0	4	1	1	3	4	3	3	5
8	46	44	45	62	51	54	0	0	1	2	0	5	4	5	3	5
9	39	56	42	40	47	37	0	0	1	2	0	3	8	4	6	7
10	60	41	64	54	62	59	1	0	3	2	1	2	5	3	4	6
11	57	49	56	54	46	49	1	0	4	2	0	2	9	5	5	6
12	34	65	44	47	49	60	0	0	4	2	0	3	9	5	6	9
13	55	66	68	60	64	49	0	0	2	2	1	3	7	5	4	5
14	51	41	61	54	47	52	1	1	4	1	1	2	8	3	6	6
15	63	61	54	59	64	62	0	0	2	2	1	3	3	4	3	6
16	49	50	56	54	58	51	1	0	4	3	0	4	7	5	3	5
17	60	61	64	62	53	54	0	0	4	2	1	3	6	5	5	6
18	66	41	50	52	50	52	0	0	3	3	1	3	6	6	6	6
19	54	38	59	61	53	49	1	0	4	2	0	2	5	5	6	5
20	54	58	56	49	49	60	1	0	1	2	0	2	5	6	5	4
21	54	45	46	43	29	48	1	1	2	1	1	5	8	6	6	6
22	36	58	64	59	60	58	1	0	2	1	1	2	7	6	3	4
23	51	43	37	36	42	53	0	0	2	2	0	5	6	4	6	5
24	51	46	54	48	53	55	0	0	3	3	1	4	7	4	6	6
25	58	49	64	48	62	50	1	0	1	2	1	5	6	4	6	8
26	69	39	66	46	65	49	0	0	2	3	1	3	6	3	3	7
27	60	64	54	51	55	41	1	0	1	1	1	3	5	3	6	5
28	43	52	50	58	55	51	1	0	3	2	1	3	5	3	6	8
29	43	59	59	64	59	64	1	1	1	1	0	2	3	3	2	4
30	39	64	39	55	51	54	1	1	1	3	0	6	3	6	4	4
31	48	59	61	59	54	51	1	0	2	2	1	3	3	5	5	5
32	51	56	57	59	60	59	1	0	3	2	1	3	6	6	3	6

33	60	66	64	55	65	48	0	0	2	3	1	2	5	4	5	7
34	60	53	44	32	50	38	0	0	3	2	1	3	5	5	4	7
35	48	63	59	59	58	60	0	0	3	3	1	2	8	4	5	4
36	57	58	37	49	55	51	0	0	2	3	0	3	6	4	4	4
37	69	66	64	64	67	53	0	0	3	3	1	1	9	4	6	8
38	36	52	38	52	39	23	1	1	4	1	0	4	6	5	6	8
39	69	39	68	56	51	51	1	0	3	2	0	2	6	5	5	4
40	57	41	42	61	49	53	0	0	3	2	0	4	8	5	6	8
41	39	46	30	42	36	41	0	1	1	2	1	4	5	5	5	9
42	42	49	56	55	55	59	0	0	3	2	1	3	7	5	6	7
43	55	49	56	50	44	53	1	0	3	3	0	2	8	4	6	3
44	60	61	61	52	65	62	1	0	3	2	0	1	8	4	5	6
45	61	49	60	46	52	52	1	0	2	3	1	4	7	4	6	7
46	49	61	66	58	67	62	0	0	2	3	1	3	6	4	5	4
47	63	50	59	52	64	58	1	1	4	2	1	1	8	4	5	5
48	48	42	49	59	55	51	1	0	4	3	1	4	7	3	6	5
49	48	49	46	57	47	61	1	1	3	1	1	3	5	5	5	6
50	49	53	58	52	44	56	1	0	4	2	1	4	5	3	4	6
51	49	50	42	51	48	53	0	1	4	2	0	7	6	4	4	7
52	54	40	49	42	53	46	0	0	4	2	0	4	8	4	6	7
53	48	45	51	48	42	56	1	0	4	2	0	4	8	6	6	5
54	57	51	59	63	64	49	0	0	3	2	1	2	4	4	3	6
55	54	64	52	58	59	54	1	1	3	3	1	3	6	5	3	4
56	39	38	42	51	53	57	0	0	2	2	1	2	3	3	3	4
57	66	66	68	55	67	49	0	0	3	3	1	1	4	3	4	5
58	66	55	64	63	58	61	1	0	4	2	1	2	5	3	4	6
59	54	41	49	58	49	60	0	0	4	2	0	4	7	6	4	8
60	69	43	56	54	53	59	1	0	2	3	0	4	9	4	6	5
61	48	44	52	46	38	35	0	1	4	2	1	2	6	5	5	6
62	60	48	64	63	58	51	0	0	2	2	1	3	4	3	4	6
63	39	52	46	49	40	43	1	0	3	2	1	3	8	4	6	9
64	51	57	46	49	55	65	0	1	4	2	0	3	5	5	3	5
65	54	41	54	59	56	52	1	0	2	2	1	2	7	4	6	5
66	66	60	68	59	62	55	0	0	3	3	1	1	8	4	5	3
67	46	65	57	52	65	58	0	1	3	1	1	1	8	4	6	9
68	42	46	40	45	42	40	1	0	1	2	0	3	4	4	6	8

(continued)

APPENDIX (Continued)

ID	*SCVOCSC*	*SCPICT*	*SCRDSC*	*SCLGSC*	*SCMATSC*	*SCMSCMT*	*SEX*	*RACE*	*COLLEGE*	*SES*	*HSPGM*	*HSGRDS*	*CREATIVE*	*PRESSURE*	*PEOPLE*	*PRESTIGE*
69	63	57	61	63	64	71	0	0	3	3	1	1	7	3	6	4
70	54	30	34	48	44	58	1	0	4	2	0	3	5	4	4	6
71	45	53	44	61	47	50	1	0	1	2	0	3	5	5	4	7
72	52	49	42	49	58	50	0	0	1	2	1	4	4	2	3	4
73	63	54	59	57	65	52	0	0	4	1	1	4	8	5	6	7
74	30	57	44	47	58	51	0	0	4	2	0	5	6	4	4	6
75	61	50	60	54	53	59	1	0	1	1	0	2	8	6	4	9
76	48	38	49	45	56	48	1	1	4	2	1	4	8	5	6	7
77	66	66	64	62	55	53	1	0	4	2	0	2	5	3	6	7
78	57	54	62	63	62	54	1	0	4	2	0	2	7	5	4	6
79	46	66	61	58	51	48	1	1	3	3	1	4	6	5	5	5
80	54	66	49	52	58	53	0	1	4	1	1	3	5	4	6	7
81	51	56	47	53	53	48	0	1	2	1	0	4	5	6	5	6
82	48	38	51	47	44	55	0	0	4	2	0	4	7	3	4	6
83	72	66	66	63	67	52	1	0	3	3	1	1	7	3	5	8
84	42	30	43	55	42	43	1	0	2	3	0	5	8	4	5	4
85	51	60	61	55	60	54	1	0	2	3	1	2	7	6	6	5
86	66	66	59	57	58	53	1	0	3	3	0	1	4	5	3	4
87	41	58	48	59	53	59	1	0	2	2	0	4	5	4	5	6
88	42	53	46	57	46	51	1	0	2	2	0	4	5	4	5	6
89	51	62	56	53	56	56	0	0	4	3	0	5	8	5	5	8
90	48	54	56	51	60	49	0	0	3	3	1	3	7	4	3	5
91	45	49	36	45	37	49	1	1	4	2	0	4	4	3	2	4
92	55	65	61	62	65	66	1	0	3	3	1	1	7	5	5	6
93	51	44	56	60	49	48	0	0	3	2	1	5	5	4	6	6
94	63	62	51	55	62	50	0	0	4	2	1	3	9	6	6	8
95	48	43	42	49	39	49	1	0	1	3	0	4	9	5	6	8
96	66	64	64	51	51	57	1	0	3	3	1	2	5	2	6	4
97	66	66	66	62	65	65	0	0	3	3	0	2	9	5	6	3
98	48	44	38	56	41	49	1	1	4	1	0	3	8	4	6	5
99	45	46	51	51	64	46	0	0	3	3	1	3	6	4	5	6
100	43	43	38	47	51	42	0	0	1	1	0	5	5	4	3	4
101	69	66	61	60	64	50	1	0	3	2	1	5	8	5	6	3
102	54	42	61	59	56	49	1	0	3	3	0	4	7	5	6	4
103	42	39	59	61	56	61	1	0	2	2	1	2	7	4	6	8
104	36	33	40	28	40	36	0	1	2	1	0	4	7	4	5	6

105	57	45	52	53	46	50	0	1	3	1	1	3	6	4	5	9
106	48	61	44	50	42	49	0	0	2	3	0	4	4	5	4	8
107	45	35	37	45	40	48	1	0	1	2	0	3	7	3	6	7
108	57	36	37	45	49	55	0	0	3	3	1	4	9	6	6	9
109	48	56	52	45	57	60	0	0	3	3	1	4	5	4	4	4
110	51	42	59	51	53	50	1	1	3	2	1	3	3	5	5	5
111	69	52	61	52	64	66	0	0	3	3	1	2	5	2	2	3
112	45	49	49	57	62	48	0	0	1	2	1	2	6	5	5	6
113	51	49	49	57	60	61	0	0	4	3	0	4	8	5	4	4
114	60	66	54	55	62	56	0	0	3	2	0	3	6	5	5	5
115	41	64	53	50	43	45	1	0	1	2	1	3	7	4	6	4
116	39	39	32	36	38	47	0	1	4	1	0	5	7	5	6	9
117	48	42	56	57	49	50	1	0	4	1	0	4	5	6	4	5
118	49	60	54	57	67	53	1	0	3	3	1	2	7	5	5	6
119	49	59	52	50	60	53	0	0	3	1	1	4	8	4	6	6
120	49	52	47	52	42	43	1	1	3	1	1	4	8	4	5	7
121	69	64	62	63	62	55	1	0	3	3	1	3	4	4	6	4
122	57	66	56	61	65	59	0	0	3	3	1	3	8	5	6	4
123	66	54	52	53	60	54	0	0	2	2	1	4	7	4	4	7
124	42	61	39	49	42	47	0	0	4	1	1	4	8	4	4	3
125	35	42	33	31	31	27	1	1	1	1	1	3	6	3	4	3
126	63	56	61	24	49	24	0	0	4	3	0	4	6	2	3	5
127	43	64	46	53	60	60	0	0	4	2	1	3	5	6	5	8
128	66	66	59	63	53	50	1	0	3	3	1	1	7	4	6	5
129	33	37	42	51	38	49	1	1	2	1	0	4	5	5	6	8
130	53	66	55	60	65	64	0	0	3	3	1	3	6	5	5	6
131	48	57	51	62	60	52	0	0	2	2	1	3	6	3	4	6
132	51	66	64	58	64	47	1	0	4	1	1	1	6	4	6	4
133	45	34	54	55	62	59	0	0	2	1	1	4	6	6	4	5
134	72	50	68	61	65	58	0	0	3	3	1	1	8	4	6	5
135	51	52	54	57	47	50	1	0	4	1	0	5	5	4	6	5
136	48	44	51	45	56	65	1	0	3	2	0	3	8	4	4	7
137	47	40	66	53	47	53	1	0	2	1	1	2	7	5	6	7
138	32	34	37	26	45	28	0	1	3	1	0	3	8	6	5	9
139	33	33	33	38	42	40	0	0	1	2	0	4	9	4	5	6
140	37	36	48	38	49	50	0	0	2	3	0	4	7	4	4	8

(continued)

APPENDIX (Continued)

ID	*SCVOCSC*	*SCPICT*	*SCRDSC*	*SCLGSC*	*SCMATSC*	*SCMSCMT*	*SEX*	*RACE*	*COLLEGE*	*SES*	*HSPGM*	*HSGRDS*	*CREATIVE*	*PRESSURE*	*PEOPLE*	*PRESTIGE*
141	40	40	37	37	37	52	1	1	4	1	1	4	9	5	6	8
142	42	60	49	57	56	45	0	0	2	2	1	4	9	6	5	8
143	63	65	68	61	58	63	1	0	3	2	1	2	8	4	6	5
144	40	60	54	53	53	50	1	0	4	2	0	4	8	5	5	5
145	36	49	42	42	42	48	1	1	4	2	1	5	7	5	6	5
146	54	60	59	55	51	63	1	0	3	2	0	1	8	4	6	5
147	61	63	49	50	51	52	0	0	4	1	0	4	7	5	3	4
148	46	57	46	53	56	63	0	0	2	3	1	4	6	6	4	8
149	66	53	66	59	67	57	0	0	3	3	1	1	7	2	6	4
150	39	66	42	48	39	40	1	1	4	1	0	4	3	4	2	3
151	57	41	56	45	64	49	0	0	2	2	1	3	7	4	3	5
152	45	51	47	46	51	55	1	0	4	2	0	2	8	6	3	5
153	45	49	59	57	55	47	0	0	2	3	1	4	8	4	4	5
154	60	64	59	63	62	52	0	0	3	2	1	3	6	5	3	6
155	66	48	68	64	60	52	1	0	3	3	1	2	8	4	6	3
156	60	64	51	57	64	78	0	0	3	3	1	2	5	4	4	7
157	66	65	68	59	67	63	1	0	3	3	1	1	7	5	6	7
158	48	47	46	45	47	50	1	0	2	3	1	3	9	5	6	5
159	61	49	44	54	45	52	1	0	3	2	1	6	6	5	6	3
160	36	45	34	33	48	41	1	1	3	1	1	2	9	6	6	9
161	55	59	52	59	62	48	0	1	3	3	1	2	8	5	4	5
162	48	42	59	45	44	53	0	0	3	2	1	3	9	6	5	8
163	66	45	54	52	53	47	1	0	2	3	1	4	5	4	6	6
164	60	43	59	57	65	57	1	0	4	1	0	2	6	4	5	5
165	51	43	37	39	35	41	1	0	1	2	0	5	7	6	6	4
166	42	40	46	56	41	67	1	0	1	2	0	3	5	5	5	5
167	39	43	55	58	58	49	0	0	4	2	0	4	6	5	4	6
168	66	40	54	57	60	52	0	0	3	3	1	5	8	4	4	4
169	36	35	37	38	40	35	0	1	4	1	0	4	5	3	4	7
170	45	57	46	50	60	52	0	1	3	1	1	2	9	4	6	9
171	39	47	44	37	46	54	0	0	3	2	1	5	3	4	6	5
172	47	37	58	42	37	38	1	0	4	2	0	5	8	6	6	5
173	66	56	68	61	67	23	0	0	3	3	1	2	5	2	6	8
174	60	66	68	60	65	56	1	0	3	3	1	1	3	6	5	6

175	48	45	31	47	39	40	0	1	4	2	0	6	5	4	6	6
176	60	57	56	57	64	56	0	0	4	1	0	4	6	4	3	4
177	60	65	46	51	46	58	0	1	4	2	1	6	9	6	6	8
178	60	37	56	60	62	59	1	0	3	2	1	2	4	2	4	3
179	66	57	61	59	58	62	1	0	3	3	1	1	8	5	6	6
180	60	44	66	59	62	52	0	0	3	2	1	3	7	5	5	6
181	69	44	64	62	64	54	0	0	3	3	1	3	9	4	6	6
182	63	62	54	63	51	49	1	0	3	3	1	2	7	5	6	6
183	51	65	51	58	60	50	0	0	4	3	0	2	6	6	4	6
184	39	53	59	43	58	44	0	0	3	2	1	3	7	4	6	6
185	39	66	61	55	59	47	1	0	2	2	1	2	6	5	5	6
186	63	64	54	59	40	93	1	0	4	2	1	3	5	4	4	5
187	51	59	42	55	51	43	0	0	2	2	0	4	6	4	4	6
188	42	35	51	36	53	32	0	1	3	2	1	5	8	5	5	7
189	54	41	42	40	35	44	1	0	4	2	0	5	8	4	6	6
190	45	64	61	62	64	53	0	1	3	2	1	5	7	4	3	6
191	45	46	32	37	29	35	1	1	4	1	0	4	7	5	6	8
192	50	49	59	49	58	41	0	0	3	2	1	2	6	4	4	8
193	45	29	35	28	37	34	1	0	1	1	0	3	7	3	6	6
194	58	56	54	57	56	55	1	0	3	2	1	1	7	5	5	7
195	39	63	46	43	44	62	0	1	3	1	1	3	5	4	6	7
196	63	64	47	56	56	56	1	0	2	2	1	2	5	6	6	6
197	48	56	44	34	45	55	0	0	2	2	1	4	9	5	6	7
198	33	47	37	49	53	36	1	1	1	1	0	4	7	3	6	7
199	52	50	64	59	64	54	0	0	2	2	1	2	6	4	3	7
200	69	58	59	60	56	55	1	0	4	3	1	2	5	2	6	6
201	57	59	59	59	58	65	1	1	2	3	0	2	4	3	4	4
202	41	55	37	59	46	58	0	1	3	1	0	3	5	3	4	4
203	52	46	52	53	53	42	0	0	4	2	1	4	8	5	6	6
204	72	65	64	50	62	51	0	0	3	3	1	1	5	3	6	8
205	54	34	45	44	42	41	0	0	3	2	1	3	6	4	5	6
206	39	46	36	38	42	47	0	1	4	1	0	5	9	6	4	6
207	45	36	42	32	38	37	1	1	1	1	0	3	8	6	6	9
208	46	58	40	57	40	61	0	1	2	1	0	6	4	3	3	4
209	69	51	68	61	64	93	1	0	3	2	1	1	7	6	6	4
210	36	43	54	22	35	38	1	0	4	2	0	4	6	5	4	6

(continued)

APPENDIX (Continued)

ID	*SCVOCSC*	*SCPICT*	*SCRDSC*	*SCLGSC*	*SCMATSC*	*SCMSCMT*	*SEX*	*RACE*	*COLLEGE*	*SES*	*HSPGM*	*HSGRDS*	*CREATIVE*	*PRESSURE*	*PEOPLE*	*PRESTIGE*
211	48	53	57	48	58	59	1	0	3	3	1	3	8	6	6	5
212	69	40	61	64	62	61	1	0	3	2	0	1	7	4	6	5
213	57	39	54	39	58	40	1	0	4	2	0	3	7	4	3	3
214	49	50	51	52	51	44	1	0	2	2	1	3	9	6	6	7
215	57	62	44	40	51	49	1	0	3	3	1	4	3	3	6	3
216	46	51	51	63	65	67	1	0	2	3	0	3	3	4	4	5
217	54	40	49	51	53	46	0	0	2	2	1	3	7	5	6	6
218	54	49	56	61	62	55	0	0	3	3	0	4	7	4	3	5
219	54	65	64	59	60	57	1	0	3	3	1	1	8	3	6	5
220	48	56	44	60	56	50	0	0	4	2	1	5	4	4	4	7
221	47	54	58	60	58	49	0	1	4	1	1	2	9	5	6	8
222	63	45	49	61	48	69	0	0	4	2	1	3	4	4	4	6
223	66	41	61	51	58	65	0	0	3	2	1	3	9	5	6	9
224	36	49	44	41	56	49	0	1	3	2	0	5	6	5	5	6
225	55	50	49	51	55	57	0	0	4	2	1	2	8	4	6	8
226	48	38	49	37	42	60	1	1	4	1	0	4	5	4	3	6
227	60	46	51	42	56	53	0	0	2	3	1	4	8	3	2	6
228	46	45	51	41	44	62	0	1	4	1	1	3	6	4	6	7
229	57	55	61	65	64	45	0	0	3	3	1	3	6	2	5	6
230	69	53	68	62	67	54	1	0	3	3	1	2	7	5	3	4
231	42	59	59	49	53	91	1	0	4	2	0	2	4	3	4	4
232	38	30	35	22	35	33	0	1	4	2	0	4	6	4	4	6
233	54	57	59	55	56	62	0	0	3	2	1	4	5	4	4	4
234	72	41	68	60	62	48	0	0	2	3	1	5	7	2	3	6
235	57	48	51	49	55	41	0	0	3	3	1	4	4	4	2	5
236	45	50	36	59	56	61	1	0	2	2	1	4	6	5	4	7
237	69	35	66	62	67	55	0	0	3	3	1	2	6	4	3	5
238	36	34	44	36	44	40	0	0	4	3	0	3	7	6	4	9
239	51	66	57	63	62	59	1	0	3	2	0	1	7	6	5	6
240	42	49	39	40	29	29	1	1	2	2	1	4	8	4	6	5
241	66	65	66	64	65	57	0	0	3	3	1	2	6	2	4	7
242	47	64	56	60	65	65	1	0	3	2	1	3	7	2	4	7
243	57	43	51	59	53	46	0	0	1	1	0	2	6	5	4	7
244	60	53	64	52	58	52	0	0	3	3	1	4	8	2	4	7

245	69	38	68	56	67	45	0	1	3	2	1	3	5	2	5	6
246	66	42	56	57	56	45	0	0	1	2	0	4	7	4	4	8
247	45	66	51	47	63	47	0	0	3	2	1	3	4	6	4	5
248	63	66	50	58	66	63	0	0	3	2	1	1	3	4	3	6
249	60	54	56	53	56	48	1	0	2	2	1	1	7	3	6	7
250	66	56	58	57	62	63	0	0	3	3	1	3	6	3	3	5
251	63	66	64	64	67	57	0	0	3	2	1	1	5	3	3	4
252	66	56	46	51	51	23	0	0	3	3	1	4	7	4	4	9
253	54	58	46	61	55	55	0	0	4	2	1	4	7	5	6	6
254	51	51	32	57	58	45	1	0	4	3	0	2	6	5	4	6
255	43	54	54	55	53	41	0	1	3	2	0	2	8	6	6	8
256	49	65	44	53	56	44	0	0	3	1	0	6	3	4	3	4
257	39	42	33	40	44	33	1	0	2	1	0	4	5	5	5	4
258	60	66	42	54	58	56	1	0	3	3	1	2	6	2	6	5
259	61	56	57	54	59	49	1	0	2	2	1	2	9	6	6	4
260	61	66	57	57	55	67	1	0	2	2	1	3	8	4	5	6
261	63	51	64	36	46	60	0	0	2	3	0	5	6	5	3	5
262	54	36	45	39	46	44	1	0	2	2	1	3	7	4	2	4
263	63	56	61	52	54	52	1	0	3	3	1	4	7	4	6	4
264	43	49	50	49	51	65	0	1	3	2	1	2	5	5	4	6
265	69	61	66	58	67	54	0	0	2	2	1	1	6	4	6	8
266	36	64	29	32	38	45	1	0	4	1	0	4	6	5	6	8
267	61	40	62	64	54	65	1	0	3	3	1	2	6	6	5	5
268	44	37	31	50	42	40	0	0	3	1	1	3	6	3	5	7
269	39	62	49	47	46	52	1	0	4	1	0	6	7	4	5	6
270	51	37	61	53	62	55	0	0	4	2	1	3	7	6	6	4
271	45	48	46	59	44	58	0	0	2	3	0	3	7	4	6	8
272	66	49	49	65	56	63	1	0	3	3	1	3	5	6	6	7
273	54	63	57	52	62	51	0	0	4	3	1	5	6	2	6	5
274	72	57	64	52	60	49	0	0	3	3	1	2	7	4	5	6
275	45	65	59	55	62	54	1	0	3	3	1	2	5	4	3	4
276	69	49	66	58	64	61	0	1	4	3	1	2	8	5	3	3
277	54	51	61	54	42	47	1	0	4	2	1	4	9	5	3	4
278	60	52	54	59	58	66	0	0	3	3	1	3	4	4	4	6
279	54	35	49	47	47	49	0	0	2	2	1	5	8	5	6	7
280	55	52	61	54	64	32	0	1	3	2	1	4	7	6	5	6

(continued)

APPENDIX (Continued)

ID	SCVOCSC	SCPICT	SCRDSC	SCLGSC	SCMATSC	SCMSCMT	SEX	RACE	COLLEGE	SES	HSPGM	HSGRDS	CREATIVE	PRESSURE	PEOPLE	PRESTIGE
281	42	36	29	61	55	48	0	0	2	1	0	4	5	4	5	5
282	47	48	49	51	55	46	1	0	4	2	0	3	3	6	6	5
283	57	59	52	52	47	54	1	0	2	2	0	3	7	4	5	8
284	48	40	46	51	55	59	0	0	4	2	1	5	9	6	6	9
285	42	47	51	47	31	59	1	0	4	1	0	4	5	2	6	5
286	63	59	56	59	49	54	1	0	2	2	1	2	3	5	6	5
287	48	54	52	61	51	40	1	0	1	2	1	4	9	4	5	5
288	58	66	59	64	64	68	1	0	3	2	1	2	5	4	6	7
289	64	61	56	57	58	49	1	0	3	3	1	4	5	4	6	4
290	48	61	51	42	40	50	0	0	4	2	0	4	5	5	3	6
291	66	65	68	60	65	54	1	0	4	3	1	2	6	5	4	3
292	52	64	64	59	64	56	0	0	3	3	1	3	8	5	4	5
293	60	53	56	55	47	52	0	0	1	2	0	4	7	3	6	6
294	51	47	54	53	42	73	0	0	1	1	0	3	7	6	6	8
295	46	37	38	47	50	46	1	0	2	2	0	3	5	4	6	6
296	69	49	59	57	55	48	0	0	4	3	0	2	6	5	2	4
297	54	64	64	42	43	57	1	0	2	3	1	4	8	6	6	7
298	54	57	59	60	64	65	1	0	2	2	1	1	6	4	6	6
299	69	63	68	64	67	61	1	0	3	3	1	1	6	4	3	4
300	48	65	64	63	65	46	1	0	3	1	1	2	8	5	4	8

References

Bartlett, M. S. Multivariate analysis. *Journal of Royal Statistical Society*, 1947, *16*, 176–197.

Birren, J. E., & Morrison, D. F. Analysis of WAIS subtests in relation to age and education. *Journal of Gerontology*, 1961, *16*, 363–369.

Cattell, R. B. The scree test for the number of factors. *Multivariate Behavioral Research*, 1966, *1*, 245–276.

Crano, W. D., Kenny, D. A., & Campbell, D. T. Does intellegence cause achievement? A cross-lagged panel analysis. *Journal of Educational Psychology*, 1972, *63*, 258–275.

Dunteman, G. H. Discriminant analysis of the Strong Vocational Interest Blank for female students in five college curricula. *Journal of Applied Psychology*, 1966, *50*, 509–515.

Dunteman, G. H., & Bailey, J. P., Jr. A canonical correlation analysis of the Strong Vocational Interest Blank and the Minnesota Multiphasic Personality Inventory for a female college population. *Educational and Psychological Measurement*, 1967, *27*, 631–642.

Fisher, R. A. The use of multiple measurements in taxonomic problems. *Annals of Eugenics*, 1939, *9*, 238–249.

Forsyth, R., & Sadava, S. W. Criteria measures of drug-using behavior: Multivariate analysis. *Educational and Psychological Measurement*, 1977, *37*, 641–658.

Glass, D. V. (Ed.). *Social mobility in Britain*. London: Routledge & Kegan Paul, 1954.

Grizzle, J. E., & Allen, D. M. Analysis of growth and dose response curves. *Biometrics*, 1969, *25*, 357–381.

Harman, H. H. *Modern factor analysis*. Chicago: University of Chicago Press, 1967.

Hauser, R. M. Disaggregating a social-psychological model of educational attainment. In A. S. Goldberger & O. D. Duncan (Eds.), *Structural equation models in the social sciences*. New York: Seminar, 1973.

Heck, D. L. Charts of some upper percentage points of the distribution of the largest characteristic root. *Annals of Mathematical Statistics*, 1960, *31*, 625–642.

Hotelling, H. The most predictable criterion. *Journal of Educational Psychology*, 1935, *26*, 139–142.

Kaiser, H. F. The varimax criterion for analytic rotation in factor analysis. *Psychometrika*, 1958, *23*, 187–200.

Kenny, D. A. *Correlation and causality*. New York: John Wiley, 1979.

Klein, A. E. *Impact of Saturday school* (2nd ed.). Ferguson, MO: Ferguson-Florissant School District, 1977.

Klein, A. E. Further evidence on the redundancy of the Stanford Achievement Test. *Educational and Psychological Measurement*, 1979, *39*, 1061–1065.

Kleinbaum, D. G. A generalization of the growth curve model which allows missing data. *Journal of Multivariate Analysis*, 1973, *3*, 117–124.

Lawley, D. N., & Maxwell, A. E. *Factor analysis as a statistical method*. New York: Elsevier, 1971.

Mardia, K. V., Kent, J. T., & Bibby, J. M. *Multivariate analysis*. New York: Academic, 1979.

Milburn, M. A. *Process analysis of mass media campaigns*. Unpublished doctoral dissertation, Harvard University, 1978.

Morrison, D. F. *Multivariate statistical methods.* New York: McGraw-Hill, 1976.

Newhaus, J. O., & Wrigley, C. The quartimax method, an analytical approach to orthogonal simple structure. *British Journal of Psychology*, 1954, *7*, 81–91.

Nie, N. H., Hull, C. H., Jenkins, J. G. Steinbrenner, K., & Bent, D. H. *Statistical package for the social sciences.* New York: McGraw-Hill, 1975.

Rao, C. R., & Slater, P. Multivariate analysis applied to differences between neurotic groups. *British Journal of Psychology,* 1949, *2*, 17–29.

SAS Institute, Inc. *SAS user's guide: Statistics.* Cary, NY: Author, 1982.

Spearman, C. General intelligence, objectively determined and measured. *American Journal of Psychology*, 1904, *15*, 201–293.

Stewart, D. K., & Love, W. A. A general canonical correlation index, *Psychological Bulletin*, 1968, *70*, 160–163.

Thurstone, L. L. *Multiple factor analysis.* Chicago: University of Chicago Press, 1947.

Wood, D. A., & Erskine, J. A. Strategies in canonical correlation with application to behavioral data. *Educational and Psychological Measurement*, 1976, *36*, 861–878.

Index

Distribution function, 24
Dunteman, G. H., 148, 206
Dummy variable, 151-152, 216-217

About the Author

GEORGE H. DUNTEMAN is currently Chief Scientist at the Research Triangle Institute, where he is actively involved in applied research, primarily in the social and behavioral sciences. He has previously held research appointments at the Educational Testing Service and the U.S. Army Research Institute. He has also held assistant and associate professorships at the University of Rochester and the University of Florida, respectively. Dr. Dunteman received his Ph.D. from Louisiana State University in industrial/organizational psychology with a minor in industrial engineering. He also has an M.S. degree from Iowa State University with a major in industrial psychology and a minor in statistics. His B.A. degree from St. Lawrence University is in sociology. He is currently on the editorial board of Educational and Psychological Measurement *and has published widely in professional Journals.*